Nevile Davidson

# Nevile Davidson

*A Life to Be Lived*

*by* ANDREW G. RALSTON

*foreword by* DAVID M. BECKETT

*Best wishes from Andrew Ralston*

WIPF & STOCK · Eugene, Oregon

NEVILE DAVIDSON
A Life to Be Lived

Wipf & Stock
An Imprint of Wipf and Stock Publishers
199 W. 8th Ave., Suite 3
Eugene, OR 97401

www.wipfandstock.com

PAPERBACK ISBN: 978-1-5326-8780-8
HARDCOVER ISBN: 978-1-5326-8781-5
EBOOK ISBN: 978-1-5326-8782-2

Manufactured in the U.S.A.                    SEPTEMBER 13, 2019

"Christianity is not only a creed to be believed—it is a life to be lived."

—Nevile Davidson, September 1938

Dr. A. Nevile Davidson as Moderator of the General Assembly of the Church of Scotland in Edinburgh in 1962, accompanied by his wife Peggy. (Photo: Falkirk Herald)

# Contents

# Foreword

VISITORS TO GLASGOW CATHEDRAL will not always realize how much its beauty and its atmosphere owe to the vision of one man who was its minister in the central decades of the twentieth century. It is excellent news that Andrew Ralston has now given us a full account of that man's life and achievement.

Many of us are fortunate to be able to look back on one or two people who had a profound impact on our early life and helped to shape what became of us later. Nevile Davidson was one such for me. As well as being our minister he was a close friend of my parents and a frequent visitor to our home in Milngavie. From as far back as I can remember I enjoyed and looked forward to his visits, not because he played children's games or took me out to kick a ball around, but because he had an amazing faculty for enabling my sister and me to meet him on what felt like common ground. In his company it seemed natural for a grown-up and a small child to talk about things on equal terms. It was the start of a relationship that was precious to me for the rest of his life, and I gained much from his guidance and his wisdom.

With his patrician appearance, elegant manners and unfailing courtesy, Nevile may have given an initial impression of remoteness, and indeed he never quite outgrew the mould of Edwardian gentleman in which he had been cast. To those who engaged with him, though, he was not in the least remote. My father's elder's district was Townhead, where many of the poorest members of the Cathedral lived, often in severely sub-standard housing. He told us how much the minister enjoyed visiting those homes, and how much his visits were enjoyed.

The distinguished churchman who convened influential Assembly committees, served as president of several societies, was appointed moderator of the General Assembly and awarded the St. Mungo Prize for service to the City of Glasgow, held in some respects a simple and uncomplicated faith. I recall him stating, during a discussion of common cups and individual glasses at communion services, his absolute conviction that no-one had ever, or would ever, come to harm through participation in the sacrament. Arguments based on fear or concerns about hygiene were, to him, irrelevant. Yet he had a formidable intellect, and was well able to debate deep theological and philosophical issues, especially in the ecumenical endeavor to which he was passionately committed.

Andrew Ralston has spent several years making regular visits to the National Library of Scotland to study Nevile's diaries and other papers stored there. It is wonderful that Andrew's work has now resulted in the fullest account so far published of a man who is now directly remembered by only a few, but who was for many of my generation the ideal model of a parish minister.

—DAVID M. BECKETT

# Acknowledgements

I AM GRATEFUL TO many people who contributed in various ways to the production of this book:

Dr. James Macaulay, Ailene Hunter and Alison Gifford of the Society of Friends of Glasgow Cathedral for their interest in and support for the project;

Heather Beadling (Glasgow Cathedral administrator), Elizabeth I'Anson (Glasgow Cathedral librarian), Sheila Allan, Shona French and Jessie Summers for the use of archive material and photographs;

Dr. Margaret Beckett, Henty and Alan Diack, Alex and Ellen Findlay, Margaret Hamilton, Rev. Hugh Kerr, Rev. Dr. Johnston McKay, David Martin, Patricia Miller and Rev. Dr. Henry Sefton for sharing personal memories of Nevile Davidson;

Gregor Smith for original artwork depicting buildings associated with Dr. Davidson;

Jill Buchanan for permission to reproduce photographs of Nevile Davidson which originally appeared in the *Falkirk Herald;*

The Herald and Times Group for permission to reproduce photographs of Nevile Davidson which originally appeared in the *Glasgow Herald;*

David Palmer (www.photoscot.co.uk) for converting slides into digital images;

Sandra Kramer (Wild Goose Publications) for the photograph of Lord MacLeod of Fuinary;

Jack Stevenson for the photograph of the Nativity painting which hangs in the nave of Glasgow Cathedral;

Dr. Neil A. Macdonald, Norman F. Shead and Rev. Dr. Sandy Forsyth for their advice on chapters of the book in draft form. Any errors are, of course, my own responsibility;

Rev. David M. Beckett and Emeritus Professor W. Ian P. Hazlett who not only read and commented on much of the manuscript but have been unstinting in their encouragement throughout the whole process;

and, finally, my wife Hazel for sharing the task of working through the many volumes of Dr. Davidson's diaries held in the Special Collections Department of the National Library of Scotland, Edinburgh.

# Introduction

"No-one can write the life of a man but himself, but in writing it he disguises it; he shows himself as he wants to be seen."

—JEAN-JACQUES ROUSSEAU, 1712–1778: CONFESSIONS

ONE SATURDAY EVENING IN March 1923, a twenty-four year old student set off from the family home in North Berwick on the east coast of Scotland to put his recently acquired motorcycle through its paces. There were few cars around in those days but when he encountered a Model T Ford on the road to Haddington he decided to race the driver for the next five miles. The young man already had quite a reputation for daring exploits on two wheels: as a schoolboy he used to impress his friends by fearlessly riding his bicycle along the top of a wall, a trick which earned him the nickname "Nevile the Devil."

Those who later knew the Very Rev. Dr. A. Nevile Davidson as the minister of Glasgow Cathedral would find it extremely difficult to imagine him taking part in such youthful escapades. During his thirty-two years at the Cathedral Davidson acquired a formidable reputation as a dignified— some even thought saintly—man of the cloth. His appearance, speech and manner were characterized by formality and he always conducted himself with the greatest of decorum. One elder who turned up at a kirk session meeting dressed in sports jacket and flannels instead of a suit was taken aside by the minister at the end and politely reminded, "country clothes for the country, town clothes for the town." No member of the congregation would have dreamed of addressing Nevile Davidson by his Christian name. After one Sunday service, people shaking hands with the minister were taken aback to hear someone greet him as "Nevile"—only to breathe a sigh of relief when it later emerged that the visitor was in fact his cousin. Even his wife, when giving a talk to a ladies' group about the couple's world tour in 1962, referred throughout to "my husband" and never once mentioned him by name.

But there was more to Dr. Davidson than dignity and distance. One of his successors as minister of the Cathedral, the late Rev. Dr. Laurence Whitley, remarked that "Nevile Davidson always struck me as something of an enigma. He seemed on the outside to be austere and yet was very good with people and they always warmed to him." Many of those who met him came away saying, "he would listen to you in a way that made you feel you were the only person there."

Any quest to find the man behind the public image is likely to begin with the two books that came from his pen: *Reflections of a Scottish Churchman* (1965), a selection of sermons and addresses which gives some idea of Nevile Davidson's theological views, and the autobiography finished shortly before his sudden death in 1976 which appeared posthumously under the title *Beginnings but no Ending*. This provides a straightforward narrative of his career. Born in North Berwick in 1899, he studied at Edinburgh University and followed his father into the ministry of the United Free Church of Scotland in 1924.[1] His first charge was St. Mary's, Aberdeen, and during his time there the reunion of the United Free Church and the Church of Scotland took place, so that he became a minister of the latter denomination. After two years at St. Enoch's Church in Dundee (1932–4) he was called to Glasgow Cathedral, where he remained until he retired in 1967, apart from a short period as an army chaplain during the second World War. He served as moderator of the General Assembly in 1962 and traveled worldwide representing the Church of Scotland. In retirement he returned to live in the East Lothian area where he had been brought up and continued to be very active in church affairs, particularly in the field of ecumenical relations, regularly attending committee meetings in Edinburgh and doing pulpit supply.

Yet *Beginnings but no Ending* does not tell the full story. Writing in the Foreword, his friend Rev. Dr. James Bulloch notes that "a great deal is

---

1. Throughout this book, frequent reference is made to the various Presbyterian denominations in Scotland. Readers unfamiliar with these are referred the Appendix on page 199 for an explanation of the terminology used.

left untold in these pages."[2] Conversations and correspondence with former colleagues and parishioners reveal a very human figure, with a sense of humor, a love of nature and animals, and an almost child-like pleasure in simple things. On a visit to friends in the West End of Glasgow one November 5—bonfire night—his hostess remembers him running to the window to watch the fireworks as excitedly as any schoolboy. He delighted in telling stories about amusing experiences, such as the time on a family outing near the Davidsons' holiday home at Nethy Bridge when their entire picnic was eaten by a cow. This he found so hilarious that it did not bother him in the least that there was nothing to eat!

As well as drawing on people's reminiscences, the present volume makes use of a largely unexplored archive of written material in the form of Nevile Davidson's correspondence files and the personal diaries he kept between 1920–9 and 1942–1976 which meticulously chronicle every detail of his daily activities, from the books he read to when he had a haircut. Three years after his death, his wife Peggy deposited this extensive collection in the National Library of Scotland in Edinburgh where it has lain ever since.

These documents shed light on a very different side of one of the most distinguished Scottish churchmen of the twentieth century and show him to be someone who still has much of value to say to the church today.

2. Davidson, *Beginnings, vii*

# 1

# "Not Enough of a Scholar"

## CHILDHOOD AND STUDENT DAYS, 1899–1924

NEAR THE VILLAGE OF Inchture, about nine miles west of Dundee, lies the historic seat of the Kinnaird family—a fine nineteenth century country house known as Rossie Priory, surrounded by a 2000 acre estate.

Some time in the 1890s the Rev. James Davidson (1853–1930), a minister of the Free Church of Scotland, received an invitation to stay there. He was not a member of the landed gentry but what used to be described in Scotland as a "lad o' pairts"—a gifted individual from humble origins who succeeds in life through education. Brought up in the "bracing, simple surroundings" of his father's small farm at Mains of Dudwick, near Ellon, James excelled as a pupil at New Pitsligo Parish School and, in spite of financial hardship, went on to gain degrees from the Universities of Edinburgh and Aberdeen. During his visit to Rossie Priory, he met a young lady from a very different social background: Rosina Constance Agnew, daughter of Sir Andrew Agnew (1818–92), MP for Wigtownshire. Sir Andrew had five sons and eight daughters, one of whom (Mary) had married Arthur Fitzgerald, the 11th Lord Kinnaird—hence the house party at Rossie. Although Constance had been brought up as an Episcopalian at her home at Lochnaw Castle, Wigtownshire, the Agnew family had connections with the Free Church and Sir Andrew's younger brother, the Rev. David Agnew, had been ordained by the Free Presbytery of Ayr shortly after the Disruption of 1843 when nearly a third of the ministers and members of the Established Church left to form the Free Church.

1

Nowadays, it is very difficult to imagine the opulence of the great aristocratic houses of more than a century ago. Rossie Priory was a vast edifice in Regency Gothic style, described in the *Ordnance Survey Gazetteer of Scotland* for 1885 as "a superb, monastic-looking pile, spacious and elegant within, [containing] a valuable collection of antiquities, chiefly Roman."[1] Arthur, the 11th Lord Kinnaird (1847–1923), spent much of his time in London but returned each year for the shooting season; a typical season's "bag" comprised 5,000 rabbits, 698 partridges, 1,215 pheasants and six roe deer. Educated at Eton and Cambridge, Kinnaird is remembered above all for his skill as a footballer and for being a key figure in the Football Association. He was a keen cricketer, too, and employed a professional to teach his estate workers the game so that his friends from England would have someone to play against.[2] He also espoused the "muscular Christianity" popular in the late nineteenth century, valuing athleticism and patriotic duty over intellectualism. His sister Emily played a prominent part in the early days of the YWCA (Young Women's Christian Association) and later served as a missionary in India where she became a friend of Mahatma Gandhi.

Rossie Priory in Perthshire, the seat of the Kinnaird family. Started in 1807, the building was successively enlarged during the nineteenth century but much of it has been demolished and the house today is considerably less elaborate than it would have been in Nevile Davidson's youth, when he regularly visited his aunt who had married the 11th Lord Kinnaird.

1. Groome, *Gazetteer of Scotland*, 264
2. www.scottishsporthistory.com/rossie-priory.html

Even in the 1920s an indoor staff of thirty was employed in Arthur Kinnaird's sprawling house, in addition to all the tenants of his farming land, but by the time of the second World War Rossie was hopelessly impractical to run, riddled with dry rot and much of it had to be demolished. With no surviving male heir, the Kinnaird title eventually became dormant in 1997 on the death of the 13th Lord. In his youth, Nevile made regular visits to his Kinnaird cousins at Rossie and it is tempting to speculate that the 11th Lord's manly brand of Christianity may have had some influence on him; certainly, his cousin Emily's connections with India would prove extremely useful many years later when he toured that country after it achieved independence in 1947.

Rev. James Davidson and Constance Agnew were married in April 1898 in London and their son, Andrew Nevile Davidson, was born on February 13, 1899, followed two years later by his sister, Louisa Margaret Constance, who was always known as "Cois" (pronounced to rhyme with "Joyce"). Mr. Davidson was minister of Blackadder Church in North Berwick but the privileged upbringing his two children received at the family home at 76 Westbourne Terrace was far from typical of a Scottish manse: Nevile writes in his autobiography that "as I grew up the household included a cook, a young housemaid, an elderly laundry maid, and my sister's governess,"[3] all of whom were closely supervised by his mother who was "determined and autocratic, never hesitating to rebuke or express disapproval . . . For us children, her word was law."[4] As well as enjoying a comfortable manse provided by his church, Mr. Davidson Senior was able—thanks to his advantageous marriage—to acquire some land at Nethy Bridge for the sum of £2,000 and he built Forest House there in 1910. His son wrote: "Completely secluded, the house had three sitting rooms and eight bedrooms and so allowed us to have many friends and relations to stay. For the next sixty years it was to be my second home."[5]

3. Davidson, *Beginnings*, 2
4. Davidson, *Beginnings*, 4
5. Davidson, *Beginnings*, 6

Nevile Davidson's father was minister of Blackadder Free Church which became part of the new United Free Church in 1900. The building still stands and is now North Berwick Baptist Church.

Between his aristocratic relatives in Perthshire and his father's congregation in North Berwick, young Nevile soon learnt to move easily in all social circles, a skill which stood him in good stead in later life when he felt equally at home mixing with royalty as he did with his parishioners in the crowded tenements of Glasgow's Townhead.

Other than sketching his family background, Nevile Davidson's autobiography *Beginnings but no Ending* says little else about his early years. It does not mention, for example, that in 1912, at the age of thirteen, he spent three months traveling through France with his family. This was the first occasion on which he kept a diary which chronicles a lengthy trip beginning on January 30 with a train journey to York where "we went to the Minster service. It was perfectly beautiful to hear the little boys singing." In York he bought a copy of Charles Dickens's *The Pickwick Papers*, no doubt to read on the next stage of the journey to London where the Davidsons stayed with relatives before crossing to France on February 6. In Paris the family visited the Louvre and the church of the Madeleine and attended services at the American church in the morning and the French Protestant church in the evening. Young Nevile also took French lessons and spent a long time looking round the shops where he bought himself a walking stick. Then it was on to Limoges, Orleans, Lourdes, San Sebastian, St. Jean de Luz ("a nice quiet little place") and Biarritz ("a very ugly town"). The journey continued through Angoulême, Bordeaux and Blois until, by April 16, he was back in Paris going round the department stores again. "In one of the shops," he notes, "we went up a little moving staircase and it was very amusing."[6]

The diary stops at this point, but these early reflections of a thirteen year old are interesting because they hint at certain themes which recur in his later life. His comments on York Minster reveal that, even as a child, he felt the attraction of a more elaborate and ritualistic service than he would have been used to in his father's United Free Church, while the purchase of a walking stick suggests a degree of vanity about his appearance. As a young man he spent a good deal of money on clothes.

Until the age of sixteen Nevile attended North Berwick High School; apparently, sending him to a boarding school was not something his father approved of. At school he preferred subjects that dealt with ideas rather than facts, particularly disliking mathematics, and claimed he did only the minimum of work to get by. Even so, in his fifth year Nevile was writing in depth about texts such as Thomas Carlyle's *The French Revolution: A History*, Milton's *Paradise Lost*, Shakespeare's *Much Ado About Nothing*, and Horace's *Odes* and his surviving essays reveal a facility with words and a breadth of reading far beyond the level of the average teenager today.

6. NOTE: unless the source is specifically acknowledged in a footnote, all short quotations throughout this book in Nevile Davidson's own words come from the pages of his personal diaries.

His flair for sentence structures which build to a climax and other rhetorical devices may well have been influenced by the pulpit oratory he would hear week by week from his father and other preachers, while the content of one (untitled) effort dated May 1914 reveals a youthful awareness of a spiritual dimension to life, even if only vaguely defined in terms reminiscent of Wordsworth's "dim and undetermined sense/Of unknown modes of being":

> There are times when the soul of man seems to be roused from a temporary sleep in which it has been indulging; when, as if at the call of some great power, it leaps to a high level and, soaring 'through realms unknown'; leaves behind the things of this world, stretching, yearning towards the infinite. The call comes at divers times according to condition and circumstance, but almost every soul must feel this impulsive longing at one time or another.

The essay goes on (at considerable length) to explain how this "call" may be experienced in mountains, beside lochs or out on the moors and concludes with a poetic flourish that is not unlike the closing appeal of a sermon:

> If you be but a beggar in some great dark city, even then you have your little patch of blue sky between the roofs and your little beam of sun which finds its way into every miserable garret and hovel. Look up, then! And as you look the bird of hope will descend, borne on wings of gold and alight on *your* shoulder; yea, and carry you up beyond the roofs and chimneys and the world will seem a cheerier place thereafter and life not quite so hopeless.

Nevile Davidson left school in 1915 to matriculate at Edinburgh University—something he later regretted, realizing that he was too immature for the experience. As a future preacher and moderator of the General Assembly, he might have been expected to show early promise as a debater but he claims to have been too shy to join the Debating Society. At university he studied Latin, History and his favorite subject, English Literature but, like many young men of his generation, his course was interrupted by the first World War. While a member of the university OTC (Officers' Training Corps) he attended Barry Camp near Carnoustie—where, in September 1917, he took ill and had to be sent home for an appendix operation—and thereafter applied for a commission in the Royal Artillery, undergoing training at cadet school on the Isle of Wight. But hostilities came to an end before he saw active service and in 1919 he went back to Edinburgh

University, having now decided to study Philosophy, partly because he did not like the English course as it placed too much emphasis on Anglo-Saxon texts. Philosophy, he wrote,

> took me into a field of study concerned not with facts, but with thoughts, ideas and speculations; the place of man in the universe, the existence of God, the possibility of immortality, different kinds of reasoning and of knowledge.[7]

However, his autobiography reveals more about his opinions of his professors and the content of their lectures than about himself, saying only that, because he continued to live at home and commute to Edinburgh, "I took little part in the wider life of the university and simply attended classes."[8] He also considers himself to have been a poor scholar, lacking in academic ambition and self-discipline and suffering from the "besetting sin of idleness." He confesses that he did not read all the prescribed texts and when the final exams came round he failed to achieve first class honors as expected. This temporarily cast a cloud over his normally close relationship with his father. "When I told my father the news he made no comment, but walked out of the room and scarcely spoke to me for the next few days."[9]

A much fuller picture of how Nevile Davidson spent his time as a student can be gained from the series of diaries which he began writing in 1920. A typical day might involve attendance at lectures, lunch with friends at the Students' Union or the restaurant in Jenner's department store in Princes Street, a visit to friends or members of his extended family and perhaps a game of golf and some hours reading. This latter activity he did at least undertake in a methodical manner, recording in his diary the books he was reading for each assignment. From these entries, it is clear that he read widely and did not confine himself to his textbooks. In the spring of 1920, for example, he had various weighty historical and literary works on the go: David Hume's *Dialogues Concerning Natural Religion*, Thomas Carlyle's *Frederick the Great* ("I wonder if I shall ever finish it!"), Lytton Strachey's *Eminent Victorians*; H.G. Wells's *The Outline of History* and—for light relief—Wells's novel about anarchism, *The Man who was Thursday*. Essay assignments would be preceded by a couple of weeks' intensive reading in preparation for answering searching questions like "Why is it better

---

7. Davidson, *Beginnings*, 6
8. Davidson, *Beginnings*, 5
9. Davidson, *Beginnings*, 7

to be Socrates dissatisfied than a fool satisfied?" or "The Deity: his existence and his attributes." Sometimes he fell behind with his work and on at least one occasion managed to persuade his professor to give him an extension until the following Monday. That Friday night, he sat up working on his essay from 11 p.m. until 3.15 a.m.

He also had literary ambitions of his own and began writing a novel entitled *The Education of Michael Fothringham,* about an only child aged sixteen living in a large house called "the Hermitage." Brought up by his mother after the death of his father, Michael is a lonely boy who had been "early initiated into the world of books" and loves to ramble in the extensive grounds of the estate. Suddenly, the "impenetrable security" of his life is interrupted by the death of his mother. Though nominally brought up in the Church of Scotland, Michael has no faith to draw on to support him in "this first great crisis in his life" and after a further two years he begins to feel the need of a change of scene. Sadly, the manuscript stops at this point and Nevile seems to have abandoned the project.

In addition to his studies and his writing, Nevile was teaching a Sunday School class at his father's church and had to prepare his lessons, but his efforts do not appear to have been appreciated by the pupils. His diary entry on June 6, 1920 reads: "Prepared lesson and went to church and Sunday School. Again had only two; so never again!" Nevertheless, by October he had once more offered to take classes and he not only drew up a series of lessons on "Heroes of the Old Testament" but wrote personal letters to eleven prospective members of his Bible class and cycled round to deliver them by hand.

These demands on his time did not prevent the young Nevile Davidson from enjoying life. In December 1920 he and his fellow students treated themselves to a visit to the carnival where they saw "the Ugliest Woman on Earth" and "The World's Fattest Boy." He sometimes sat up late playing the gramophone and even attended dances on occasions. High spirits were in evidence when he and a friend were at the house of their tutor, the Rev. Mr. Moir where, he writes, "We fooled about, tried on Mr. Moir's gown and I went out and posted a letter [wearing] his clerical hat."

When not trying on other people's clothes, he spent a good deal of time choosing his own. Asked to do readings in church, he felt it necessary to go out and order some new shirts. He noted in his diary on January 1, 1922 that "My second overcoat came from Burberry's and didn't fit much better than the first." By March he was worried about "money affairs which have reached a point uncomfortably near zero" but still went ahead and ordered some patterns for a new suit. "I bought several pairs of socks and stockings at wonderful prices. There are sales everywhere." With an eye to further bargains, he was often to be found going round shops in Edinburgh in search of books, pictures and antiques—something he enjoyed doing throughout his life.

The young man was always taking up new hobbies and he would read up on the subject or take lessons to improve his skills. He became interested in photography after receiving a Kodak "Autographic" camera for his twenty-first birthday. In 1920 he was going regularly to the swimming baths where he had diving lessons. In 1921 he was practicing the piano every day and taking lessons from Marjorie Kennedy-Fraser (1857–1930), the Scottish musician famous for collecting and arranging the traditional songs of the Hebrides. In 1923 he developed an enthusiasm for birdwatching, spending the huge sum of five guineas on a book called *Game Birds and Wild Fowl of Great Britain*. Another passion that year was antique furniture and he spent time with a local furniture trader named Willie Auld adding to his knowledge. He paid £22 and ten shillings for a walnut bureau from Mr Auld and arranged to have the top inlaid instead of green baize. Nevile still had much to learn, though: when Auld came round to see a table he had purchased, the verdict was that it was pretty but not a genuine period piece, and when he contacted Sotheby's with a view to selling some Bohemian glasses he was disappointed to be told that they were "not suitable for inclusion in one of their sales."

In addition to all these pastimes, he had a busy social life with his Kinnaird and Agnew cousins and his numerous friends—many of them girls. During the summer months he played a good deal of tennis and went long cycling excursions into the countryside around North Berwick. "Tea at Eastfield", reads an intriguing diary entry dated July 8, 1922. "Suzan and Penelope there too. Dined at St. Margaret's! A *very* pleasant evening." The Davidson family would often travel north to stay at Rossie Priory, particularly over the festive season, where Nevile enthusiastically joined in the leisure activities of his well-heeled cousins. "Kenneth, Teddy and I shot in the morning", he writes in December 1923. "A mixed bag of pheasants, woodcock, pigeons, hares, rabbits (I shot very badly and only killed a hare and a rabbit)." Class distinctions were temporarily laid aside on Christmas Eve when "after tea about ten of the maids came to the Picture Gallery and we played Blind Man's Buff, Fox and Geese, etc." and on Boxing Day when everyone attended a big party for all the estate workers.

Then there was his motorcycle. On January 27, 1923 he ordered a 2¾ horsepower Bradbury and, with typical enthusiasm, started teaching himself motor mechanics. By March he knew how to dismantle the carburetor and, more importantly, how to reassemble it. But the Bradbury proved to be a source of endless trouble. Once, the exhaust fell off and he had to wheel it ignominiously home; another time, a valve broke four miles from Jedburgh and he had to leave the bike in charge of an AA (Automobile Association) officer. In May he had an accident in Murrayfield Place, Edinburgh, where, he writes, "I tore my only respectable dark suit badly." Worst of all, he found himself at the Sheriff Court in Edinburgh in October where he was fined £1 for having his number plate covered and ten shillings for failing to show his license!

But the youthful Nevile Davidson was not spending all of his time on frivolous pursuits. After his finals in June 1921 the family immediately set off on a trip abroad, sailing from Southampton to Rotterdam and visiting towns in Holland, but by August he was back home systematically reading through the books of the Old Testament and turning his thoughts towards the future. As was common at the time, his parents assumed he would follow in his father's footsteps, but he was as yet unsure of any strong sense of a calling to the ministry. He nevertheless sat, and passed, the entrance exam for the Divinity course at New College, Edinburgh, which was followed by much soul-searching. At one point he even considered whether he ought to be a sheep farmer.

Nevile had always been close to his father, particularly after the loss of his mother, who died at home from cancer in June 1920 after a lengthy illness. Strangely, he says nothing about her death in his diary, other than describing how, towards the end of her life, a group of elders joined the family in the manse for a service of communion at which his mother was anointed with oil in strict obedience to James 5:14: "Is anyone among you sick? Let them call the elders of the church to pray over them and anoint them with oil in the name of the Lord."

Whenever father and son were apart, they kept each other fully informed of their activities. During World War I Mr. Davidson volunteered with the YMCA (Young Men's Christian Association) in France and two letters to his "darling Nevile" have survived from that time. From these it is clear that he closely monitored every step of his son's studies, constantly instilling into him the need to fulfil his potential and urging him—as Polonius did Laertes—to "thine own self be true." The following extract from a letter sent from Dieppe on YMCA notepaper, dated September 20, 1918, is typical:

> Above all things shun those who only drift with the mob, who follow the rout—seek to be individual, singular, a born leader. It may be a hard road at the outset but it is the heroic and the happy road . . . I know you have splendid abilities, charm of manner—high ideals and loyalty to the Lord and if you add to it this one thing more—scorn mob leadership—your battle is won. It is the first step that counts. Distrust your own strength—Pray about everything and God bless you my darling boy.

Another (undated) letter urges Nevile to "honestly labour to discover what God would have you do and having discovered do not look back. I am praying for you all the time so that you may not by any mischance miss the best."

Nevile's dilemma about whether to embark on a Divinity course was temporarily resolved when he received a letter from Professor Kemp Smith (1872–1958), under whom he had studied Logic and Metaphysics, offering him a part-time assistantship in Philosophy, at a salary of £100. He decided to accept the post and put off entering New College for a year. He was also awarded a prestigious Vans Dunlop scholarship and these two sources of income made him feel he was financially independent and had "no need to ask father for help"—though, like many a student, he conveniently forgot that he was benefiting from free board and lodging at home.

The work mainly involved relieving his academic colleagues of the drudgery of routine correction of essays and exam scripts, a task which Nevile found fairly time-consuming. At the same time, he was taking a considerable interest in church matters and looking ahead to his future ministry. Sometimes he went to St. John's Episcopal Church in Princes Street where "I enjoyed the Church of England service, as always" but he also attended Charlotte (Baptist) Chapel in Edinburgh's Rose Street, a major center of evangelistic preaching. The minister of Charlotte Chapel was W. Graham Scroggie (1877–1958), well-known as a speaker at the Keswick Convention, a large Christian gathering held each summer in the Lake District. Nevile commented on one "very inspiring sermon (fifty minutes!)" by Scroggie and sometimes visited him at home. In 1920 Scroggie formed the Charlotte Chapel Evangelistic Association to hold meetings outside Edinburgh and in January 1922 Nevile attended a series of daily meetings held in the North Berwick area "in the hope of causing a religious revival."

Even in these early years Nevile's breadth of theological outlook is apparent. While instinctively a high churchman, he was equally sympathetic to the evangelical wing of the church and a recurring theme of his long ministry is his awareness of the need to take the message of the gospel to those outside the institutional church.

But he was not only listening to other preachers; he preached his own first sermon on the evening of the first Sunday of the New Year in 1922 in the United Free Church at Nethy Bridge, choosing as his text the Apostle Paul's words in Philippians 3:13: "forgetting those things which are behind and reaching forth unto those things which are before." He read his draft aloud to his father and sister, and then rewrote it. On January 1, he "got thro' the service somehow." Later that month, after reading the biographies of great Scottish churchmen like Thomas Chalmers and Robert Murray McCheyne, he decided that he "really must at once read the Shorter Catechism and the Westminster Confession of Faith!!"

In October 1922 Nevile Davidson began his Divinity course at New College and resumed his student routine. In the mornings there were three classes: Natural Science at 10 a.m., Old Testament at 11 and Apologetics at 12—"all going to be interesting I think." Though he self-deprecatingly writes that "I was not enough of a scholar to feel the fascination of detailed textual criticism," he did respond imaginatively to the lectures in theology: "The field of thought, for the philosopher, is dominated by reason, but in Christian theology a new concept appears, revelation, made supremely in a Person, Jesus Christ."[10] As in his undergraduate years, after classes he would lunch out, visit, go home to North Berwick, read, walk, play golf or badminton or indulge in his favorite activity: long conversations with his friends. One he was particularly close to at this time was Ian Simpson, who later became minister of Ceres in Fife and many a diary entry recalls their late night discussions: "Ian came back to supper as usual and we talked theology afterwards, he still being absorbed in his 'Controversial Exercise' on the Kenotic Theories[11] and a paper on the Holy Spirit in St. John's Gospel."

10. Davidson, *Beginnings*, 9

11. "The kenotic theory of Christ's incarnation—drawing from Philippians

In addition to such abstruse intellectual speculations, Divinity students were expected to become involved in more down-to-earth activities that would prepare them for the pastoral side of their ministry. Nevile attended meetings of the New College Missionary Society and did some work in connection with the Edinburgh University Settlement, part of a wider movement that was popular at this period, the idea being to bring students from the more privileged sections of society into contact with their less fortunate brethren. He found helping out at Saturday night Settlement concerts to be "great fun." After one of these, he went back to Ian Simpson's, where "we talked till 12.45 a.m. and ate grapefruit and drank Sanatogen [a tonic wine]."

The future minister continued to take a fairly relaxed attitude to his studies and his diary frequently gives an insight into the tension he felt between duty and pleasure:

> Tried to get on with my paper on "Sin" but thought it an unsuitable subject of meditation for a sunny spring day. So rode over the hill to Haddington; found a moorhen's nest just behind the abbey in the stream, and then bought a charming old colored print of the Bass Rock (£2) at Leslie's. In the afternoon went round to Willie Auld's and had 1½ hours of instruction in old furniture. Started writing my paper on 'Sin' in the evening (having committed the sin of idleness all day!)

The same point is summed up even more succinctly on May 30, 1923 when he wrote, "Discussed immortality with father and read my book on old furniture." Eventually, on March 11, 1924, he was able to record: "Last day of classes!" A week later the results were announced, and he achieved a respectable 84% in Dogmatics, 77% in Christian Ethics and 71% in Church History.

The next day the family set off on holiday for Cornwall. Nevile's sister Cois had by this time started to take an interest in the Roman Catholic church, and much to her father's dismay, insisted on attending RC services while they were away. This caused a good deal of tension as in these days "a convert to Roman Catholicism was inevitably separated in some degree

---

2—articulates a doctrine of the incarnation in terms of Christ emptying himself and becoming a servant. According to kenotic theory, Christ abandoned aspects of his omniscience, omnipresence, and omnipotence in order to 'humble himself' and become a human being." *(www.logos.com/resourcesLLS_HALLDOGTH15/the-kenotic-theory)* One can readily appreciate how this would provide two Divinity students with plenty of material for late-night discussions.

from other members of the family at the deepest level."[12] A diary entry from this period states that "Cousin Agneta (who is here for a short visit) came in after tea and debated as violently as ever about Roman Catholicism (and left quite convinced that I was practically a Jesuit already!)" Another Kinnaird cousin, seventy-five year old Louisa, wrote to Nevile that she had heard the "sad news" about Cois, and attributed it to her being "under the spell" of two Catholic friends from the aristocratic Lothian family. "How *can* she believe in the Pope as the Vicar of God upon earth and in transubstantiation and in absolution by a man tho' he calls himself a priest?" lamented Louisa. "It makes life so much more difficult for you all . . . You can no longer rely on Cois' sympathy in your work and your aspirations. It is a sad loss."

Cois entered a Carmelite Convent in London and Nevile records an occasion when there was "great excitement over a telephone call from Cois proposing to come home for a few days but father sadly refused." It seems that in due course Mr. Davidson relented to the extent that Cois was allowed to make visits home, but she never again lived permanently with her father and the terms of his will make it clear that he never fully got over what he saw as her betrayal. His estate was to be divided equally between his son and daughter, but Cois was to receive only the interest on her half as income, with the capital going to Nevile on her death (although, in the event, Nevile predeceased her).[13] This action was taken as it was felt that any capital inherited by Cois would have been handed over to the Catholic Church authorities. Still handling the matter in 1940, a decade after her father's death, the family solicitors made reference in a letter to "the great sorrow that was Mr Davidson's, so heroically borne, caused by his daughter's action."

The effects of Cois' conversion on her brother were more complex and profound, and Nevile chose not to discuss the subject in public. However, among his papers in the National Library of Scotland there are some random sheets of notes, jotted down when he first began to consider writing his autobiography but never used and these are considerably more forthcoming than the guarded comments he makes in the published book, and even in his private diaries. Referring to Cois' conversion to Catholicism, he says:

> this unexpected happening in our family circle with all its implications brought home to me, as perhaps nothing else could have

12. Davidson, *Beginnings,* 10
13. Cois died in 1989

done, the realization that there are many different gates in the city of God, that different branches of the church have different distinctive insights and customs, and that all have much to learn from each other.

Nevile continues by explaining that what attracted Cois to the Catholic church was the beauty of the ritual, the sense of ancient tradition and the deep spiritual quality of certain biographies she had been reading—all factors to which he, too, felt emotionally drawn. Moreover, in the early years of his ministry he read books which are very likely to have been passed onto him by his sister, such as Ignatius Loyola's *Spiritual Exercises* and works by Friedrich von Hügel, an influential Austrian Roman Catholic layman, and the German theologian Friedrich Heiler, who originally came from an RC family.

> These and similar books took me into a wider field of theological reading than I had till then discovered. In all of them [there was] a new sense of the importance of the inner life of prayer and worship and a new sense of the supernatural and transcendent. Here was an approach which could do much to deepen the individual life of the Christian and also to enrich and deepen public worship. [This] led me to the idea of the value of Retreat, almost unknown in the life of our church.

All of this goes a long way to explaining why the son of a former Free Church minister developed into a "Scoto-Catholic"[14] Presbyterian and ideas which would play a key role in the younger Davidson's later ministry—his emphasis on the aesthetic qualities of worship, his fondness for liturgy and ceremony and his enthusiasm for ecumenical co-operation—may well owe their origins to his sister's influence. For whatever reason, though, Nevile did not include any of this in his autobiography.

In spite of Louisa Kinnaird's fears, brother and sister always remained close. Cois suffered from a bad back and various internal ailments and on one occasion required an emergency operation for appendicitis. By September 1929 a surgeon had declared her medically unfit for convent life and she returned to Scotland and lived in Aberdeen for some years. For the rest of his life, Nevile was always ready to help his sister and on numerous occasions dropped everything and traveled to see her when she was ill or in some kind of difficulty. A somewhat eccentric individual, Cois would

---

14. See Chapter 12

impulsively give away her money and possessions to the needy—and then ask her brother for money to buy herself a coat.

Although there were no strict rules about serving a probationary year before ordination in these days, it was clearly wise to have a period of pastoral apprenticeship under some experienced minister, and Nevile was invited to become assistant to the Rev. Dr. James Black (1879–1949) of Free St. George's (later St. George's West) in Shandwick Place, Edinburgh. April 6 1924 was a significant day: "put on my dog collar for the first time." Three weeks later, he wore gown, cassock and bands while taking services at Fountainbridge Church where he "felt more at ease in the pulpit than ever before."

As well as dressing for the part, the young preacher was developing the skill of self-evaluation. Speaking again at Fountainbridge in July, instead of using a fully-scripted sermon he "preached from notes (tho' pretty full ones) for the first time: much too fast and a good deal of repetition, but felt it much easier to hold their attention." He also bought some notebooks in which he collected "references, illustrations and beautiful phrases." At St. George's, he carried out parish visitation, conducted funerals and took charge of prayers and readings on Sundays but was rarely allowed to preach. He found the ostentatious wealth of the St. George's congregation "alarming" and the atmosphere of complacency "disturbing." Nor was he impressed by the famous Dr. Black's over-dramatic preaching style. Nevile Davidson was never a flamboyant preacher and one of his colleagues later remarked that his spell at St. George's had made him react against the theatrical type of preaching popular at the time. By February 1925 he was writing to his father telling him that he felt depressed and mentally tired, and could not stand another month at St. George's.

Nevile Davidson had served his apprenticeship. The time had come for him to take on the challenge of a church of his own.

# 2

# "Something a Little More Strenuous"

## MINISTRIES AT ABERDEEN AND DUNDEE, 1925–1934

1925 WAS A TURNING-POINT in the lives of both James and Nevile Davidson, marking the end of one ministry and the beginning of another.

In January a number of vacancies came to the attention of the aspiring preacher, among them the United Free congregations of Greenlaw in Berwickshire, Callander and Old Aberdeen. On February 8 he preached at Greenlaw but felt he was "rather dull." One of the church elders showed him round the village and manse and he stayed overnight at the Blackadder Temperance Hotel, where there was only a young English commercial traveler for company. The following week Nevile wrote to the interim moderator at St. Mary's, Old Aberdeen regarding arrangements for preaching there on March 1, noting in his diary that he had decided not to pursue the Greenlaw option as "I thought I ought to look out for something a little more strenuous."

So, on February 28, he took the train to Aberdeen, arriving on a "grey day with drizzling rain." He stayed with his aunts, had tea with the interim moderator and on the Sunday preached on "The Kingdom of God is within you" in the morning and the rich young ruler (Matthew 19) in the evening. The vacancy committee was impressed and invited him to preach as sole nominee on March 22.

Meanwhile, the health of James Davidson, who was now in his late sixties, had deteriorated and he was beginning to have memory lapses. His doctor strongly recommended that the time had come for him to retire and when Nevile received a unanimous call to Aberdeen, it was decided that his father would come and live with him. The contents of the manse at North Berwick were hastily packed up and at 8.30 a.m. on March 28 a cart called to collect six trunks and kit bags to be sent by train to Aberdeen. With some sadness, the Davidsons vacated the house where brother and sister had lived all their lives.

A few months earlier Nevile had acquired his first car. Having nearly decided on a Morris Cowley he took a trial run in the latest Swift model—the first one to arrive in Edinburgh—and bought it for £250. The garage gave him some lessons on how to drive and maintain it but Nevile proved to be a reckless driver: after owning the Swift for little over a week he took off on his own "to test her, and did 44 m.p.h. still accelerating." A few days later the car rolled off the road and nearly overturned and he had to call on five men working in a nearby nursery garden for assistance. Before long he found himself in trouble with the law again, for failing to stop in time, which led to another £1 fine at the Burgh Court.

Once the elder Mr. Davidson had been safely sent up to Rossie Priory at the end of March 1925 to stay with the Kinnairds, Nevile and Cois set off on the long drive to Aberdeen, taking turns at the wheel. Unable to get overnight accommodation at Tyndrum, they crossed Rannoch Moor but again found no vacancies at the Kingshouse Hotel. So the intrepid pair pressed on through Glencoe "in pouring rain and a hurricane of wind," reaching the Clachaig Inn at Ballachulish at midnight where, after much knocking and a conversation through the letterbox, the door was at last opened by two women and a man wielding a large stick.

Sunday was spent at Fort William, where Nevile attended the parish church and Cois the Catholic one. Next day, on the moors near Inverness, they were caught in a blinding snow storm which made driving difficult but the Swift finally made it to the Aberdeen manse at 9 p.m., where brother and sister were greeted by two newly-employed maids.

Before taking up his new duties, Nevile had time for a holiday in the Aberdeen area, playing golf and visiting relations. There was also much discussion about wallpapers, chintzes, curtains and furniture to ensure that the décor of the manse at 92 High Street suited his fastidious tastes.

St. Mary's Church, Aberdeen, was Nevile Davidson's first charge. It closed in 1944 when the congregation re-united with St. Machar's Cathedral from which it had split a century earlier at the Disruption. The building was subsequently purchased by the University of Aberdeen.

The ordination and induction took place on May 14, with a social gathering the next evening attended by 730 people. The new minister preached for the first time at the evening service on the following Sunday, delivering a sermon lasting thirty minutes and, as an indication of his intention to take the pastoral side of his role seriously, met with the kirk session immediately afterwards to collect the names of members of the congregation who were ill. His senior elder was no less a figure than Sir George Adam Smith (1856–1942), Old Testament scholar and Principal of Aberdeen University, but the session was made up of a cross-section of men from all social classes. No women elders in these days, of course.

So began a new routine of mornings usually spent on sermon preparation, a pre-lunchtime stroll with his father, parish visitation or social calls in the afternoon and frequent church meetings or other functions in the evenings. One early domestic mishap that he had to deal with involved his new cook, who went out one evening and failed to return. Nevile went to her home, to the hospital and to the police station but could find no trace of what had happened to her and it was only when he called back at her house the following morning that the explanation became clear: "she had obviously been drinking."

The cook is not mentioned again in the diaries, but one comment that does recur frequently is that sermon writing did not come easily to him. Often he would be putting the finishing touches to the next day's addresses on the Saturday morning. In his preaching, the new minister strove to follow the example of his Master who "showed us how it is possible to speak on the profoundest themes in simple and homely language."[1] It is said that the famous nineteenth century Edinburgh Free Church preacher Dr. Thomas Guthrie used to call his maid into his study to listen to him rehearsing his sermon, after which he would cut out any difficult words she had not understood. The equivalent for Nevile Davidson was a "fine working man" called John Cowie, "a carter of meagre education but of upright character and strong faith,"[2] whom he used as a representative of the kind of parishioner who should be able to benefit from his preaching. Sermons were generally based on texts taken from anywhere in the Scriptures but as time went on they tended to form part of a series, starting with "Foundations of Faith: Fundamental Doctrines of Christianity." Later came a series on the Lord's Prayer and on "Essential Elements in the Christian Life" (these being defined as suffering, joy and effort), the life of Jacob and a "Christological course" on various aspects of Christ's character.

Clearly, the preacher's desire that his sermons should be intelligible to ordinary people did not imply any "dumbing down" of the subject matter.

Nevile Davidson always favored order and decorum and emphasized the aesthetic dimension of worship—priorities that would soon become apparent in various changes he made to his Aberdeen church. But he was equally aware of the need to take the Christian message beyond the church walls and after barely a month's experience as a minister was thrown in at the deep end when he took part in an outreach campaign run by Aberdeen United Free Church Presbytery on summer Sunday evenings. This involved standing on the platform of a horse-drawn lorry in Castlegate, addressing any passers-by who might stop to listen and attempting to answer their questions.

1. Davidson, *Beginnings,* 14
2. Davidson, *Beginnings,* 14

In these days before television, public meetings were well-attended and heckling was all part of the fun, so the ministers braced themselves for something similar—and they were not disappointed.

At the first event in June Nevile presided while his colleague, Rev. John Rankine of Trinity UF church faced a barrage of questions. After doing his best for forty minutes, Mr. Rankine was asked by a man at the back: "Can you tell us what a miracle is?" Beginning to lose his patience by this stage, Rankine rather unwisely retorted, "He's asking me to tell him what a miracle is. I'm beginning to think it will be a miracle if I get a sensible question!"

"Is that the way you answer a question?" fired back his interrogator. "In Parliament they never turn their backs on a speaker, minister. It is a terrible cheap-jack way you are talking."

"Do you really want me to answer your question?" asked Rankine. "A miracle is something that goes beyond our understanding."

But the questioner was still not satisfied. "If a miracle happened to-night," he continued, "and the same thing happened tomorrow, would it be a miracle then?"

"Yes," replied Rankine.

"Oh, dear! I never heard the like of such nonsense!" exclaimed the questioner. "A miracle can only occur once, man!"[3]

Though his legs were shaking when he first stood up to speak on the back of the lorry, Nevile Davidson seems to have had an easier ride than the hapless Mr. Rankine when he spoke on the question: "Is there a judgment?" Hardly anyone nowadays paid any attention to this subject, he said, partly because they did not like it, but the Bible left no doubt that there would be a final judgment. Men had found it difficult to reconcile the doctrine of eternal punishment with a God of love but God, having given us freewill, could not prevent us choosing evil if we want to choose it.[4]

It was an impeccably orthodox explanation which showed the young minister had conscientiously studied his Divinity textbooks.

Not all of the questioners raised issues of such theological depth: when one asked facetiously whether celibacy was the best way of getting into Heaven, Davidson said that was a difficult question for him to answer as he was a bachelor. The question and answer sessions usually lasted about forty

---

3. *Aberdeen Press and Journal*, June 17 1929
4. *Aberdeen Press and Journal*, August 12 1929

minutes and the preacher often had to compete with a rival Communist orator to gain the attention of the large crowds who invariably turned up.

These open-air sessions were just one example of how the young Nevile Davidson played his part in the wider church affairs of Aberdeen. He also supported by his presence a mission campaign in October 1925, when hundreds queued outside the Music Hall to hear the evangelist Rodney Smith (1860–1947), better known as "Gipsy" Smith on account of his upbringing. In March of the following year, he met with other Aberdeen clergy to protest against a license to open on a Sunday being granted to the Palais de Dance, though he clearly did not object to dances in principle, as his deacons' court voted later that year to allow the congregation's women's social to hold them. St. Mary's also held regular social events for new members and in addition to the usual youth organizations there was a badminton club, at which the minister sometimes joined in. He was also happy to play Santa Claus at Sunday School Christmas parties!

At the same time, Nevile was keen to introduce a number of innovations of his own. One of these was his belief that the sanctuary should be open every day and in August 1925, about three months after taking up his new charge, he persuaded his kirk session to agree to this by offering personally to unlock the doors each morning. A noticeboard was erected stating that "This House of God is open daily for prayer and meditation"— though on one occasion the sign was stolen by some high-spirited students, who later returned it. Nevile developed the habit of spending time in quiet devotional reading each morning in the empty church. At times he followed the *Spiritual Exercises* of Ignatius Loyola, founder of the Jesuit Order in the sixteenth century—of whom his cousin had earlier suspected him of being a disciple. In 1928 he turned to Loyola again during Lent, only to record a few days later in his diary: "Alas! Have not been able to keep up the *Spiritual Exercises* at all, owing to pressure of work."

One can only guess at the elder Mr. Davidson's reaction to his son's choice of reading material. He would have been still more horrified in February 1928 when Nevile received "a letter and a miraculous picture of the Blessed Virgin from Cois from the Carmelite convent in London."

But the United Free Church of Scotland wasn't quite ready for pictures of the Virgin Mary, as Nevile discovered the following January when he returned from a visit to London. He had purchased a reproduction of *The Adoration of the Magi* by the fifteenth century Florentine Renaissance artist Fra Filippo Lippi which he had taken to the Medici Society's gallery for framing, with the intention of hanging it in his "children's corner" in the church. But a painting by an Italian friar depicting the Madonna and Child did not meet with the approval of the church elders. A kirk session meeting was held to discuss the matter which decided that picture should be removed. Nevile's diary comment was a single word: "disappointing."

In spite of this setback, the young minister did succeed in taking small steps towards the introduction of a more visual dimension to his rather austere sanctuary, especially with a view to appealing to children. In 1927 he held a big Christmas service for children which attracted a congregation of about 450. At this, he set up a large picture of the cradle scene surrounded by holly and lights. And those who abhor modern styles of worship using screens might be surprised that Nevile sometimes employed the equivalent technology of his day: for another children's service in 1928 a magic lantern was hired from Lizar's photographic shop and he showed slides of the Easter story.

Nevile was also able to carry his congregation with him in his desire to beautify the church building. After taking a break at the house at Nethy Bridge in April 1928, he returned to find the lower part of the walls of the church had been painted cream, "as I had long wanted," and the pulpit seat reupholstered in brown by some of the ladies as a surprise for him. Endearingly, they left a card on the pulpit that said "with love from the ladies of your congregation." It is safe to assume that more than a few of these ladies saw the young bachelor minister as an eminently suitable match for their daughters!

After redecoration came the matter of replacing the carpets. Nevile, his father and various ladies spent much time viewing samples and after endless debate the deacons' court finally, and unanimously, decided on a blue material. Around this time Nevile was working on the preparation of a paper he was to deliver to the local ministers' fraternal on "the Problem of Suffering" and there was a certain irony that, when he returned home after giving his talk, he discovered his father had suffered "a tiresome visit" from two of the ladies of the church. They had come to complain about the color of the carpet.

Nevile Davidson had made an energetic start in his first charge. There is ample evidence from his diaries that he was conscientious in sermon preparation, assiduous in pastoral visitation and genuinely concerned for individuals in need. His diary for Christmas Day 1928 records that, after preaching at a joint service in St. Machar's Cathedral, he visited "some of my poorest families with some money and some little plum puddings."

But one noticeable characteristic of his life was that periods of busyness were often punctuated by times of poor health. Indeed, he seems to have been something of a worrier about his fitness and well-being. This may stem from his childhood when, according to his autobiography, "owing to periodic bouts of asthma and bronchitis I was not sent to school at the usual age."[5] Diaries from his student days indicate that he was still prone to asthma attacks which sometimes gave him sleepless nights and numerous entries suggest that whenever he felt under the weather he was not slow to take to his bed and even to dramatize conditions that hardly sound life-threatening:

> Ill in bed all day with cold, cough, temperature and headache. Took aspirin and dozed most of the time . . . A nephew of Mrs Charleson's, a chemist, looked at me and said I had a slight attack of the prevailing influenza and prescribed a cough mixture.

Whether it was a recurrence of the asthma or simply exhaustion he does not say, but in September 1926, after just fifteen months in his charge, Nevile was recommended by his doctor to take two months off. He took the advice and set off a week later for London where in the course of his stay, in spite of frequent headaches, he visited St. Martin-in-the-Fields and St. Columba's Pont Street Church of Scotland, heard a sermon by a Jesuit priest at Westminster Cathedral and received communion at Westminster Abbey. During this time he missed the wedding of his friend Ian Simpson at Ceres, Fife at which he was to have been the best man. He does not seem to have resumed his preaching duties until December, only to interrupt them again in the new year when, on January 8, with a temperature of over 100°, he had to arrange for a substitute to preach and for a nurse to come and look after him. He did not preach on the two following Sundays either, and by the end of January he was staying at the manse of the newly-weds in Ceres to recuperate. Not until February 20 did he climb the steps of his own pulpit again for the morning service, noting that "everybody seemed pleased to see me back." It was a pattern that would recur in years to come.

5. Davidson, *Beginnings*, 3

Perhaps his visits to the Anglican and Catholic churches in London strengthened Nevile Davidson's determination to bring about his next innovation at Aberdeen. He was a passionate believer in more frequent celebrations of communion, something not particularly controversial today but unusual in Scottish Presbyterian churches at that time. Traditionally communion took place only once a year and in the period leading up to it communion tokens (small metal tablets) would be distributed to those who, in the opinion of minister and kirk session, were fit to receive the sacrament, which would be served at a long table erected for the purpose in the church sanctuary. Prior to the event there would be a preparatory service, and a thanksgiving service after it.

By the twentieth century the tokens had been replaced by cards and the spiritual state of those communicating was subject to less scrutiny; in fact, right up until the 1970s communion services in Church of Scotland parishes tended to bring out the least faithful members who wanted to retain some tenuous link with the church and turned up at communion to avoid being removed from the membership roll. Conversely, in the Scottish Highlands there were those who stayed away from communion services in the belief that they were unworthy to partake of the elements. All this was very different from the practice in Roman Catholic and Episcopalian churches where Mass or the Eucharist would be a feature of the main service of worship each Sunday.

Yet infrequent celebration of communion was not originally intended to be a distinctive feature of the reformed faith. In his monumental work *Institutes of the Christian Religion,* John Calvin (1509–1564) argued that "the Lord's Table should have been spread at least once a week for the assembly of Christians, and the promises declared in it should feed us spiritually."[6] Similarly, John Knox's liturgy of 1564, known as *The Book of Common Order,* provides a liturgy for "The Day when the Lordes supper is ministered, which Commonlye is used once a month."[7] The ideas of Calvin and Knox on the frequency of communion were never fully realized in the Presbyterian system, and Nevile Davidson considered that celebrating communion more often would enrich the connections of the Scottish church with both its reformed heritage and with the wider church.

As a first step, he proposed to Aberdeen Presbytery that congregations should hold a communion service on Easter Day, and in March 1927 wrote

6. Calvin, *Institutes,* 113
7. *The Liturgy of John Knox,* 138

a letter to *The Scotsman* appealing for as many churches as possible to do so. The Easter communion seemed to go down well in his own congregation, where 179 people communicated, leading him to go further and suggest to his kirk session that communion should be held once a month—having taken the precaution of making an advance visit to his senior elder, Sir George Adam Smith, to secure his support. Apart from a "wild protest" from one elder, the session agreed to the idea.

The young preacher was also becoming involved in the church at a national level through his work on General Assembly committees. In June 1928 he joined both the "Faith and Order Committee" and the Committee on *The Book of Common Order*, where he proposed three small recommendations which were carried, though he "felt rather overwhelmed," being at least ten years younger than the other members who were all ex-moderators, professors and doctors of Divinity.

Even more significant for Nevile's future reputation was his pioneering work with the new medium of "the wireless." His autobiography states that in October 1927 he was "engaged for the first time" in conducting a broadcast service but he must have forgotten that, according to a diary entry for August 1926, he had already broadcast a wireless sermon from the Aberdeen BBC studios. Nevile was soon included on a panel of preachers that the BBC could call on, and in future years he made many similar broadcasts.

This came about through his friendship with Rev. Melville Dinwiddie (1892–1975) a former army officer who was minister of Aberdeen's St. Machar's Cathedral. In 1933 Dinwiddie was offered the post of Scottish Director of the BBC. "I felt that the tremendous possibilities and influence of broadcasting in these days required my giving it most serious consideration and as I believe it is a call from God to serve him in this wider sphere, I have accepted it,"[8] he announced to his congregation in July. He remained in this post for nearly twenty-four years.

In these early days of wireless, the idea of transmitting church services caused a good deal of controversy. While the benefits to the housebound were acknowledged, some clergy felt that it would deter people from attending church in person. Others worried that a broadcast service might be listened to without the proper degree of reverence. In 1923 the BBC was not permitted to broadcast the wedding of the late Queen Mother from Westminster Abbey on the grounds that "the services would be received by

8. Dinwiddie, *Religion by Radio*, 20

a considerable number of persons in an irreverent manner, and might even be heard by persons in public houses with their hats on."[9] All such objections, however, were soon overcome.

Nevile Davidson described Dinwiddie as "my neighbour and friend" and regularly played golf with him. Both their congregations worshiped together for a time in St. Mary's while St. Machar's was undergoing renovation work, and the two ministers shared the preaching. In January 1929 joint kirk session meetings were held to discuss an ambitious campaign in which every house in the parish would receive a visit. All this paved the way for the eventual amalgamation of the two congregations in 1944—appropriately enough, as St. Mary's had originally been founded almost 100 years earlier as a Free Church by those who seceded from the Cathedral at the time of the Disruption. After the two congregations reunited the St. Mary's premises were purchased by the University of Aberdeen.

If Davidson and Dinwiddie were instrumental in bringing religion into the public sphere via broadcasting, they were equally concerned to develop their inner spiritual lives. Together they organized an annual retreat from 1928 onwards, the idea being to offer a small group of like-minded ministers the opportunity for meditation, self-examination, silence and prayer. No general publicity was issued, participation being by private invitation only. The first gathering took place in Bonskeid House in Pitlochry which at that time was used by the YMCA but in subsequent years the retreat was held in the old Cathedral city of Dunkeld. By 1936 a "Fellowship of Dunkeld" had been formed by those who attended each year, the aim being defined as promoting "a deeper experimental knowledge of God the Father in Jesus Christ, a more faithful and self-denying service in His kingdom, and more Christ-like relationships to one another." Yet private spirituality and public proclamation were in reality two sides of the same coin: according to one long-standing participant, many of the preachers invited by Dinwiddie to take part in broadcast services were drawn from those who attended the Dunkeld Fellowship. A typical day at the retreat followed a strict, almost monastic, timetable:

9. Dinwiddie, *Religion by Radio*, 20

| | |
|---|---|
| 7.45 a.m. | Holy Communion |
| 8.30 a.m. | Breakfast |
| 9.30 a.m. | Morning Devotions |
| 10.30 a.m. | Discussion |
| 12 noon—1 p.m. | Silence and Meditation |
| Afternoon | Free Time |
| 5 p.m. | Discussion |
| 6.30 p.m.—7.30 p.m. | Silence and Meditation |
| 10 p.m.—10.30 p.m. | Evening Devotions |
| 11 p.m. | Retire |

Soon this order was slightly modified to make it stricter still, with silence being maintained all evening until 10 p.m. except for one of the group reading aloud during supper. Communion took place at night: "very quiet and impressive, no lights in the Cathedral except those at each side of the Communion table." Here was a group of Scottish Presbyterian ministers recreating the atmosphere of a medieval monastery.

The discussion periods would center around a selected book. At the first gathering the chosen text was *The Soul of Prayer*, a devotional classic published in 1916 by the distinguished theologian P.T. Forsyth (1848–1921), the son of an Aberdeen postman. This closely argued and sometimes difficult work encouraged readers to "probe into their motivation and values as they commune with God"[10] and would certainly have provided plenty of material for thoughtful discussion.

These early gatherings took place against a background of hope for the future of the church in Scotland for, after years of discussion and negotiation, the reunion of the United Free and Established churches had finally been achieved in May 1929, largely healing the divisions caused by the Disruption of 1843. The merger was a result of a number of different factors: the UF and Established churches were fairly similar in terms of theology and practice; the union of the Free Church and United Presbyterian Church in 1900 had set a powerful precedent; the heat had gone out of the earlier conflicts over the relations between church and state and the question of patronage, while the 1914–18 war had seen the churches working together more closely at home and at the front. Thus, as Andrew Muirhead points out in his history of the Scottish church between the Reformation

10. www.ccel.org/ccel/forsyth/prayer.html

and the 1960s, "for the first time in nearly two hundred years, the great majority of Presbyterians were members of the same denomination."[11]

The reunited Church of Scotland had nearly 1.3 million members and wildly optimistic predictions were made that in a few years time the figure could be doubled. Sadly, this never materialized in the difficult economic climate of the 1930s; moreover, at a local level, the union was often difficult to implement, as the Kirk now comprised some 3000 congregations and parish divisions had to be redrawn to accommodate them, leading to inevitable mergers. As J.H.S. Burleigh says, it is one thing to unite denominations, and quite another to unite congregations . . .[12]

Issues such as these would occupy Nevile Davidson's time in the future as he became increasingly prominent as a national churchman, but his father did not live to see how the new denomination would develop. Father and son walked side by side in the great procession in Edinburgh from New College to the High Kirk of St. Giles for the united thanksgiving service, "deeply moved and happy, and conscious that we were taking part in an event which would transform the whole religious life of Scotland."[13] By the following spring, however, James Davidson's health had declined and he died peacefully in his sleep.

Himself confined to bed through illness, Nevile did not travel back to North Berwick for the funeral but a memorial service was held in St. Mary's in December 1930 at which two of his father's favorite hymns, Psalm 23 and *Lead kindly Light,* were sung and a tribute delivered by Principal David Cairns of Aberdeen University.[14] Inevitably, the death of his father made a huge impact on Nevile's life at the manse in Aberdeen where they had both lived for the last five years. His aunts and cousins were nearby and he had plenty of friends who would invite him for meals but, without his father's daily companionship, "I felt a loneliness which until then I had never known."[15] Apart from his servants, Nevile had only his pets to share his manse with. Over the years he had quite a variety: cats, a tortoise, a dog called Jude and Marquita the parrot, who used to perch on his master's shoulder during mealtimes, looking for morsels of food. Sadly, Marquita

11. Muirhead, *Reformation, Dissent and Diversity,* 207

12. Burleigh, *Church History,* 410. For a detailed account of the stages in the reunion process, see Burleigh, 394–421

13. Davidson, *Beginnings,* 23

14. *Aberdeen Press and Journal,* December 15 1930

15. Davidson, *Beginnings,* 25

took ill over Christmas 1928 and, although Nevile and Cois nursed her all day and gave her a mixture of brandy and milk, she died during the night.

Altered domestic circumstances may well have made Nevile more receptive to a change of scene and a fresh challenge in a larger charge, and he responded positively to a "completely unexpected invitation"[16] from St. Enoch's Church, Dundee. Surviving correspondence shows how simply these things were done in that era. On January 18, 1932 the convener of the selection committee at St. Enoch's wrote asking if Nevile would be interested in the charge. His name had been recommended by Rev. Dr. Charles Warr of St. Giles' Cathedral, Edinburgh, and the convener gave a broad hint that the job was practically his for the taking: "I may say that the policy of the congregation as regards the last two appointments has been to avoid competition for the ministry." On offer was "possibly the most beautiful church in Dundee" and an unequaled "atmosphere of goodwill." This was followed on February 3 with an official nomination, an assurance that no other name would be put forward and an invitation to come and preach.

The selection process, such as it was, was over. Nevile Davidson had the job.

At a farewell gathering in his Aberdeen church on March 29, he was presented with a state-of-the-art "portable wireless set"—an appropriate gift for someone with an interest in broadcasting, though a newspaper photograph shows him looking at the object with a puzzled expression, perhaps wondering how "portable" this unwieldy contraption really was.

16. Davidson, *Beginnings*, 26

St .Enoch's Church, Nethergate, Dundee originated as a Free Church in 1865. It closed in 1963 and the building was demolished during redevelopment of the area in the 1970s.

True to his rather reserved nature, Nevile made a conventional speech in which he talked about developments in the parish and said he felt it "a wrench to leave" after being there for seven years. But the interim moderator appointed in his place, Rev. W. W. Gauld of Queen's Cross church, delivered a more forthright assessment of his ministry:

> Ministers are a drab lot but now and then they have the good fortune to produce amongst them a man with a bit of colour and originality, and St. Mary's was lucky enough to hit on him. But more than being a man of colour, Mr. Davidson was sound to the core in the central truths of their great faith. His ministry would be fragrant in all their memories.[17]

Dundee in the early 1930s was certainly in need of "a bit of colour." Since the nineteenth century most of the city's working population had been employed in mills making products from jute, a rough fiber imported from India and used for sacks, twine and canvas. But global recession and foreign competition had caused the industry to decline and in the year Nevile Davidson moved to the city 70% of jute workers were unemployed. The introduction of means testing that September led to unrest in the city, with riots and charges by mounted police. As an indication of his concern for those suffering poverty in Dundee, the new minister was elected as a member of the executive council of the Dundee Charity Organisation Society which sought to supplement state assistance to the unemployed by offering advice and support.

The lot of Nevile Davidson was much more fortunate than the jute workers: he enjoyed a stipend of £620 and a spacious house at the western end of Magdalene Green, with a magnificent outlook up the wide River Tay. It was here that he first employed a Highland lady, Flora Cant, as his cook and she became "a devoted and well-loved friend of the family,"[18] remaining with him for the rest of her life. Dundee was also conveniently close to relatives like Colonel Quentin Agnew, his uncle, while Rossie Priory was only half an hour away in his four-seater Morris Cowley (the Swift having being sold for just £55, which sounds like a rather high rate of depreciation considering that it originally cost £250).

17. *Aberdeen Press and Journal*, March 30 1932
18. Davidson, *Beginnings*, 26

Nevile at once embarked on a methodical program of visitation in his new parish, aiming to visit the homes of all 700 members at least once a year. St. Enoch's was a larger and more ornate building than his previous one, and was notable for its musical tradition, making it an ideal place to extend some of the changes he had made in Aberdeen, particularly with regard to observing the festivals of the Christian year. One of his innovations was to set up a Christmas tree in the church but even this was too radical for some. In an echo of the dispute at Aberdeen over the Filippo Lippi painting, *Beginnings but no Ending* relates how Nevile

> was astonished to receive a letter from one of our older members saying that she never expected to see Popery in this form in St. Enoch's and that never in future would she feel able to attend Christmas services. A long and friendly conversation persuaded her to change her views and to reconcile her to her new minister.[19]

Nativity plays were just as controversial in a Presbyterian Scotland where even Christmas Day was not a public holiday (and would not become one until 1958). However, in 1934, the Christmas story was re-enacted by the Munich Marionette Theatre in the hall of Dundee's Teacher Training College. To a full house of children and parents, Nevile Davidson read the relevant Bible passages before each scene, and the audience found the eloquent gestures of the puppets particularly affecting in the scene where Joseph and Mary pleaded with the innkeeper to provide shelter.[20]

As in Aberdeen, he joined with local ministers at outreach meetings, held in the Westport area, where Communists would often interrupt with challenging questions. Davidson would certainly have had no sympathy with them: when he ran a series of monthly talks by prominent laymen at St. Enoch's, one was entitled "The Dangers of Communism" and it was delivered by the 8th Earl of Glasgow, supporter of Oswald Mosley and leader of British Fascist units in Scotland. According to newspaper reports, the idea of inviting laymen to occupy the pulpit "created considerable interest in church circles at the time"[21] as in these days it was rare for an elder or other lay person even to read the lesson in a Church of Scotland.

When it came to the role of women in the church, however, Nevile Davidson took a much more conservative stance. Though women were not eligible to serve as elders, there was already a small but significant minority

19. Davidson, *Beginnings*, 28
20. *Dundee Courier,* December 3 1934
21. *Dundee Courier,* November 4 1933

who believed in the ordination of female ministers and the issue raised its head early in Nevile's ministry at St. Enoch's at the opening of a sale of work organized by the Women's Guild in March 1933. In a remark guaranteed to enrage feminists, he referred to the fact that

> Last year at the [General] Assembly several women had applied for admission to the ministry and to the eldership. That application had not yet been granted, and he did not believe in the Church of Scotland it ever would be.

He went on to dig a bigger hole for himself by praising the ladies of the church in a manner which, by today's standards, would be seen as patronizing:

> From some departments women might feel they were excluded— they might not enter the pulpit nor might they sit on the kirk session—but there was one department which was entirely their own: the sale of work. That was women's province.[22]

This was something of a *faux pas* on Nevile's part as the dignitary performing the opening ceremony was Mrs W. H. Buist, the Lady Provost, who happened to be a member of the committee of the Church of Scotland appointed to consider that very subject. Politely but firmly rebuking the minister, she told him that "I think we shall just wait."

The waiting took much longer than expected, as it was not until 1968 that the General Assembly permitted women to be ordained.

Mrs Buist's rebuke obviously didn't change Nevile Davidson's mind, as he returned to the theme later in 1933 during a debate at a Dundee Presbytery meeting at which it was agreed that women could serve as deacons, but not as elders or ministers. "Nobody owes more that I do to the ladies of my own congregation and parish," he said, "and I think it is their very devoutness which would encourage men to push them forward if they were eligible for office, and I think it would be a loss to the Church if that took place. The time is not opportune."[23] In fairness to Nevile, other speakers in the debate took up more extreme positions. "The proper place for women is in the home," declared the Rev. McIntosh Mowat adding, with dubious logic, that "If you are going to have women elders and women ministers, I maintain strongly that they must be celibate."[24] As an aside, it is

22. *Dundee Courier,* March 27 1933
23. *Dundee Evening Telegraph,* December 6 1933
24. *Dundee Evening Telegraph,* December 6 1933

worth noting that Dr. Maude Royden of the nonconformist City Temple in London had already preached at Glasgow Cathedral in 1931, possibly the first woman to do so in the building's 800 year history.

Although he was only in his early thirties, Nevile Davidson was already becoming a well-known figure, not only in Aberdeen and Dundee but nationally, thanks to his regular broadcasting. This growing reputation—assisted, no doubt, by his impeccable social connections and by a recommendation from Charles Warr, Dean of the Order of the Thistle and Dean of the Chapel Royal in Scotland—led to an invitation to preach before King George V at Crathie church in September 1935, preceded by a dinner with the royal family at Balmoral Castle. Nevile took as his theme "The Simplicity of Christianity." He had little choice other than to keep it simple: he had been told to keep his address down to twelve minutes because the king did not like long sermons.

In the autumn of 1934 Nevile Davidson's ministry at Dundee came to an unexpectedly early end. If his own account is to be taken at face value, this occurred in much the same way as his departure from Aberdeen, as the result of an unsolicited approach. "To my astonishment I received a letter from the session clerk [of Glasgow Cathedral], Gavin Boyd, saying that the vacancy committee would like to hear me preach."[25] An arrangement was made for the committee to hear him in Edinburgh at St. Giles, resulting in a unanimous invitation to preach in Glasgow as sole nominee. Clearly, it was unusual for a minister to move on after only two and a half years, though his predecessor at St. Enoch's, the Rev. Professor J. H. S. Burleigh, had only served there for three, but Nevile was convinced that "it was a call in the true and deep sense of the word." He left Dundee in January 1935, with the gift of an oval-shaped dining table to join the portable wireless set donated by his Aberdeen parishioners.

He left with mixed feelings of "trepidation and exhilaration,"[26] but it proved to be the right decision: Nevile Davidson would remain minister of Glasgow Cathedral until his retirement thirty two years later.

25. Davidson, *Beginnings,* 30
26. Davidson, *Beginnings,* 31

# 3

# "A Call I Could Not Refuse"

## GLASGOW CATHEDRAL, 1935–1939

LIKE MOST CATHEDRALS, GLASGOW has guides on duty each day to show visitors round the building, parts of which date back to the thirteenth century. After being taken on the tour, a group of nuns chatted pleasantly with their guide and, on their way out, signed the visitor book, as people do. Only later did the guide notice what they had written: "Give us back our cathedral."

The story is a reminder of the checkered history of the building. At the time of the Reformation in the sixteenth century altars, images and furnishings associated with Roman Catholicism were removed. Although papal authority was rejected, various attempts were made to retain or reinstate an episcopal system of church government until the eventual triumph of Presbyterianism with the Revolution Settlement of 1690. Consequently—as some are still keen to point out—the church is no longer a cathedral in the sense of being the seat of a bishop, and should technically be referred to as St. Mungo's or the High Church of Glasgow.

Nevertheless, Glasgow Cathedral continues to be called Glasgow Cathedral and it has never ceased to be at the center of the spiritual life of the city. To this day, public bodies such as the city council, Glasgow University, the Trades House and the Merchants House continue a long tradition of holding annual services there and it is the natural venue for special ceremonies commemorating significant national occasions. Though Glasgow has, of course, plenty of other parish churches, the Cathedral's role is such an important one that its minister is entitled to call himself simply "Minister of Glasgow." There is a story that Nevile Davidson, when signing in at a meeting of the Presbytery of Glasgow, wrote after his name "Minister of Glasgow." The colleague behind him in the queue, considering this an affectation, added the word "Cathedral."

No wonder Nevile, at the age of thirty-six, felt he had been given "a call I could not refuse."[1]

Glasgow Cathedral was begun in the middle of the thirteenth century and completed around 1500. (Photo by the author).

He was inducted to the charge on January 30, 1935 and later recalled that "as I walked slowly towards the church and suddenly saw the great spire coming to view above the surrounding rooftops an almost overwhelming sense of responsibility swept over me, followed by a silent but intense prayer that I might be given the much needed strength to be equal to it."[2] That feeling of awe has been experienced by many a visitor to the ancient building before and since. It is difficult to put into words but few have expressed it better than Nevile Davidson's predecessor as minister, Lauchlan

1. Davidson, *Beginnings,* 30
2. Davidson, *Beginnings,* 30

MacLean Watt (1867–1957), in a letter written to Nevile during the second World War, by which time MacLean Watt had been living in retirement for many years in his Highland home at Lochcarron. In his richly poetic prose, he describes taking a distinguished visitor, the Sultan of Zanzibar, round the Cathedral.

> The great high solemn stillness, stepped into from the street, the silence settling like snowfall in the mountains, impressed him very deeply. I took him through it all, and he said, "Now this is the peace of Heaven." . . . That's exactly what I used to feel—often—standing there, and feeling the centuries soundlessly environing my soul. That dear old place has a touch of the spirit of eternity about it. It's a great privilege to have as a shelter and tabernacle and whispering gallery of the thought of God.

Fortunately for the minister and congregation, the huge responsibility of maintaining this venerable structure has, since the mid-nineteenth century, lain with the Crown and is today in the hands of Historic Environment Scotland. The congregation and its governing body, the kirk session, makes decisions about improvements to the furnishing and fittings of the building but in the years before Nevile's arrival little appears to have been done in this respect and his efforts to beautify the Cathedral have proved to be his most enduring legacy.

Indeed, the issue of improvements to the building emerged on the very day of his induction when, at a lunch for the kirk session held after the service and attended by the Lord Provost and bailies (magistrates) of the city, Charles Warr provocatively stated that if he were the minister of St. Mungo's he would take down the rood screen and send it to the Kelvingrove Museum and thereby "fling the whole of the magnificent interior open." He was referring to the stone screen or pulpitum dividing the nave from the quire which dates from the early 1400s and is reckoned to be the only one of its type left in any secular (i.e. non-monastic) church of the pre-Reformation period in Scotland. This remark plunged the new minister into controversy from day one and at another public meeting the following month he repudiated any suggestion that he was associated with the proposal. "No-one who knew the history of the Cathedral . . . could ever contemplate for a moment such an act of sacrilege."[3]

While Warr's suggestion was never a serious option, it is true that in 1935 full use was not being made of the interior of the Cathedral. The nave,

3. *The Scotsman*, February 25 1935

the lower church or crypt and the Blacader aisle on the south side of the building were virtually unfurnished. There was no lighting downstairs and even the nave lacked electric lights until as recently as 1923. Furthermore, the nineteenth century German painted glass used for many of the windows was in poor condition and let in little light, giving the interior a gloomy air.

Nevile longed to see the building restored to its original splendor. Barely four months into his ministry he reported to his kirk session that he had met with the Lord Provost who had agreed to convene a meeting in the autumn with a view to forming a Society of Friends of Glasgow Cathedral, following the model of a similar organization at Dunblane Cathedral. Among the stated aims of the Society—still pursued today—were "the adornment and furnishing of the Cathedral . . . , the installation of stained glass of worthy quality, the safeguarding of the Cathedral's amenity and the beautifying of its surroundings."[4]

A letter signed by the minister and Lord Provost Alexander Swan appeared in the *Glasgow Herald* inviting citizens to an inaugural meeting in the Merchants Hall on October 31 where Nevile reiterated, to applause, that there was absolutely no intention to remove the ancient rood screen. There was, however, general agreement that the stained glass urgently needed replaced and it seems that work on this was already in hand, as in February 1936 the first new window, depicting Moses as the central figure, was installed to a design by Douglas Strachan (1875–1950) who had the reputation of being the best designer of stained glass in Scotland. A complete scheme for the renewal of glass was drawn up and approved by the Royal Fine Art Commission for Scotland, the initial plan being to replace ten windows in the quire. Of course, as *The Scotsman* noted, "the carrying out of the scheme will depend upon the generosity of future donors."[5] Nevile Davidson soon had key figures on board, such as Sir John Stirling-Maxwell (1866–1956), the politician, philanthropist and patron of the arts and Sir Steven (later Lord) Bilsland (1892–1970), businessman and future chairman of the Scottish National Trust. The plans were backed by public bodies such as the Trades and Merchants Houses and the Duke and Duchess of York—soon to be King George and Queen Elizabeth—agreed to be the Society's first members and royal patrons. By the end of the Society's first year, as many as 577 members had joined and £3000 had been raised in

4. www.glasgowcathedral.org/society-of-friends
5. *The Scotsman*, February 24 1936

subscriptions and donations. The new minister was a man who could get things done.

To Nevile the beautification of the sanctuary was not merely a matter of aesthetics but a means of evangelism. Echoing the well-known saying of the medieval Abbot Suger of St. Denis that "the dull mind rises to truth through that which is material," he argued that many people worshiped through the eye rather than the ear; if the Cathedral's beauty was restored then "naturally it would be full." Sir David Young Cameron (1865–1945), the King's Painter in Scotland, expressed this noble aim in a more trenchant manner, telling the inaugural meeting of the Friends that

> Man was not going to be continually taken up with motor toys on Sundays and with caramels and cigarettes and the froth of life. Man was going to come back to greater things and the Cathedral would once again be the great heart of our people.[6]

Appropriately enough, this was all happening in the year of the 800th anniversary of the dedication of an earlier Cathedral building in 1136 during the reign of King David I. A further incentive to upgrade the Cathedral and encourage more visitors was the Empire Exhibition held at Bellahouston Park in 1938, attended by over twelve million people. In 1932 the Cathedral's provision for tourists had been so poor that there was only one small plan of the building hidden in an inconspicuous corner and no sign to indicate the whereabouts of the tomb of the city's patron saint, Mungo. By the end of 1937 notices had been placed at each point of interest; postcards and a new guidebook written by the minister himself (priced at threepence, or just over 1p in today's currency) were on sale; guided tours were offered and opening hours extended so that tourists could visit on Sunday afternoons during the time of the exhibition. Earlier the same year, the Blacader aisle—at that time referred to, somewhat inaccurately, as Blacader's crypt—had been reopened and dedicated as a chapel for worship.

Other improvements envisaged by the Society of Friends, such as a competition for the remodeling of the chancel area with stalls as in medieval times, had to be put on hold because of the outbreak of war, although some work did go ahead: as late as May 1940 new windows gifted by Sir John Stirling-Maxwell were installed.

6. *Glasgow Herald*, October 31 1935

Passionate though he was about restoring the Cathedral to its former glory, Nevile Davidson firmly believed that "a cathedral church should never be thought of simply as a magnificent monument but always as a living centre of worship, prayer and spiritual life."[7] Hence, in his early years in Glasgow he sought not only to beautify the sanctuary but to use the experience gained in his first two charges to minister to his parishioners and find ways of reaching those outside the church.

He did not have to go far to find them, for just across the road from the Cathedral were the overcrowded, soot-blackened tenements of the Townhead area where in the early 1930s as many as 35,000 people lived in poverty. Undaunted by the challenge, the new minister started by getting to know the members of his congregation, announcing in his first pastoral letter in the church magazine, *The Chronicle*, that "I hope in succeeding months, as time and strength permit, to visit all of you in your homes."[8] Well aware that women are sometimes more receptive to ministerial visits than men, he added the following month that "I will try to visit between the hours of 6 and 9 p.m. so as to have the pleasure of meeting the husbands, fathers and brothers."[9] With a membership roll of 1202, this was obviously a large undertaking and, predictably, by December he had found that the visitation program "was taking longer than first anticipated."

One contributory factor was that he had been involved in "a rather bad motor accident" while visiting Aberdeen in July when he collided with another car at a junction. Both vehicles were badly damaged and Nevile suffered a back injury, only returning to "light duty" in September. In between, he took his customary six week summer break. "How good it is," he enthused to his parishioners, "sometimes just to sit and allow the noise and rush, and even the sense of the passing of time, to subside out of one's soul, and leave one absolutely passive and quiet inwardly as well as outwardly."[10] This, no doubt, would be an indulgence afforded to few of those struggling to make ends meet in the Townhead tenements. We might smile, too, at his advice to his flock to give up luxuries for Lent: "It is good, at least now and again, deliberately to deny oneself some pleasure, however

7. Davidson, *Beginnings*, 51
8. *Chronicle*, February 1935
9. *Chronicle*, March 1935
10. *Chronicle*, September 1935

harmless—whether it be cigarettes, or sweets, or rich food, or even the use of too comfortable an armchair!"[11]

Such statements might lead some to consider Nevile Davidson to be rather detached from the grim reality of daily life as it was for ordinary folk in the thirties. And yet, there are many who would testify to his genuine concern for people. As he went about his visits in the tenements, there would often be ground floor dwellers who, in Glasgow parlance, were "hinging oot" their windows, and he made a habit of stopping and talking to them without any sign of condescension.

Although Nevile kept a diary from his student days right up until his death, for some reason the volumes covering the years 1930 to 1942 are missing. Having written up his daily activities in such a methodical manner, it seems unlikely that he would suddenly stop doing so for over a decade. Did his wife dispose of these volumes because they contained comments she did not want to put into the public domain? Or were they simply lost for some reason?

Fortunately, kirk session minutes give some insight into his priorities during the early years of his Cathedral ministry prior to the second World War. Compared to his previous charges, there were many more civic and other special services to conduct. In 1936, for example, organizations holding their annual services in the Cathedral included the Sir Walter Scott Club, the City of Glasgow Police, the Highland Light Infantry and Cameronians, the Faculty of Physicians and Surgeons, the Salvation Army and the Trades House, in addition to the annual "Kirking of Magistrates" when the town council paraded at a morning service. In such a large congregation the minister could not be expected to oversee every activity personally; numerous committees managed the Sunday schools, mission, halls, choir, parish magazine and seat letting, and he usually had two assistant ministers to help him, the first two being Rev. James Hay Hamilton and the Rev. George P. Innes. The assistants came and went frequently when they finished their studies or found charges of their own.

Attempts at change in any congregation are bound to be resisted by traditionalists and it wasn't long before Nevile found himself embroiled in a type of dispute only too familiar in churches. In 1935 he persuaded the choir committee that a boys' choir should be introduced and this led to the dismissal of six of the adult members—and the resignation of the convener of the choir committee in protest, after forty years' service. But the six

11. *Chronicle*, March 1935

refused to go quietly, and turned up at the Cathedral on the Sunday after they were sacked. They had, moreover, supporters within the choir and, after the dispute had rumbled on over the summer and into the autumn, twenty-eight choir members signed a letter in November asking that the notice of dismissal be withdrawn on the grounds that it would stigmatize the individuals concerned and prejudice their future careers. This was agreed, on condition that the six voluntarily resigned and abstained from attending services.

The experience seems to have been enough for Nevile Davidson and he quickly indicated his desire[12] to be relieved of involvement in the choir committee. The following year the organist, R. H. Clifford Smith, resigned, as did the church treasurer and the captain of the Boys' Brigade company, but the reasons for these departures, and whether they were connected, are lost in the mists of time. From later references, however, it does seem that the boys' choir went ahead.

Early in his ministry Nevile showed a willingness to experiment with different timings and formats of services. In his first year, he changed the daily services during Holy Week in April from 3 p.m. to 8 p.m., presumably to enable more people who were working to attend. The reopening of the Blacader crypt allowed a daily service to be instituted, at which the minister and his assistants shared the duties with the minister of the neighboring Barony congregation. Even though there were sometimes only one or two people present, to Nevile Davidson it was important to revive the idea of daily worship being offered within the Cathedral.

Nevile's first campaign to reach the unchurched was carried out in the run up to Christmas during November and December 1936 making use of the nave, which now had the benefit of 400 chairs donated by the Society of Friends. A series of "Special Services for the Man in the Street" was planned, to be held at 7.45 p.m., straight after the regular Sunday evening service, and consisting of simpler prayers, a more informal style of address "on a subject of living interest and importance" and popular hymns like *Nearer my God to Thee* for which the congregation remained seated to allow those unfamiliar with church to feel more at ease. Instead of choral music with organ accompaniment, music was provided by the orchestra of the Glasgow Society for Community Service in Unemployment. A Christmas tree was put up in the nave at which gifts in money or kind could be left for the needy together with toys for children. Scotland's recovery of Christmas

12. *Glasgow Cathedral Kirk Session Minutes*, November 8 1935

customs in the last ten years had been "wonderful", in Nevile Davidson's opinion—though, significantly, the distribution of the gifts to families of unemployed men took place not on Christmas Day but at New Year.

Another Christmas innovation followed in 1938: a nativity play in the form of ten tableaux enacted in the nave by members of George MacLeod's Govan Old Parish Church, assisted by the boys' choirs from Govan and the Cathedral. This, Nevile believed, was similar to the way the church presented the gospel drama to the people in medieval times.

Midnight Christmas Eve services were a novelty in Scotland in these days and Nevile Davidson claimed to be the first to hold one (though MacLeod had actually beaten him to it in Govan in 1934). Indulging his love of pomp, he began the service with a procession of choir and clergy round the building during the opening hymn and, after a series of carols and readings, started his address at 11.45 p.m. with the whole building in darkness apart from the pulpit and Christmas tree. As midnight struck the lights came on, the bell rang out in celebration and the service ended with *O Come, all Ye Faithful*. It was a huge success and even in today's secular climate the crowds still flock to the Cathedral on Christmas Eve.

But Nevile wanted to go still further in reaching the unchurched. "If the people will not come to the church, then the church must go to the people," he declared in a powerful address at the annual meeting of the Lodging House Mission:

> For too long [churchgoers] had lingered within the walls of their churches on comfortable, cushioned seats, lulled by the soft sound of organ music, while outside crowds drifted by in their thousands. I know of no more exciting or exhilarating experience than to stand on a lorry and speak to perhaps 200 or 300 working men without collars or ties, as I did in Aberdeen and in Dundee. Open-air preaching was work that could be undertaken by laymen as well as by clergymen if they possessed a good voice and were sincere in heart.[13]

Thus, when the second series of People's Services commenced in May 1937, they were held outside in the churchyard, the first one being addressed by MacLeod who tackled the question: "Can we accept the authority of Christ?" Of course, outdoor events in Scotland are dependent on the weather, and in June rain meant the gathering had to go back indoors. There was a third series of these popular services in the winter and further

13. *The Scotsman*, April 2 1936

special events designed to bring others into the Cathedral, such as a service in February 1937 marking the centenary of the birth of the American
evangelist D. L. Moody (1837–99) who, accompanied by gospel singer Ira
D. Sankey (1840–1908), had carried out campaigns in the UK, including
Scotland. Moody died in the year of Nevile's birth, but his mother had been
a great admirer of him. The commemoration took the form of an address
on the life of the evangelist and all the hymns were taken from Sankey's
*Sacred Songs and Solos*, which cannot have pleased some of the more staid
members of the Cathedral.

Nevile's outward-looking approach was very much in tune with
the mood of the national church at the time, which was embarking on a
"Recall to Religion" campaign held, at Nevile's suggestion, during Lent in
1938. The title in fact came from a plea issued in England by Cosmo Lang,
Archbishop of Canterbury, in December 1936, but the new emphasis on
mission in the Church of Scotland was also a by-product of the 1929 union
with the United Free Church which had had a noticeably more evangelistic
ethos than the "Auld Kirk" and the lead was taken by Rev. R. J. Drummond,
a former UF moderator.[14] In Glasgow, the city was divided up into districts
and meetings were held in nearby Townhead by Rev. D. P. Thomson (1896–
1974), the Church of Scotland's official evangelist. In the March issue of
*The Chronicle*, Nevile's message to his flock took the form of an evangelistic
appeal:

> Now God is calling us back to Himself. Don't let this chance go
> unheeded. Don't let any false pride or selfish sloth keep you from
> listening to His call. Are you conscious of sin? Come and find for-
> giveness. Are you troubled by doubts and perplexities? Come and
> pray for light. Are you growing "weary in well-doing and tired in
> spirit?" Come and receive new inspiration. Are you lonely? Come
> and take your place in the fellowship of the church. "Today, if ye
> will hear His voice, harden not your hearts."[15]

But you cannot please all of the people all of the time. Nevile's fondness
for the seasons of the Christian year aroused the ire of extreme Protestants
who were more numerous in pre-war Scotland than they are now and
Alexander Ratcliffe, Leader of the Scottish Protestant League, complained
in November 1935 that "whispers are going the rounds that you are a Jesuit
in disguise." He advised the Cathedral minister to "get away from Papist

14. Bardgett, *Scotland's Evangelist*, 152–53
15. *Chronicle*, March 1938

Ritualism and . . . consider that you are a paid minister of the Protestant Church and well-paid at that."[16]

Ratcliffe and his ilk proved to be a thorn in Davidson's flesh on many more occasions, interrupting the Good Friday service in 1937 and accusing him of encouraging "pagan and Roman Catholic observances" and of being "a traitor to Protestantism." The service had just started when Ratcliffe stood up and read out a protest against the "Papist institutions known as Lent, Palm Sunday, Good Friday and Easter, and also the so-called Holy Week. Some 400 years ago John Knox and the other reformers swept those things out of this very church."[17] With that, he led 150 of his supporters out of the building. Nevile made no direct response but later told journalists that "I think it is most regrettable that anyone who calls himself a Christian should interrupt another Christian in his own church."[18] By the end of the year it was necessary to post a policeman on duty at the door of the Cathedral during the staging of the nativity play after Ratcliffe's supporters had disrupted a similar event at a church in nearby Dennistoun.

History repeats itself and many years later Nevile's successor, Dr. William Morris, had a similar experience when an ecumenical service in 1968 was interrupted by the Protestant campaigner Pastor Jack Glass.

Occasional local opposition did not stop Nevile Davidson's profile from growing nationally and internationally. In the summer of 1936 he spent a month in the USA where he occupied the pulpit of the fashionable Fifth Avenue Presbyterian church on three Sundays. Here, he was "somewhat startled" to be faced with a congregation of a thousand people calmly waving straw fans throughout the service as the temperature was in the 90s and there was no air conditioning. The New York press reported on one of his sermons praising the League of Nations which the preacher optimistically believed would "eventually lead to a world in which all nations and races will live side by side in peace." Those who considered such efforts to be idealistic, he added, should remember that "Jesus was the greatest idealist the world has ever seen."

But it was above all through broadcasting that Nevile was making a name for himself beyond Glasgow. In the time of the previous Cathedral minister, Lauchlan MacLean Watt, the kirk session had unanimously

16. Letter addressed to Davidson and published in *Vanguard*, the newspaper of the Scottish Protestant League in November 1935.

17. *Glasgow Herald*, March 27 1937

18. *Glasgow Herald*, March 27 1937

turned down a request from John (later Lord) Reith of the BBC (British Broadcasting Company) to broadcast services on the radio. The objection seems to have been based mainly on a fear that the Cathedral would incur additional expenses or liabilities but broadcasting was finally allowed in 1929 when the service to mark the reunion of the United Free Church and Church of Scotland took place. Soon after Nevile's arrival, the session agreed to allow a BBC transmission of Scottish psalm tunes (for which the Cathedral was paid a fee of fifteen guineas) and a series of organ recitals; by 1937 the minister's broadcast talks and sermons were bringing him fan mail from all over the country. One correspondent who wrote to compliment him added that he found "churches on the whole very useless nowadays. So many of the clergy have nothing to give." The writer knew what he was talking about: he was an Anglican vicar. Recordings of these talks were, sadly, not preserved but the comments in a letter from an ordinary layman from Wrexham, North Wales, convey some impression of what it must have been like to listen to Nevile's dignified and sonorous delivery.

> As soon as I heard you I understood by your splendid voice and tone that you are a real servant of Our Lord and I wish there were many more like you. Most of the clergys (sic) and the chapels never mention anything about the spiritual word so the poor people have been kept in darkness for hundreds of years.

At the start of his ministry, Nevile Davidson had been looking for "something a little more strenuous" than a country parish. With a full program of preaching, visiting, broadcasting and managing improvements to the building, he had certainly found it at Glasgow Cathedral. But a still greater challenge lay ahead. The shadow of war was looming, even if in October 1938 Nevile wrote in his pastoral letter that "it looks at the moment as though such an appalling catastrophe may still be averted."[19]

Like the Prime Minister who shared his Christian name, the minister of Glasgow Cathedral was sadly mistaken.

19. *Chronicle,* October 1938

# 4

## "A Difficult Choice"

### WARTIME SERVICE, 1939–1943

IN OCTOBER 1939 NEVILE Davidson told his flock that "the catastrophe has come upon us and as a nation we are engaged in a gigantic struggle, the end of which none can see."[1] He was, of course, referring to Britain's declaration of war on September 3, 1939 as a consequence of Germany's failure to withdraw its troops from Poland.

Glasgow Cathedral, like other public venues, was immediately subject to various practical measures: lighting restrictions meant that the evening service was replaced by an afternoon one; worshipers were reminded to bring their gas masks and the lower church served as an air raid shelter. During the services the fire wardens listened for air raid warnings and if necessary office bearers would usher the congregation to shelter in the lower church. But Nevile Davidson was determined that the daily service should continue. "This," he said, "is at least as vital and valuable a service to the nation as keeping watch in an ARP shelter or knitting comforts for the troops."[2]

The minister now faced "a difficult choice" about his own wartime role. The clergy were exempt from military service and, in any case, he was over the age of forty, so there was no requirement for him to do anything other than continue to minister to his people. On the other hand, he wrote,

1. *Chronicle*, October 1939
2. *Chronicle*, April 1940

48

"I felt a growing discomfort at seeing men day by day preparing for war while not offering to take some share."[3]

He therefore told his kirk session in October that he had volunteered his services as a military chaplain. There was opposition to this, with some elders feeling that his first duty was to remain at the Cathedral "to minister to the many cares, anxieties and spiritual needs which were likely to arise as a result of the war." Eventually, though, the session "warmly endorsed the moderator's courageous action" and on his last Sunday, May 27, 1940, hundreds queued up to shake hands with him before he left. Thereafter, the two assistant ministers at the time, James Bulloch and William Syme, carried out preaching and pastoral duties, with help from Roy Sanderson of the nearby Barony church as interim moderator.

Few outside the kirk session knew that during his absence Nevile donated £300 per annum to help with the shortfall in the Cathedral's offerings when so many were away on war service, stipulating that £70 of this sum was to be paid as an extra bonus to the two assistants.

The story of the British Expeditionary Force (BEF), sent to assist the French army at the outbreak of the war and evacuated from Dunkirk in May 1940, is well-known. But there was also a second BEF, sent immediately afterwards "to stand alongside the retreating French armies and save a foothold for the allies in Europe."

Among these troops were the 4th and 5th battalions of the King's Own Scottish Borderers, and it was to the 5th that Nevile Davidson was sent as a chaplain in the spring of 1940. This was a territorial unit made up of recruits from the south of Scotland who met in drill halls in places like Gatehouse of Fleet, Dumfries and Castle Douglas. For some months training had been carried out locally and thereafter in the south of England and the new chaplain was told to report to Kingsclere, near Newbury. He arrived just in time to be greeted by the commanding officer who asked if he would like to join the others who were about to set off on an exercise in the North Wessex Downs, which he did.

The new padre got his first—and only—taste of action when his battalion sailed from Southampton to St. Malo on the evening of June 12. On arrival the soldiers immediately started to march but, as one later recalled,

3. Davidson, *Beginnings*, 39

"we had no idea where we were going and we were never told anything. We marched along those long straight roads and it was a relief to see a corner coming up until we were round it, only to find another great long straight."[4] Time at a camp near the fishing port of Cancale was followed by a train journey inland to Sillé-le-Guillaume in the Pays de la Loire region, in turn followed by another long march. After camping in a forest, the chaplain decided to hold an outdoor communion service which was well attended.

Some senior officers had considered that sending out another BEF after the withdrawal from Dunkirk was a pointless gesture. And so it proved. In spite of RAF raids to support the French troops, the German armies advanced towards the coast and the decision was taken to evacuate the outnumbered and outgunned British forces. In his usual sober style, Nevile describes in his autobiography how he was sent by his senior officer to investigate whether the various routes to the port of Cherbourg were clear. He learnt that French troops were blowing up bridges to hinder the German advance and, on reaching the headquarters of the Norman forces, demanded to speak to the commander, Major-General James Marshall-Cornwall, and persuaded him to halt the destruction of bridges on the last remaining open road to the port until the 5th battalion had passed. But Nevile played down the importance of his own role in this. As his battalion made its way to Cherbourg he went on ahead with the wounded and discovered that French sappers were about to blow up a bridge that the party had just crossed, leaving the remainder of the battalion stranded. He remonstrated with them verbally and then took up his stance on the bridge to prevent them destroying it until the rest of the British troops caught up.[5] It was this incident that Dr. Ronald Selby Wright had in mind when, delivering the eulogy at Nevile's funeral many years later, he observed that "his courage and enterprise saved at least half a Battalion of the King's Own Scottish Borderers one June day in France in 1940."[6]

Nevile's own verdict on his time in France was more muted: "The ending of another phase of the war with seemingly little achieved."[7]

The remainder of Nevile Davidson's military service was spent in the UK where the 5th Battalion undertook intensive training for possible future action as mountain troops and airborne infantry, initially stationed

4. www.bbc.co.uk/history/ww2peopleswar/stories/96/a1107596.shtml
5. *Life and Work*, February 1977, 36
6. *Chronicle*, January 1977
7. Davidson, *Beginnings*, 41

in Cambridge and Norfolk and then moving back to Scotland in October 1940, at first to Kirkintilloch then to East Lothian, Callander, Banff and Buckie. On Sundays Nevile would be kept busy with several church parades in different locations. His other duties included meeting new recruits and giving them copies of the Service New Testament, delivering educational talks, visiting hospitals and generally offering help and support as required. This might involve simple, practical measures like distributing cigarettes, chocolate and writing materials and spending time getting to know the men. While based in Dunbar, one private, James McQuarrie, received a telegram to say that his daughter had been born and he was granted forty-eight hours leave to go home to see her. To cover the cost of travel the padre lent him ten shillings; many years later, McQuarrie recalled that he still hadn't paid it back! Even though the battalion was not in the thick of action in Europe at this point, tragic situations still occurred where pastoral care was required as, for example, when six men guarding the beach at Dunbar were killed by a mine.[8]

As it had done so often in the pulpit and on the airwaves, Nevile's preaching made a powerful impact on the troops. At that time, church parades were compulsory and many attended under sufferance but, like the leper who turned back to thank Jesus, one ordinary soldier wrote to express his gratitude to the padre for "all he had done for chaps like me":

> At first I thought "Blast, this is a Sunday and another Church Parade" and before long I would not have missed a Sunday Parade for love or money. It has taken me a long time to sum up [sic] enough courage to write you because outwardly . . . I am not a Churchman because I swear a good deal occasionally and because I take a drink now and then but believe me since I first heard you preach I have never once looked back and I never shall.

Part of Nevile's appeal to such men no doubt lay in his brand of "muscular Christianity", as he seems to have played a full role in battalion activities, rising at 7.15 a.m. when in Banff to take part in strenuous physical training conducted by a strict sergeant and going on twelve and fifteen mile route marches. In January 1942 he was involved in the "Big Scottish Command Exercise" which took place around Stirling, Dunblane and Callander. The camaraderie of all this obviously appealed to him, and he was also able to indulge his love of motorcycling when he took part in an officers' ten mile cross-country race in June 1942:

8. www.bbc.co.uk/history/ww2peopleswar/stories/96/a1107596.shtml

We started at 10 a.m. on Cullen golf course, over pretty rough steep tracks, two water splashes, mud splash, etc.—great fun. My clutch broke just as I was starting and I had to take the umpire's BSA instead but got round, finishing 7th.

In other respects, Nevile managed to continue many of his ordinary routines while serving as padre. He still had time to devote to writing and sermon preparation and returned to Glasgow periodically to take services or weddings. He sometimes had evenings off and could go to the cinema (his diary entry for May 11 1942 reads: "saw Walt Disney's 'Dumbo'—rather sweet") and had spells of leave when he could visit friends and relations and travel by sleeper train to London, where he was shocked to see the extent of bomb damage.

As a broadcaster, his reputation was spreading far beyond the British Isles as his wireless addresses could now be picked up worldwide. Letters of appreciation flooded in from places as far away as Canada, Jamaica, India, South Africa and the US, where his voice sounded "so clear and plain one would have thought it was only a few miles away." A listener from Rangoon even wrote offering to cover the costs of putting his latest broadcast onto a gramophone record—which would, in fact, have been a good idea, as none of this material was preserved by the BBC.

All in all, Nevile Davidson's spell as an army chaplain was not an unpleasant one. "Monotony," he wrote, "was the chief enemy."[9]

Eventually the monotony would end for the 5th Battalion which saw action again in 1944 in the assault landings on Walcheren Island in the Low Countries and thereafter fought its way into Germany. However, by then Nevile Davidson had returned to Glasgow Cathedral. Having felt in 1939 that it was his duty to serve with the forces, by the spring of 1942 he believed he should resume his original role. What changed his mind was a meeting with two Cathedral representatives when he was visiting Glasgow. One of the assistant ministers, James Bulloch, had been overwhelmed with work and had fallen seriously ill, and the kirk session urged Nevile to come back. He detected the providence of God in this request, and confided to his diary: "decided very clear duty was to apply for release from the army to return to Glasgow. It seems what mother wd. have called a 'leading' undoubtedly."

9. Davidson, *Beginnings,* 44

Consequently, on June 28 he took his last church parade as an army chaplain and attended a farewell dinner in the officers' mess at which he was presented with a silver salver. By the beginning of July he was back in Glasgow where he "changed into a black suit again and felt very strange after a year in uniform." Routine matters had to be attended to, such as arranging food and clothing coupons and an ID card. He also needed to find somewhere to live. Unlike most Scottish ministers, Nevile Davidson was not provided with a manse and when he first came to Glasgow in 1935 he had bought a three story corner house near the University at 69 Oakfield Avenue for the sum of £600. Here he had a maid and his housekeeper, Flora Cant, to look after him. However, when he went on active service he put his furniture and belongings into storage and let the house to the American Ambulance Association, a charity founded by Americans living in the UK with the aim of providing emergency vehicles and staff in wartime. During this period, Flora worked for David Beckett's maternal grandparents in Falkirk.

On release from army duties Nevile Davidson checked into the Bath Hotel while looking around for a suitable flat, frequently dining at the exclusive Western Club of which he was a member and working on his sermons there, especially on Saturday evenings when it was very quiet. By the end of July he had found a flat at 278 St. Vincent Street, opposite the "Greek" Thomson Church. Consisting of three rooms, a kitchen and a bathroom, this was offered at a rent of £55 per annum and the factor arranged for plastering, redecoration and the installation of a new bath. He also got his car—a Vauxhall—back on the road. By mid-August he was able to move his possessions out of storage as the painters were nearly finished in the flat and once everything was in place he thought "it is really going to be quite cosy and attractive." Before sleeping there for the first time on August 28, he made a trip to London and Sussex, bringing back with him two small crosses for chapels in the Cathedral and an antique mahogany "what-not." Flora returned to look after his every need—to such an extent that he thought it worth recording in his diary that he made a cup of tea for himself when she had a day off!

Not that Nevile had any intention of retreating into comfortable domesticity. Characteristically, as soon as he arrived back in Glasgow he sought out opportunities to serve the people of the city, enrolling for fire watching duties and making arrangements with the Ministry of Works for the lower church to be used as emergency accommodation for servicemen on leave who required it. As there had been an outbreak of smallpox, he wrote to the City Medical Officer offering to visit any serious cases. He also contacted the naval hostel in Rottenrow, near the Cathedral, to make arrangements with the officer in charge to hold a special service for the men and met with the Lord Provost to plan for the National Day of Prayer to be held on September 3.

Many other important national services would take place in the Cathedral in the months that followed, such as the service of thanksgiving for the work of the Civil Defence League in November 1942, when 1600 members marched through the city from Blythswood Square to the Cathedral, and the memorial service in July 1943 for the Polish Prime Minister in exile, General Sikorski, who died in a plane crash at Gibraltar. Nevile Davidson was also on the platform at the spectacular opening ceremony of "Wings for Victory" week in May 1943, designed to encourage the public to contribute towards the cost of aircraft for the RAF. A Lancaster bomber was displayed in George Square and 1350 pigeons were released, representing Glasgow's target figure of £13.5 million—a target which was in fact comfortably exceeded, as much as £15 million being raised by the city.

But Nevile's contribution to national life during wartime was not confined to carrying out ceremonial duties. His concern for the state of the nation led him to write letters to the press whenever he felt strongly about an issue and his correspondence files reveal that he spent a vast amount of time trying to persuade prominent clerics, academics and aristocrats to support him, unsuccessfully in some cases. One letter appeared in several newspapers in both Scotland and England on September 1, 1942—significantly, two days before the National Day of Prayer scheduled to take place, at the request of the King, on the third anniversary of the declaration of war. The carefully drafted letter argued that "our nation has reached what is perhaps the most critical hour of its history" and contrasted the national response to the invasion threat of 1940 with the current situation where "a greater spirit of dedication" was called for. In fact, the signatories of the letter went as far as to say that the nation required "a rude awakening" as "the destiny of our whole Christian civilisation hangs in the balance."[10] The letter does not go into specifics but readers would naturally be aware that at this stage of the war the whole of Europe lay under German domination,

10. *Glasgow Herald,* September 1 1942

Japan was advancing in the East and in India Ghandi was leading mass protests demanding British withdrawal.

In October 1942 the Cathedral minister was concerned about the need to provide recreation and entertainment for members of the forces who found themselves in the city for a time. He was nevertheless uneasy at a proposal to allow cinemas to open on Sundays, making the rather impractical suggestion that access should be for men and women in the services only, rather than the general public—an arrangement which, predictably, did not materialize. He further made a plea that any such Sunday entertainment should be "worthy of our Scottish religious heritage and traditions" and suggested that a better idea would be for church members to offer hospitality in their own homes to service personnel.

A fortnight later, Nevile took to the correspondence columns once more, this time to criticize Winston Churchill over the question of putting prisoners of war in shackles, a policy being proposed by way of retaliation for the treatment of British prisoners by the Germans. Nevile argued powerfully that if this action on the part of the enemy amounted to a breach of the Geneva Convention, Britain should not behave in a similar manner. This, he said, was "a morally perilous course." "If as a nation we have certain principles and standards, let us not be tempted to compromise them, whatever the enemy may do."[11] He returned to the theme of reprisals when preaching to the congregation of St. Columba's Church of Scotland, Pont Street, London at New Year 1943 (then meeting in temporary accommodation as the church had been destroyed in an air raid) in a sermon entitled "the Preservation of the Gentler Virtues in Time of War."

Frequent newspaper letters and pronouncements on public issues of this kind suggest that Nevile Davidson was emerging as a spokesman for the national church and at this stage of his life he was becoming more actively involved in the committee work of the Church of Scotland. Particularly important at the time was the Huts and Canteens committee, chaired by Charles Warr, who invited Nevile to participate. Building on a scheme used during the First World War, the committee raised funds to provide places of rest for soldiers where refreshments and reading and writing materials were provided. Free copies of the New Testament in modern speech were available for those who wanted them and numerous ministers who were not official army chaplains volunteered their services to provide spiritual support. One key difference between the conflicts of 1914–18 and 1939–45

11. *Glasgow Herald,* October 15 1942

was that much of the former took place in static positions whereas action in the latter was far more mobile, and the Huts and Canteens committee responded by not only providing temporary premises but supplying specially-adapted mobile refreshment vans. Where chaplains were not available, Huts and Canteens staff would lead services of worship and often the hut would be affectionately nicknamed the "Kirk o' Jocks."

Recognition of Nevile Davidson's increasingly high profile came in the form of a letter from the Clerk to the Senate of Glasgow University in March 1943 offering him the honorary degree of Doctor of Divinity—the youngest minister in Scotland to have that honor conferred on him, though he confessed that "I don't really feel as old or as dignified as 'Dr' would suggest!" He was inundated with letters and cards and received so many congratulatory phone calls that he ended up taking the receiver off. At a celebration in June in the Ca' D'Oro restaurant at the corner of Gordon Street and Union Street attended by 200 members of the congregation, he was presented with his DD gown which he wore on the following Sunday as "I gathered that many people were expecting and hoping I would. It was so sumptuous that I felt rather shy."

The comment is an indication that, notwithstanding academic glory and public adulation, Nevile Davidson retained his humility. On his forty-fourth birthday on February 13, he recorded in his diary that "[I] spent a little longer than usual in meditation and prayer. May I get more, and not less, conscious of the tremendous importance and wonderful comfort of constant communion with God as life goes on." And, in spite of all his important public engagements, he continued to carry out routine parish duties which others might have been happy to delegate entirely to an assistant. He would always take his turn conducting the Cathedral daily service and most days saw him making home or hospital visits. After leading the big Civil Defence League service in November 1942, he might have been forgiven for taking a day off; instead, he "visited a poor family where a tiny boy had been burned to death."

Yet another role taken on by Nevile Davidson was as a trustee of Iona Abbey. George MacLeod (1895–1991) had resigned from Govan Old Parish Church in 1938 to pursue his dream of setting up a community consisting of ministers, students and unemployed men working together to rebuild the ancient abbey. The pacifist and socialist MacLeod was regarded as something of a maverick within the Church of Scotland, believed by some to be "halfway to Rome and halfway to Moscow," yet he got on well with the more conventional Davidson, who came from a similar privileged background. Once, he stood in when Nevile was preaching elsewhere and when Nevile came back to the Cathedral after taking the service he found that MacLeod was still in full flight in the pulpit.

In July 1943 Nevile had occasion to travel to the island of Iona in his capacity as a trustee. It was a long journey: breakfast at 6 a.m., train from Buchanan Street station to Oban at 7.15 a.m., a steamer to Mull, a drive in a hired car from Craignure along the Ross of Mull and finally the ferry across to the island. "A dull rainy morning," he wrote in his diary, "but the mist lifted and we had grand views of the islands and mountains."

The purpose of the visit was to meet with MacLeod and others to discuss new furnishings for the Abbey. But Nevile Davidson was not to know that he was about to meet someone else who would change his life for ever.

# 5

## "Happiness Beyond All My Dreams"

### MARRIED LIFE, 1943–1945

THERE ARE STILL SOME members of the congregation of Glasgow Cathedral old enough to remember that one of Nevile Davidson's favorite hymns was *Summer Suns are Glowing*.

The sun was certainly glowing for him on July 26, 1943 as he boarded the ferry to Iona. He noticed a "charming, quiet and reserved girl" about to carry a large suitcase on board and gallantly offered to assist. When the ferry reached the jetty at the other side, Nevile was greeted by Sir David Russell (1872–1956), the driving force behind the papermaking company Tullis Russell, and a generous benefactor of Iona Abbey and many other causes. Russell and his wife invited him to lunch the next day and then, to his surprise, escorted the young lady up the hill.

The young lady in question was Margaret (Peggy) Martin, the twenty-four year old daughter of Colonel Charles de Carteret Martin, a doctor in the Indian medical service serving in the Jubbulpore division of the Central Provinces of British India, and grand-daughter of General Sir Malcolm H. S. Grover. After leaving boarding school, Peggy had lived abroad as her father was on active service but at the time of her Iona trip she was staying in the family home in Yateley in Hampshire with her mother and younger brother Peter who himself would have a distinguished military career, serving all over the world with the Cheshire Regiment and ending up as a Major General.

After meeting for lunch, Sir David Russell's party on Iona went on an expedition to the west side of the island where Peggy picked wild flowers to send to her mother. The next day, they visited the south end and Nevile and Peggy spent a long time "searching for pebbles and lying on the sands and talking in the sun." But the idyll was short-lived. By July 30 the minister had to catch the ferry at 6 a.m. on a "wet, grey morning" to make his way back to Glasgow. He later acknowledged that his mind had been on other things than the furnishings of Iona Abbey.

Back in his St. Vincent Street flat, Nevile sat down and confided his feelings to his diary, but what exactly he wrote will never be known, for the pages covering the next few days have been torn out. For her part, Peggy Martin returned and told her mother all about Nevile. She must have approved as about a week later he received a "charming letter" inviting him to stay with them for a weekend. He wrote a long reply accepting and on his next trip south to visit relatives rang up Peggy at Yateley where he arrived on August 27.

Corner Cottage, where the Martins lived, was described by Nevile as "a Queen Anne house with very low ceilings, old bare rafters and meandering passages." Peggy was currently working as the manager of a canteen in a nearby war factory with a staff of twenty under her and each day she cycled there and back, a round trip of some twenty-four miles.

Peggy and Nevile spent a "perfect" weekend together, strolling in the grounds of the house, walking and cycling in the surrounding countryside and sitting up talking late at night. Before he left, he asked Peggy for a photograph of herself. On the Monday morning, Peggy set off for her factory while Nevile headed back to London and booked the night sleeper north. While he was waiting, he "began a very important letter to Peggy" and once on the train "took two aspirins and slept marvellously."

Throughout his life, Nevile always had plenty of female friends whom he met through the many social events arranged by his extended family, and much of his leisure time as a youth had been occupied with cycling, playing tennis and having picnics with his companions, though there are few hints in his diaries of him being especially close to any one particular girl. With Peggy, it was clearly a case of love at first sight; the relationship developed rapidly and the fact that he was twenty years older than she was does not seem to have been an issue.

The day Nevile arrived back to Glasgow happened to be Peggy's twenty-fifth birthday and he spent time, unsuccessfully, trying to find a brooch or bracelet to send her. It was not until a week later that he found something suitable: a lizard-skin handbag. On September 6 Peggy replied to his "very important letter" in very encouraging terms, but "she didn't give her final answer."

Perhaps it was the strain of the wait, or just one of Nevile's recurring spells of worrying about his health, but during these weeks he had seen a doctor who told him he was suffering from "nervous exhaustion." He had also been more than once to an eye specialist who reassured him that there was nothing wrong with his sight other than tiredness. As a result, he arranged a stay at the Nethy Bridge house where he was joined by Cois and some family friends. It was here, on September 23, that he received the news he longed for: "a wonderful letter from Peggy accepting me!"

During this time of recuperation he returned to Glasgow periodically for Cathedral duties and on October 4 attended a huge gathering at the St. Andrew's Hall to inaugurate the opening of an evangelistic campaign. Weekdays were spent in the tranquility of Nethy Bridge, with peaceful talks in the evening and autumn afternoon walks in the woods where the river was "full and fast and a beautiful peaty brown colour."

Forest House, Nethy Bridge, now much altered from Nevile Davidson's time. Built by Rev. James Davidson in 1910, it was used by Nevile as a holiday home until 1970. (Photo by the author).

By the beginning of November he had returned to the flat and was arranging for his mother's engagement ring to be enlarged to fit Peggy, who was making a weekend visit for which, once again, diary entries are lacking. They worked on their wedding plans, booking the Grosvenor ballroom for the reception on January 19 and arranging for Charles Warr to officiate and George MacLeod to act as best man. When MacLeod heard of the engagement he wrote saying that "the news brings a (much needed) conviction that the Trustees of Iona Abbey have a place in destiny: as but for them you might not have met her."

A month later Peggy was back in Glasgow. Two ladies in the Cathedral congregation had offered the gift of a large house in University Gardens for use as a manse, but the couple decided it would not be suitable and planned to stay at the St. Vincent Street flat, at least until the end of the war. Christmas was coming up; it was the pantomime season and Nevile took Peggy to the Alhambra Theatre to see Will Fyffe, a popular Scottish music hall artist—"absolutely first class and we laughed almost without stopping. Peggy looked simply lovely in a black frock with a tiny lace collar and cuffs."

Yet Nevile was never entirely off duty, and Peggy accompanied him on the first of many pastoral visits, to Ruchill Hospital to see a young soldier who had recently come home after three years in a German prisoner of war camp, only to be hospitalized suffering from tuberculosis. He died about a year later and Nevile conducted his funeral.

Peggy had a taste of another aspect of what lay in store for her as a minister's wife when she attended a small dinner party at the flat at which the guests were Principal and Mrs Fulton of Glasgow University and Dr. H. Sloane Coffin (1877–1954), a prominent American Presbyterian. Perhaps her first appearance at the Cathedral on the Sunday morning would have been more of an ordeal as she sat in the manse pew on the north side, in full view of an inquisitive congregation, and was introduced to the elders in the sacristy afterwards.

When Peggy returned home on the night sleeper on December 21, "the flat felt terribly dull and empty." Nevile's poignant diary entry for the last day of 1943 reads as follows:

> So ends the most marvellous and memorable year of my life which has brought me happiness beyond all my dreams and infinitely beyond all my deserts. Laus Deo. And may He only make me a little more worthy of it.

While they were apart Nevile and Peggy communicated by letter and telephone as much as wartime restrictions would allow. Calls were limited to six minutes' duration ("which seemed more like six seconds!") but they soon acquired the art of getting the maximum amount of conversation into the meager time allowed and Nevile drew comfort from the fact that in a few weeks Peggy would always be by his side. Still troubled by tiredness and head pains, he was given some reassurance by his best man, George MacLeod, who said that he, too, had suffered from the same "nervous exhaustion" and had recovered with rest. A few days before the wedding, Nevile wrote in his diary that "The long wait and separation has been a great strain, but it is difficult to believe that it is so nearly over, and that on Monday I shall [have] her for always: marvellous thought, for which I gave special thanks in my evening prayer."

The wedding of Nevile Davidson and Peggy Martin at Glasgow Cathedral in January 1944. (Photo courtesy of the Herald and Times Group).

The diary entry for January 19 1944 consists of three words and two ex-
clamation marks: "Our wedding day!!" The bride was not given away by
her father who was serving in India but by her brother Peter, then an army
Major. According to the assistant minister, who at that time was the Rev.
Fred Fulton, the wedding represented a historic "first" for the Cathedral. As
he rather ponderously put it in the *Chronicle*, it was "the first instance of a
direct descendant in office of St. Mungo taking upon himself the vows of
Holy Matrimony beneath the venerable arches of the sanctuary in which he
serves." No doubt Fulton was right, but the congregation would probably
have been more interested in what the bride was wearing. The *Dundee Courier* described the outfit in some detail: "the bridal gown was of off-white
chiffon velvet cut on classical lines. A heart-shaped necklace and gathers
added distinction to the close-fitting corsage, and the softly flowing skirt
fell into a fan-shaped train." After the event, Warr wrote to his newly-mar-
ried friend saying that "The old Cathedral looked lovely on your wedding
day and the sunshine that fell on you both at the Great West Door seemed
a benediction and an augury of future joy and peace." Among the guests
was David Beckett, then a boy of seven, who, on being told that George
MacLeod was the best man, took this statement literally and inquired, "Why
is he better than anyone else?" The reception was held at the Grosvenor in
Gordon Street, one of Glasgow's most upmarket venues, and a few days
later the happy couple found themselves on honeymoon in Portree on the
Isle of Skye where they were thrilled to receive their first letter addressed to
"The Rev. and Mrs. Davidson."

At this stage of marital bliss, even minor mishaps provided a source
of fun. The weather in Skye in January was, as might have been expected,
very wet and when trying to dry out their clothes in their room after a walk,
Nevile accidentally knocked over the stand on which they were hanging,
setting fire to a pair of Peggy's stockings. Usually so meticulous about his
appearance, the new husband had forgotten to have his hair cut before he
left on honeymoon and Peggy tried to cut it herself, resulting in a good deal
of hilarity as she thought he looked like he was wearing a wig.

At Dunvegan Castle the newly-weds lunched with Mrs (later Dame)
Flora MacLeod, Chief of Clan MacLeod and, being so close to Lochcarron,
took the opportunity to cross by ferry and hire a car to call on Dr. MacLean
Watt who was "as usual full of talk and showed us all kinds of things in his
house." Now in his late seventies, MacLean Watt seemed a rather lonely
figure and Nevile was pleased to find his young grandson staying with him.

"It was cheering to see the old man and the tiny boy together. He showed us his wife's grave in the little churchyard nearby, looking up towards the mountains." Next came a visit to Grantown-on-Spey and then the couple took the train to Nethy Bridge where Peggy stayed in Forest House for the first time.

By February 8 they had reached "the last day of our perfect honeymoon" and returned to Glasgow where Peggy now had to take on the many social responsibilities expected of a minister's wife in these days. She presented the prizes at a whist drive in the Cathedral halls where she was introduced to a "bewildering number of people but quite enjoyed it." Later in the month a big congregational reception took place in the Ca' D'Oro Restaurant for about 170 guests and the Davidsons shook hands with them all as they arrived. They were presented with a check for £193 as a wedding present; throughout the evening there was "a delightful atmosphere of friendliness" and, in the opinion of her adoring husband, "Peggy looked a most lovely hostess." Peggy regularly attended the gatherings of old people (known as the Mission) in the Cathedral halls, and was persuaded to become president of the Women's Guild as well as vice president of the West of Scotland Society for Prevention of Cruelty to Animals. Members of the congregation were pleased that the minister's wife often came with him on house calls: "Peggy always gets on so beautifully with all the people, of whatever sort, that we visit." In October 1944, after opening a sale of work at a church in the Partick district, she went straight to Springburn with Nevile to visit a Mrs. Walls, who was blind and paralyzed on one side. "She was specially delighted to see Peggy and said her visit was an answer to her longing." Calling on another family, Peggy was presented with a "charming old spinning-wheel, which is supposed to be over 200 years old." She polished it up and put it beside the fireplace in the dining room.

As well as the congregation, there were many friends and relatives for her to get to know, such as the Beckett family in Milngavie, Sir John Stirling Maxwell of Pollok House (who, at the age of seventy-seven was "very frail and helpless but marvellously courteous, brave and alert in mind") and Nevile's Aunt Ella who was "very admiring" of Peggy. Ella asked her to go out of the room for a minute so that she could tell him confidentially that the doctor had assured her that Peggy would have a large family of five boys. It was just as well that she was able to give Peggy her blessing, for early in May 1944 her doctor phoned to say that she was very ill. The Davidsons reached Edinburgh in time to see her but she had lost consciousness and, two days later, she died. "It is a relief to think of her as having now really escaped from all weakness and worry and entered upon the life everlasting", reflected Nevile in his diary. Under the terms of her will, Nevile and Cois each received a sum of £3000—the equivalent of over £90,000 today.

A further financial windfall arrived in September 1945 when the house at 69 Oakfield Avenue sold for £1700—£1100 more than Nevile had paid for it ten years earlier. He had not lived in it since letting the premises to the American Ambulance Service when he took up his duties as an army chaplain. He and Peggy took a last look round in October, deciding which furniture to bring to the flat, what to put in storage and what to sell, and enjoyed a picnic lunch in the almost empty drawing room, sitting in the bay window in bright sunshine. Space for more furniture in St. Vincent Street was limited, though an extra room was freed up as Flora had decided that, with the arrival of a Mrs Davidson, it would be better to move out to a room in nearby North Street, though her daily services would continue to be relied on by the couple.

There were indications that Flora found some difficulty in coming to terms with the new regime at first. During one early trip to Nethy Bridge Flora was "being very difficult and moody and grumbling about everything so after lunch Peggy gave her a severe talking to, and she gave notice." But things must have been quickly smoothed over, as the faithful Flora remained with the Davidsons until her death at the age of seventy-four in 1970. Fiercely protective of Nevile, she could be a formidable lady who, in the words of one visitor, "could scare the hell out of you." On her days off Nevile helped Peggy to prepare dinner and to wash up, which must have been a new experience for him.

Flora had moved out but a newcomer had moved in: a nine week old dachshund puppy purchased from kennels in Bearsden at a cost of fifteen guineas. "Gentle, and not the least nervous about his new surroundings," he was to be called Dingwall—full name "Dingwall Dachshund Davidson"—and would be the couple's constant companion wherever they traveled. He had his daily walks in Kelvingrove Park and sat between husband and wife on train journeys. Sometimes he proved to be a source of worry as when, during a visit to Aberdeen, he appeared to have a fit and Nevile thought he had been poisoned, though he soon recovered. Then there was the incident at an old coaching inn near Loch Ailort in Invernessshire when Dingwall disappeared for a while and the niece of the landlady rushed in and said that he had killed one of the ducks. Nevile "made all possible apologies, but we all felt rather in disgrace."

Once married, Nevile generally followed his previous routine of sleeping late in the mornings, spending time writing, preparing sermons and making telephone calls before lunch, visiting parishioners or attending committee meetings in the afternoons and carrying out frequent evening engagements. A couple of times per week, his secretary, Miss Stewart, would report in the evenings for two hours' dictation. He greatly valued his new-found domestic contentment and when the couple found themselves free of commitments their evenings would occasionally be spent going to the theater but more often by reading aloud to each other. Nevile continued to record in his diary the books he had been reading, with a new preference for short stories and biographies of women which appealed to Peggy. During an October stay at Forest House in 1945 he read Margaret Cole's life of the pioneering economist and socialist Beatrice Webb; *Unforgettable, Unforgotten,* the newly-published autobiography of John Buchan's sister Anna, who wrote under the name of O. Douglas and *From One Century to Another,* the memoirs of Elizabeth Haldane, Scotland's first female Justice of the Peace. *The History of the Fairchild Family* by the nineteenth century children's writer Mary Martha Sherwood offered purely escapist pleasure: "it takes us into an absolutely different world of peace and simplicity and family happiness and goodness, which we both love." Another shared pastime was organizing newspaper cuttings about the Cathedral into scrapbooks.

Each week, the couple would endeavor to escape, not just through the pages of fiction, but by taking a day trip and the heading "our day off" now begins to appear in the diaries. Partly this was a reaction to the restrictions of wartime which were slowly, if not entirely, easing. In June 1945 the Davidsons celebrated the renewal of the basic petrol ration of five gallons per month by taking their first long pleasure drive into the country, traveling to Milngavie, Strathblane and Campsie and picnicking on the edge of Loch Walton, a trip that was unfortunately cut short by heavy rain. Every day Nevile and Dingwall would walk through the park to collect the car which was kept garaged at Wylie and Lochhead's in Berkeley Street. Peggy often took her turn at driving, but the Vauxhall's engine could be temperamental; finding replacement tires and parts in that era of post-war shortages proved difficult and longer trips were usually taken by train.

As ever, there were regular retreats to the Nethy Bridge house where "the silence and peace are marvellous after the noise and rush of Glasgow and neither the telephone nor the doorbell ever ring." Fresh food was more easily obtainable there, too: one January day in 1945 they picked up a dozen eggs—more than they'd had in Glasgow in the previous three months—and arranged for deliveries of fish, rabbits and vegetables. In addition to Nethy Bridge, Peggy was keen to visit other places her husband had lived before they knew each other and while in North Berwick in September 1944 for a Blackadder Church centenary meeting Nevile took her to see the graves of his parents. Aberdeen was a frequent destination as Cois had an office job there at this time, and when Nevile was asked to preach at King's College chapel at the closing service of the term in December 1945, Peggy wanted to see the inside of the former St. Mary's manse which, like the church itself, had been bought over by the university. It happened to be undergoing some renovation work and the tradesmen let them in to look around.

The Davidsons' first extended summer holiday in July 1944 started with a sail from Oban to Barra and South Uist on the MV *Lochearn*, a mail steamer operated by David MacBrayne Ltd. During this trip Peggy took up sketching and painting and, naturally, her husband thought the results "charming." On South Uist Nevile bathed in the sea then lay in the sun and read aloud while Dingwall played about—"a perfect day" for which he paid a heavy price, returning home "in agony" with severe sunburn. While Peggy did "a rather nice water colour sketch from the boat", her husband tried his hand at fishing and caught four brown trout. On the island of Barra, the Davidsons attended the local parish church where they found only fourteen in the congregation, the population being predominantly Roman Catholic. In the absence of the minister on active service, the service was taken by an elderly missionary acting as locum and was conducted in Gaelic, "except for an English prayer put in for our benefit." They left before the sermon began—presumably not as a gesture of uncharacteristic rudeness but simply because they would not have been able to understand the language. On the same trip, they met the writer Compton MacKenzie (1883–1972) who had built a house on the island. A convert to Catholicism, a romantic supporter of the Jacobites and a Scottish nationalist, MacKenzie impressed Nevile: "He was extremely pleasant and insisted on our staying to tea . . . He is very 'left' in his views and sympathies, extremely well-informed and cultured."

During all these trips Nevile was constantly on the lookout for gifts that would please Peggy. In Stirling "I bought her a rather charming little old amethyst brooch surrounded by tiny pearls." On Barra "I went to see a widow who weaves tweed and chose a beautiful light brown with dyes of sea-green and arranged for her to weave ten yards of tweed for Peggy. I am giving it to Peggy as a birthday present." While at the Orphan Homes at Bridge of Weir to address the annual meeting, he visited the workshops of what was then called the "epileptic colony" and bought her a red scarf. Most extravagantly of all, Peggy had admired a "beautiful pair of small diamond and turquoise earrings" in Aberdeen in December 1945 and when Peggy went back to Cois' room, Nevile returned to the jeweller's shop and bought the earrings to keep as a first wedding anniversary present. They cost him £95. In comparison, Peggy's gifts to him, such as a walking stick, a pipe and a knife with six different implements, seem comparatively modest, but he was always delighted with them.

Gradually, Nevile's friends began to notice how marriage changed him. One family member described the process in some detail: "Perhaps because of his bachelordom, or it may have been because of the heavy responsibilities he carried, he had tended to cultivate an image of austerity and asceticism that made him seem to ordinary folk just a little aloof. Peggy with her blithe spirit, and of course because of their mutual devotion to one another, was able to change this—quite imperceptibly, I'm sure, as far as Nevile was concerned, but she made him appreciate the value of relaxation and helped him rediscover for himself and for the benefit of others the lighter side of life."

On the last page of his 1945 diary Nevile only needed two words to sum up his feelings about the year gone by: "*Very* happy."

If these years were a time of personal happiness for Nevile Davidson, they were equally a period of national rejoicing. Peace was in sight and as minister of the Cathedral he had a key role to play in the ceremonies marking the end of hostilities.

Since the Normandy landings in June 1944, allied confidence had grown. By September Nevile had drawn up a victory thanksgiving order of service and by February of 1945 he had "made practically every arrangement except the date." VE (Victory Europe) Day at last arrived on May 8 when the Cathedral bell was rung for fifteen minutes and a congregation of 800 people gathered for a service. At midnight Nevile walked down to George Square which was filled with "an enormous and hilarious but friendly crowd." The following day he gave Flora a day off and took his place on the platform near the Cenotaph in the Square to lead a short act of thanksgiving in front of a crowd of 30,000, watched from the balcony of the City Chambers by Peggy and her mother. Another Cathedral thanksgiving service took place on Sunday May 13, with a procession of clergy and choir singing the 95th Psalm: "O come, let us sing unto the Lord: let us make a joyful noise to the rock of our salvation." All this was but a prelude to the main national service of thanksgiving in St. Giles' Cathedral, Edinburgh the following Wednesday in the presence of the King and Queen, at which Nevile took the first part of the service and Charles Warr preached.

Some insight into Nevile's organizational skills can be seen from the arrangements he made for a memorial service for President Franklin D. Roosevelt, entirely on his own initiative. Reading his *Glasgow Herald* over breakfast on April 13, Nevile learned of the President's death and immediately contacted the American consul, the Lord Provost, and the commanders of US and British forces. In the afternoon he drafted a sermon for the occasion. Two days later, the Cathedral was filled to overflowing and hundreds had to stand in the aisles. There was a parade of 250 US troops, the consul read the lesson and the service ended with the British and American national anthems. All in all, it was a remarkable logistical exercise, achieved in just forty hours.

Though he was undoubtedly a master of the ceremonial occasion, it would be wrong to see Nevile Davidson as simply an establishment figurehead. He may not have shared the radical, socialist opinions of George MacLeod, but that does not mean to say that he thought the church should remain silent on political, social and international issues. For example, he voiced strong opposition in May 1945 to the government's decree that armed forces based in Germany should not fraternize with civilians. A regular army officer stationed in Berlin wrote to him saying "we are forbidden even to say 'Good Morning' or to return the waving hands of little children. I wonder how much longer we can go on hating, or pretending to hate, our enemies." In a powerful speech to the General Assembly of the Church of Scotland, Nevile argued that non-fraternization was a form of psychological punishment to the defeated nation which was bound to breed bitterness. But the General Assembly refused to back him, maintaining that "the whole German nation, sharing in some degree at least in the guilt [of the Nazis] must, and will, share in the sufferings." Nevertheless, Nevile received many letters of support for his stance, some from ex-servicemen who said that 90% of soldiers would agree with him but had to obey the order because they feared that otherwise their release from the army would be delayed as a punishment.

Undeterred, Nevile used a broadcast service in September to preach on the theme of the Christian duty to forgive our enemies, with special reference to Germany. And when the government proposed further victory parades in June 1946, he wrote to the newspapers denouncing this as "a shocking extravagance" in view of the terrible shortage of food in parts of Europe. He had already encouraged his congregation to sign a petition urging the British government to take action on this matter and at the Cathedral halls in December 1945 people handed in second-hand clothing and gifts to send to destitute people in Holland. He had also written to the *Herald* urging the citizens of Glasgow to contribute to his "Christmas Tree Fund" for European children, resulting in £230 and twelve large cases of clothes and toys being collected.

Though Nevile may not have succeeded in stopping the victory parades, he organized something he considered more important: a "Service of Intercession for Peace and Understanding among the Nations of the World." "However inopportune the time may be for victory celebrations, it is certainly very urgent to have prayer for peace," he wrote. A 10,000 strong procession took part in the celebrations on June 8 but only sixty came to the Peace Service that evening.

A still more remarkable service took place in the Cathedral on January 5 1947 for German prisoners of war staying in camps and hostels in the Glasgow area. Having received permission from the War Office, he sent out invitations to more than 100 different places and prepared an order of service in German and English. Nevile himself delivered the bidding prayer in German to a congregation of 1000 Germans and 700 civilians and other prayers were led by Markus Barth, son of the theologian Karl Barth. The sermon was delivered in German, too, the preacher being the Rev. David H.C. Read who had spent four years as a prisoner of war in a German prisoner camp.[1] Hymns included *Stille Nacht*, *Nun Danket* and Martin Luther's *Ein Feste Burg* and the most moving moment was when everyone recited

---

1. While a prisoner of war, Rev. David H. C. Read (1910–2001) prepared a series of talks on Christian belief and when one of the guards found out about this, he confessed that before the war he himself had been a Lutheran pastor and helped Read send his manuscript home where it was published in 1944 as *A Prisoners' Quest*. Further details of Read's career can be found in *The Church of Scotland Army Chaplains in the Second World War* by D. G. Coulter (PhD diss.,University of Edinburgh, 1997). Read later became a noted preacher at Madison Avenue Presbyterian Church, New York.

the Lord's Prayer in his or her own language. It was a powerful and forward-looking symbol of reconciliation.

With the war over it was now time, as Nevile told his congregation, to turn from tasks of destruction to purposes of reconstruction. The question was, how would the church rise to the challenge?

# 6

## "Great Times and Great Tasks"

### ADAPTING TO THE POST-WAR WORLD, 1945–50

IN A SPEECH AT the kirk session lunch held after Nevile Davidson's induction to Glasgow Cathedral in 1936, Charles Warr maintained that "there never was a time when the Church of Scotland stood more broad-based upon the affection of the Scottish people . . . To talk of the waning power of the Church was mere silliness."[1] That may have been how things looked from the lofty heights of the pulpit of St. Giles in Edinburgh, but Warr was perhaps not best placed to assess what ordinary Scots really thought of the Kirk: his autobiography *The Glimmering Landscape* is so full of references to his friends in the aristocracy that cynics said it should be renamed *The Glittering Handshake.*

Other speakers at the induction service were more realistic about the future of the Scottish church. In his sermon the Rev. Sydney Still of Queen's Park West acknowledged that "there were many people today who cried insistently that the Church was an outworn and defeated institution" while the Rev. Alfred Brown of Maxwell Church, delivering the charge to the new minister, referred to the "opposing forces of the world and the worldly spirit whose grip was deep and firm."[2]

Up until the 1930s the Kirk worked on the assumption that Scotland was a Christian nation and that its role was to offer a "territorial ministry"—in

1. *The Glasgow Herald,* January 31 1935
2. *The Scotsman,* January 31 1935

other words, a network of parish churches covering the whole country. From time to time there were efforts to encourage people to attend church, such as the "Recall to Religion" campaign of 1938—a title which implies that everyone previously had some church connection and simply needed to be enticed back.

The reality was that the disconnect between the church and the masses was far more profound. Much of the urban working class had been lost during the inter-war period as a result of a perception that the Kirk had failed to speak out about social issues and had largely fallen back on the view associated with Thomas Chalmers in the nineteenth century, that poverty was caused by individual sins and failings rather than by social and economic forces.[3]

One visionary churchman who had been trying to tackle the problem head on was Nevile's friend and best man, George MacLeod, in whose Govan parish two-thirds of the men were unemployed. MacLeod challenged the notion that the Kirk was "no' for the likes o' us" by organizing a visitation of every house in the parish, backed up by a "chain of prayer" and street preaching. People began to return to church and the Sunday School and youth organizations grew. MacLeod's notion of the gospel involved a radical social dimension: he recruited unemployed volunteers to work on a war memorial garden project and this was followed by even more ambitious schemes like building a holiday center near Fenwick Moor for Govan people and, above all, the formation of the Iona Community and the restoration of Iona Abbey.[4]

In spite of everything, Sunday church attendances remained high in many parts of Scotland after World War II and members of the post-war generation still look back fondly to a time when social life centered round the church and people met their spouses in the youth fellowship. And yet, as Steve Bruce puts it in *Scottish Gods*, his study of religion in Scotland over the last hundred years, "it is difficult to exaggerate the extent to which . . . settled patterns of behaviour were disrupted by six years of war which, one way or another, mobilised most of the population."[5] One example was the erosion of the strict observance of the Sabbath which had long been characteristic of Scottish life. Small steps such as the relaxation of restrictions on

3. See Forsyth, *Mission by the People*, 75–87

4. The full story of George MacLeod and the Iona Community is told in Ronald Ferguson, *George MacLeod*.

5. Bruce, *Scottish Gods*, 100

Sunday opening of places of entertainment were the thin end of the wedge; a return in 1945 to the status quo of 1939 was simply not going to happen.

Recognizing that a new approach would be needed when peace returned, the General Assembly of 1940 had appointed John Baillie (1886–1960), Professor of Divinity at the University of Edinburgh, to chair the portentously named "Commission for the Interpretation of God's Will in the Present Crisis" and Nevile Davidson was invited to join. From 1942 onwards, he regularly traveled through to Edinburgh by train for meetings of the commission, whose annual reports were put together in 1946 under the title of *God's Will for Church and Nation* covering areas such as marriage and family life, education, social and industrial life, international reconstruction and church organization.

The Baillie Commission acknowledged the shortcomings of the pre-war church in failing to identify with the poor in society and distanced itself from the ultra-conservative and even racist stance associated with the Very Rev John White (1867–1951) who, as convener of the Church and Nation Committee in the 1920s, had condemned "the menace of the Irish race to our Scottish nationality." Baillie's reports, by contrast, presented a much wider vision of church and society, arguing that "the threat of universal secularism can be countered only by the Universal Church." Assessing the work of the commission half a century later, Professor Stewart Brown wrote that the Church of Scotland "turned to Baillie's idea of a church working to inculcate a Christian morality in a pluralistic society and a social welfare state, while recognizing the limits of influence and authority, and its need to convince rather than to instruct".[6] In other words, Bailie knew that the church would have to adapt in order to survive in a very different world.

6. Morton, *God's Will in a Time of Crisis*, 28

Lauchlan MacLean Watt (1867–1957),
predecessor of Nevile Davidson
as Minister of Glasgow Cathedral.
(Photo: Glasgow Cathedral).

Charles Warr (1892–1959),
Minister of St. Giles'
Cathedral, Edinburgh.
(Photo: Glasgow Cathedral).

George MacLeod (1895–1991),
Baron MacLeod of Fuinary and
founder of the Iona Community.
(Photo: Iona Community).

William Morris (1925–2013),
Nevile Davidson's successor as minister
of Glasgow Cathedral.
(Photo: Glasgow Cathedral).

To Nevile Davidson this changing climate "presented the Church with an immense opportunity for evangelism and the whole Christian life of the country for the next 100 years would depend upon the way the Church responded to this challenge." In July 1944 he struck a note of urgency during his address on "Preparing for the Return of Men from the Forces" at a conference on evangelism arranged in St. Andrews by Divinity professors:

> through loneliness, hardship, danger and death many service people [have] begun to take a new interest in supreme things, and when they returned to civil life they would be prepared to give the church another chance. They might give the church only a short chance. The church must be ready.

He admitted that "The church had lost hold on the majority of younger men of the working class from various causes—smug respectability, complacent conservatism, excessive caution." His solution? Preaching should be simple and straightforward and use the ordinary language of home, shop and office; it must have a note of passionate personal conviction, and the church must seek to bridge the gulf between religion and everyday life. The day of Sunday religion was finished, he said.[7]

Followers of MacLeod would have agreed—but they wanted to go much further. The Rev. T. Ralph Morton of the Iona Community argued that the church must begin creative experiments in economics and social living among its own members; what was required was not only personal faith but "a new corporate committal" or, as MacLeod would have said, not just "soul salvation" but "whole salvation." Nevile, by contrast, stuck to the more orthodox line that Christianity could only change society by first changing individuals:

> Everything we dream of, whether for ourselves or for society— from new and better housing to new and better international relationships—will follow only on first getting right with God, as the old-fashioned evangelists used to put it. [8]

This is at least part of the explanation why Nevile did not become fully involved with the Iona Community, even though he was a trustee of Iona Abbey and a great friend of George MacLeod.

During 1944 and 1945 Nevile Davidson attended many meetings of a Glasgow Presbytery committee on evangelism which eventually produced

7. *St. Andrews Citizen*, July 15 1944

8. *The Daily Record*, November 13 1945

a 25,000 word report and in January of the following year he traveled to Emmanuel College, Cambridge for another conference on the subject arranged by the British Council of Churches (where he found himself sharing a room with MacLeod). This brought together "about sixty delegates from every conceivable denomination" and the theme of the first session was "Is there a Word of God for Our Time?" Nevile's verdict on the three day event was that "although the conference did not perhaps in the end register any large or vital resolutions, it is the first inter-church conference on evangelism in this country."

The comment is significant as it points to the fact that he viewed evangelism and ecumenism as inseparably linked. In these years Nevile was a key figure in an organization called "The Christian Front in Glasgow" involving representatives of the Church of Scotland, Episcopal, Methodist, Baptist and Congregational churches. Initial meetings focused on coming up with a definition of the Christian gospel on which the churches could make a united witness. "We don't claim to say anything very new or very startling, but we are going to speak together," said Nevile. "That, perhaps, in itself is something new."[9] In November 1945 a week of public meetings took place, with mixed results. Frost and fog meant that only 100 people turned out to hear Nevile speak on "Our Common Faith" but he hoped that numbers would grow. The next meeting on "Christianity and the Home" attracted no more than sixty, and was followed by no discussion at all, but the final two evenings on "Christianity and the Social Order" and "Christianity and the International Order" were better attended and aroused some lively debate. Nevile was also able to use his position as minister of the Cathedral to contribute to ecumenical co-operation through invitations to guest preachers. 1945, for instance, saw a series of Lenten evening services on the theme of "Many Voices but One Gospel" led by speakers from different denominations.

Fundamental to these various experiments was Nevile's belief that "if the Christian Gospel was to reach the masses of the ordinary population in the country the Church must discover and use every available channel of communication."[10] His pioneering work in radio has already been noted and a key proposal of his report on evangelism was that a full-time "radio minister" should be appointed for an experimental period of one year. He also frequently made use of the columns of newspapers and in March 1947

9. *The Scotsman,* June 14 1944
10. *The Scotsman,* March 15 1947

supported a proposal that Glasgow Presbytery should hold a monthly press conference in order to pass on information about the church's initiatives. A popular discussion program at this time on radio, and later on television, was "the Brains Trust," in which a group of experts sought to answer questions submitted by the audience and the Christian Front borrowed this format for a series of similar events, held in the Lyric Theatre with Nevile acting as question master.

His desire to reach the unchurched led Nevile to adopt a pragmatic approach. "The Church, if it was wise, must adapt its own methods to the new social situation," he said; mere condemnation of social changes would achieve nothing. This was seen particularly with regard to Sunday activities. Even before the war, he had been honest enough to ask whether it was realistic to expect people to attend both morning and evening diets of worship:

> Tea-rooms are open in many places. Sunday trains and buses make it possible to visit friends at a distance. Sunday evening concerts are becoming much more common. The wireless programs doubtless offer people an added inducement to spend the evening indoors. And they can sometimes listen to a more beautiful service or a more inspiring sermon than they would find in their own Parish Church . . . We must not be narrow, or professional, if we are to understand the point of view of the plain man in the street. And in spite of our carefully thought-out sermon, prepared for delivery at 6.30 p.m., it is sometimes good to put ourselves in the position of the ordinary layman and ask ourselves, "What should I do to-night if I were he?"[11]

Hence, when Glasgow Corporation proposed to sponsor concerts for young people on Sunday evenings, Nevile argued during a Presbytery debate in February 1945 that there was little point in the church issuing protests against encroachments on Sunday observance. "Except in very limited circles, the old Puritanical Sabbath was dead—dead as the dodo—and very few of them would wish that it should be brought back to life. They wanted, not a Puritanical Sabbath, but a Christian Sunday."[12] Rather than simply objecting to the concerts, he proposed petitioning the council suggesting that they should not begin until 8 p.m. so that they did not clash with evening church services and that ministers of religion should be allowed to speak

11. *Church Service Society Annual* 1933–34, 34
12. *Glasgow Herald*, February 7 1945

for five minutes and conduct some community hymn singing. This was expecting too much, though, and the Corporation refused to co-operate.

The debate gave the fiercely Sabbatarian *Free Presbyterian Magazine* an opportunity to launch one of its frequent diatribes against the Cathedral minister:

> The Sabbath Day may be as dead to Dr. Davidson and his friends as the "dodo" but the God of the Sabbath is not dead . . . Is it any wonder then if there is such deplorable immorality and appalling iniquity going on in Glasgow! . . . We have warned our people and strongly urge upon them never worship, nor associate with the religious hypocrites of the Church of Scotland. The curse and wrath of God is upon that Church.[13]

Inevitably, Sunday entertainments began to increase and Nevile's pragmatism reached its limit when it came to Sunday cinemas. In 1948, as convener of Glasgow Presbytery's Social Problems Committee, he asked the city's magistrates—rather naïvely—to reconsider a decision to allow cinemas to open on a commercial basis on Sunday nights. "In this noisy twentieth century we needed a day of rest more than our forefathers. The opening of places of entertainment and amusement would destroy that, and if a few cinemas were opened at first, before long there would be many."[14] For better or worse, it proved to be an accurate prediction.

Though fully committed to so many aspects of the work of the church within Scotland, Nevile Davidson had so far had little involvement in the international work of the Kirk. However, in July 1947 he was unexpectedly asked whether he would be willing to represent the Church of Scotland at the inauguration of the United Church of South India in place of Professor William Manson, convener of the Inter-Church Relations Committee, who had suddenly been taken ill. The plan was to spend a fortnight in Madras and South India followed by six weeks traveling round the mission stations. Having received an encouraging response to his request for leave of absence from his kirk session, Nevile started to prepare for his adventure, reading up on Indian church affairs and, naturally, going on shopping expeditions with Peggy to acquire suitable clothing. He was excited to acquire

13. *Free Presbyterian Magazine*, April 1945, 232
14. *The Scotsman*, April 7 1948

from Wippell's, the clerical outfitters, "a wonderful garment—a cassock and Geneva gown in one, made of the thinnest material, for use in very hot weather."

Before sailing for India, however, he had various engagements to attend, notably a presentation party at the Palace of Holyrood—held indoors on July 16 because of heavy rain—at which he and Peggy were introduced to the King. The couple also managed some holiday trips, first of all to Stranraer and Glenluce in the south-west of Scotland in early August, meeting up with relatives from the Agnew family at Lochnaw Castle where Nevile's mother had been brought up. There they enjoyed a picnic in the grounds with a view across the loch. "Everything was looking serene and beautiful . . . the sun shimmering on the water and the terns diving round the little rocky island. Very sad to think it is to be sold in November and the house and land going out of the family after almost 600 years." Then they went on to Aberdeen to see Cois for a few days before arranging for typhoid inoculations and making a final appearance at the Cathedral to say goodbye to people.

The Davidsons had so much luggage that it could not be taken to the station in two taxis and they had to ask an obliging neighboring tradesman to lend his delivery van. A comfortable cabin had been secured in the Anchor Line ship *Cilicia* which had only returned to the Bombay route in May 1947 after war service. At 6 p.m. on August 30 the ship departed from Liverpool and as there were quite a few other clerical representatives sailing for the same purpose as the Davidsons, they drew up a schedule of Sunday and daily services covering the next fortnight. A stop at Port Said allowed passengers to visit Cairo and take a trip to the pyramids, mounted on camels. "Everywhere women were carrying water pots or farm produce on their heads," observed Nevile. "The standard of life is obviously low but the people seemed cheerful and vigorous." Fortunately the stop was brief: only a few days later the wireless reported anti-British demonstrations in Cairo and Port Said against the United Nations' pronouncement on maintaining British troops in the Suez Canal zone.

Meanwhile, passengers whiled away their time playing tennis or bridge but, in spite of cold showers, the heat was unbearable. With their destination of Bombay in sight on September 16, the Captain held a farewell dinner at which Nevile made a speech. He excitedly recorded details of the menu which was crammed with luxuries unobtainable in austerity

Britain: "tomato juice, soup, fish, roast turkey and braised ham, plum pudding, ice cream, pears and oranges—and coffee!!"

Arriving in Bombay early in the morning, the Davidsons faced "an hour of pandemonium" before all their luggage was taken ashore and cleared by customs. Waiting to meet them were the Rev. Dr. James Kellock and his wife who took them to stay at Wilson College, an institution founded by a Scottish missionary, where Kellock was the principal. Soon the distinguished visitors were lunching at Government House with Lady Colville, wife of the governor who himself was absent in Scotland for family reasons.

The Davidsons were visiting India at a crucial stage of the country's development. Only a month before their arrival, the country had been granted its independence from Britain, the culmination of a decades-long campaign of non-violent protest led by Mahatma Gandhi. India was now partitioned along broadly religious lines, with Pakistan being created as a Muslim state—a move which led to some fifteen million Muslims, Hindus and Sikhs relocating, a huge upheaval resulting in violent clashes and the loss of over a million lives. The Davidsons witnessed much of this unrest in the course of their travels over the subsequent months.

Almost immediately the couple embarked on a round of visits to schools and churches, with Nevile often speaking at several different events or services each day. Everywhere they went Peggy would be garlanded with flowers. Sometimes Nevile visited poor Indian congregations where a native pastor would translate his address; at other times he would be in more familiar territory, preaching in a Scots Kirk, where he would hold discussions with the ministers about their future relationship with the new United Church whose episcopal structure proved a stumbling block for some of the Presbyterians.

Saturday September 27 was "The Great Day": the ceremony inaugurating the new Church of South India. Church bells rang as crowds made their way to St. George's Cathedral and by the start of the service at 8 a.m. there were 1800 in the congregation. "Almost melted in the heat" in his robes, Nevile was "never more conscious of the power of the Holy Spirit" as he watched the consecration of fifteen new bishops and took communion during the four and a half hour long service. The only sour note occurred the following day when he preached in the Cathedral at the 8.15 a.m. Eucharist. "We had been asked to breakfast with the Chaplain, but he was so discourteous before the service that I declined to go." As a result, the Davidsons went without any breakfast.

There followed three weeks "crowded with interest" traveling across India, starting with mission stations within reach of Madras, and venturing further afield to Nagpur and Calcutta as guests of the principal of the Scottish Church College. They moved on to the hill country at Kalimpong where they visited a leper hospital and the school founded by Dr John Anderson Graham, another Church of Scotland missionary. At Allahabad there were meetings with the United Church of North India and then another long train journey from Lucknow to Ajmer, with a stop at Agra and a visit to the Taj Mahal whose grandeur "exceeded all expectations." But tensions were simmering: at Ajmer serious violence between Hindus and Muslims led to a seventy-two hour curfew and armed soldiers could be seen everywhere. Not that this put off the Davidsons. It was now nearly the end of October and they decided to stay a further month, during which Nevile went on alone to the Punjab where the fighting had been particularly intense. There were no trains but he managed, with some difficulty, to get a seat on a plane—adding yet another mode of transport to a tour which had already involved trains, buses, cars, a horse-drawn victoria and occasionally elephants.

A diary entry from January 11 1948 describing a visit to the Mission station at Jahra, Rajasthan, is typical of many:

> To church at 7.45 a.m. for the baptism of a young Indian soldier . . . Set off in the hospital wagon to a village about 7 miles away on the edge of the jungle. It is an entirely Christian community. 250 of a congregation. I preached on "The Star of Hope." Afterwards Peggy and I were given fine garlands. At 4.30 all went to the Marathi service in the Jahra church. A magnificent congregation of about 700 . . . I preached on "The Church Family of God." At 6.30 we returned to church for the English service. I preached on "The Universality of Christ": an Epiphany sermon. Felt rather tired in the evening.

In spite of the frenetic pace, Nevile found intervals in which he could indulge in one of his favorite pastimes: shopping. Browsing in the bazaar at Udaipur, "one of the most beautiful places in India", he came away with an antique brass elephant and some old brass ink pots with a pen case. Another time he picked up a "good strong leather suitcase" at a bargain price, and he would certainly have needed extra luggage to accommodate the crocodile leather handbags, elephants carved from buffalo horn and the three rugs for Mrs Martin that had already been purchased at a market in Madras.

The highlight of the trip was meeting Mahatma Gandhi and, as so often in his life, Nevile's connections opened doors for him. His cousin Emily Kinnaird, who had only recently passed away, had been a friend of Gandhi. Emily (1855–1947) had devoted her life to the YWCA, which itself had developed out of earlier organizations founded by her mother, Mary Jane Kinnaird, and had spent many years involved in missionary work in India, setting up YWCA branches. The story of her life was told in her book *My Adopted Country*, published in 1944.

It was sufficient for Nevile to contact Gandhi's secretary and arrange an appointment to see the great man at Birla House, New Delhi, where he was staying. Nevile was surprised that he could simply walk through the gates, as Gandhi, in his desire to be accessible to all, had refused any security precautions. The two men sat on the floor in "an atmosphere of stillness and peace" and talked affectionately about Emily. Nevile now had the opportunity to raise personally with Gandhi the question which summed up the purpose of his India trip:

> He wanted to know why I was in India and to hear of the mission stations. I asked him, "Is the future of Indian Christianity and mission work secure for the future?" He said, "I can't answer that question. But what I would say is, if it is God's will that the Christian missionaries remain in India, then they will go on against however terrible odds. If it is God's will that the missionaries should not remain, then they will have to go. But history doesn't suggest that it will work out in that way."

Nevile left deeply impressed with Gandhi's "combination of utter simplicity of life, shrewdness of practical judgment and spirituality of outlook." He saw him as "the one voice to which the whole of divided India listens." But that did not stop a Hindu nationalist from shooting Gandhi at point-blank range six weeks later. The assassination occurred the day before the Davidsons left India for their journey home on the *Cilicia* and, as he had done so often before at Glasgow Cathedral after the death of a prominent individual, Nevile arranged a memorial service on board for 4 p.m. to coincide with the cremation in Delhi.

The return journey offered plenty of entertainments: in addition to the tennis there was after-dinner dancing on the deck, in which Peggy briefly participated, film shows (including a "delightful Mickey Mouse film"), and a chat with the chief baker working on board who turned out to be a Cathedral member. Another quick stop at Port Said allowed Nevile to buy some Turkish Delight and Peggy "a rather nice pair of snake-skin shoes."

Looking back on a four and a half month period during which he had covered some 10,000 miles, he wrote: "we have certainly had a wonderful and unforgettable time in India and done more than we should ever have thought possible." But what conclusions had he reached about the state of the church in India? Drawing together his thoughts in a pastoral letter to his parishioners, his assessment was typically upbeat:

> Although Christians so far number only ten millions out of four hundred millions, yet Christianity has struck its root deep into the life and soil of India. Everywhere across the land we found Christian communities firmly established. The Christian Church is making its voice more clearly heard and its influence more widely felt. Many Christians are now occupying positions of importance in public life. It is a source of widespread gratification that the Governor of Bombay, Rajah Sir Maharaj Singh and his wife are both devout and enthusiastic Christians who will have a great influence for good in this great city and famous Province.[15]

At a press conference about his Indian visit held in Edinburgh, Nevile optimistically stated that in none of the Church of Scotland areas was there any thought of withdrawal or curtailment of their activities, even near the dangerous border of Kashmir. In the long term, though, the Scots kirks were absorbed into the united denominations of South and North India and their schools and hospitals taken over by other agencies. Today, the Church of Scotland's involvement in India is mainly limited to congregational or presbyterial twinnings, the provision of scholarships and support for various HIV projects.

With hindsight, Nevile's bullish predictions for the future of the Christian faith under the new Indian regime may seem naïve; however, having observed that the United Church of South India had managed to lay aside what he called "western-style division and rivalry" and bring together both episcopal and non-episcopal traditions in one denomination, he returned to Scotland with a renewed belief in the cause of church union which had long been dear to his heart.

15. *Chronicle*, February 1948

Once they had settled back into their routine after the trip to India, the Davidsons started to look for a more roomy base in Glasgow than the flat in St. Vincent Street, not in the West End of the city, but—surprisingly—in the less fashionable but centrally located Garnethill area.

The couple first viewed a flat there in May 1948, though they rejected it as "the surroundings were too sordid." The following month they looked at a big old-fashioned house in the same street, but Peggy thought it would be too difficult to run. Back in the city at the end of August after their customary summer vacation at Nethy Bridge and a trip to Shetland, they heard that a flat at the top of Hill Street was available to let for an indefinite period. It was above all the spectacular views that attracted Nevile: from the rear, the hill of Dumgoyne in the Campsie Fells could be seen and from another window the spire of the Cathedral was visible. The Davidsons immediately decided to take the lease.

In these days Hill Street housed a floating population of actors and entertainers living in digs while they were appearing at the Alhambra, the Empire and the many other theaters and dance halls to be found in postwar Glasgow. Nearby was the famous Glasgow School of Art designed by Charles Rennie Mackintosh. All this gave the area a bohemian and cosmopolitan feel and it later became the center of the city's Chinese community. But Hill Street also acquired a more sinister reputation: it was part of what the press dubbed Glasgow's "murder mile" and at least three gruesome killings took place in the vicinity during the fifties, the most notorious being the discovery of the body of four year old Betty Alexander in October 1952. In spite of a huge police operation sealing off the whole of Garnethill the killer was never brought to justice.

Occasionally, the seamier side of life in Hill Street encroached on the Davidsons' peaceful existence. Peggy used to say that after a rowdy Saturday night it was not unusual to find blood on the pavement the next morning. Early one Sunday in July 1952 they woke to the sound of smashing glass: a taxi had collided with their car parked outside. The driver made off and the taxi was found to have been stolen. It was not the first damage the car had sustained in Hill Street, though the previous occasion had been Nevile's own fault: in May 1951 he left it parked with the handbrake off and it rolled down the hill and smashed into a granite post.

158 Hill Street might have had little in common with the Queen Anne-style cottage in Yateley where she used to live, but Peggy was nothing if not adaptable. When interviewed for an *Evening Times* series on "Wives of Men at the Top", "tall, dark-haired, dark-eyed Margaret Davidson" told journalist Alice Russell that "I never really knew what it was like to have a place of my own." Sent to boarding school while her parents were serving abroad with the Indian army, she would spend her holidays with relatives in Edinburgh and Iona and it was only when she left school and joined her parents in Burma that she had a bedroom of her own. "The nine years I've been in Glasgow is the longest I've ever lived in one place," she added.[16]

When the Davidsons moved to Hill Street during October 1948, more than a few members of the Cathedral congregation expressed their disapproval. The unpromising appearance of the entrance to the close was enough to make at least one lady refuse to enter, but those who did venture inside found the flat was spacious and comfortable. It offered two sitting rooms and three bedrooms and had previously been lived in by a musician from the BBC who had incorporated musical motifs into the décor. Far from being put off by the possibility of disreputable neighbors, Nevile positively relished the vibrancy of the area. Once, a student living in the flat below came to the door to warn him politely that there was going to be a party and there might be some noise. Of course, joked the student, the minister could always come and join them. So he did!

However, a good deal of work was needed before the flat was to the Davidsons' taste. One initial shock was that the wiring was found to be in very poor condition and needed renewed. Extensive redecoration also had to be carried out: the "drawing-room in the palest sort of powder pink and our room with an old-fashioned flowered wallpaper" from Sandersons. There was a room for Flora, too. To complete the renovations, Mrs Martin offered to pay for the hall and bathroom to be painted as well, and at times things were so chaotic that up to ten tradesmen were working in the house. During a short trip north to Forest House in November, Nevile was pleased to receive a large post containing several dividend payments—"very welcome after all the heavy expenses in connection with 158 Hill Street."

Social gatherings at Hill Street were frequent. The Rev. David Beckett recollects that after the Good Friday service those who had taken part would be invited back for a frugal meal of boiled eggs and hot cross buns. On Christmas Day, after the services in the Cathedral, Flora would have the

16. *Evening Times*, November 10 1952

Christmas lunch and a roaring fire prepared so that the meal could be finished in time for the Queen's broadcast when, led by Nevile, the assembled company would spring to attention in their paper hats at the opening chord of the National Anthem. At such gatherings Nevile's sense of humor would often come through. The wife of the Cathedral's longest serving elder remembers being invited for lunch in her youth and nervously playing with her necklace while sitting at the table. This caused the string to snap and the pearls to cascade all over the floor. In these days both the assistant minister and student assistant would be present—Nevile expected them to act as waiters during the meal—and soon all three clerics were down on their knees scrambling to pick up the pearls. Was it a coincidence that later that day Nevile took as his text for the evening service the words from Matthew 7:6: "Do not cast your pearls before swine"?

At one time or another, most of those involved in the Cathedral would have been invited to Hill Street, whether to lunch, evening gatherings of groups of elders, quiz nights for younger people, or for a personal interview with the minister lasting fifteen to twenty minutes in the case of those proposing to take up church membership. But, like so much of the Charing Cross area of Glasgow, the houses at the top of Hill Street were swept away in the extensive redevelopment of the early 1970s. Today, a new block of flats stands on the site.

# 7

# "Must Try to Do More"

## CATHEDRAL MINISTRY, 1950–55

"AND SO I SUPPOSE one is quite indubitably middle-aged," wrote Nevile Davidson on February 13 1949, his fiftieth birthday, "though I don't *feel* any older than I did at thirty." He was certainly still able to draw on exceptional reserves of energy to carry out an astonishing variety of parish, civic and national duties. Halfway through the year, before setting off for a summer break at Nethy Bridge, Orkney and Shetland, he totaled up the number of tasks he had carried out in the previous six months: 191 pastoral visits, fifty-two sermons, eighty-five meetings, twenty-five speeches, not to mention the many toasts at weddings and dinners.

The renowned theologian Reinhold Niebuhr (who preached at Glasgow Cathedral in May 1943) once said, "I do not regret the years devoted to the parish" and it is to Nevile's credit that, in spite of his increasingly prominent national role, he never ceased to prioritize the pastoral side of his ministry. In a revealing diary entry from the end of June 1949 he says: "Wish I could find more time for visiting but the congregation becomes more widely scattered every year and the distances to be covered are enormous. But must try to do more." It has to be remembered that the Cathedral was not a typical Scottish parish church as the congregation was "gathered" from all parts of the city. Some ministers simply refused to pay pastoral visits outside the boundaries of their parish, but not Nevile. Post-war Glasgow saw a huge movement of population as the crowded tenements of the city center were gradually demolished and new peripheral housing schemes sprang up in Drumchapel, Castlemilk, Pollok and Easterhouse. The Cathedral minister did not neglect his parishioners who relocated to these areas, even though he sometimes had to stop his car and ask for directions. Henry Sefton became assistant minister in 1957 and when he started on a program of visitation he "soon discovered that Nevile Davidson was as well-known in the slums of Townhead as in the princely mansions of Pollokshields."

The amount of comfort and guidance dispensed during these visits can never be quantified. People would consult him about all kinds of personal problems. In January 1948 he visited a couple in Dennistoun where the husband had been offered a good job in Canada but his wife did not want to go. After discussing the matter for two hours, they agreed that he should take up the offer and, once he had found a suitable home, his wife should join him. Not every case was so clear cut. On another occasion he was approached by a parishioner who wished to marry a divorced man and was very anxious that the ceremony should take place in church but Nevile felt it his duty to "keep before the people the sanctity of marriage" and declined to give an immediate decision.

Experience taught him to distinguish between those who were genuine and those who weren't. Once, he said, "a woman came to see me and told me a long sob story which seemed very convincing. I said a prayer with her. She asked to borrow £1 which I gave her. I felt suspicious immediately afterwards and am sure I shall never hear from her again." Another time, he was approached by "a Jew" who told him a sad tale of his unhappy life and marriage, ending by saying that he had decided to become a Christian in order to escape from his wife. "He was very indignant when I refused to give him any encouragement in that direction."

Nevile's sincere sympathy for deserving cases is only too apparent. He recalled a visit to an elderly couple where the wife's memory had completely gone and she simply sat gazing into the fire with a smile. The husband bathed, dressed and fed her like a child and kept the house clean, all without a word of complaint. Bringing out a photograph of his wife as a young woman, the old man said that "she was a bonny lass when I married her." Deeply moved, Nevile wrote that "here, surely, is a 'saint in common life.'"

Such was the stature of the Cathedral minister that even a casual comment from him in passing could have a profound effect. Living amidst the chaos of a removal in 1953, a woman who had relocated to Glasgow with her five year old son felt in need of a peaceful hour and attended a service at the Cathedral. On the way out, Nevile patted the boy's head and said, "I do hope my sermon wasn't too long. The little boy was so good." These simple words had such an impact that, eighteen months later, the mother wrote him a nine page letter of thanks. Similarly, in a letter to Peggy Davidson after her husband's death, a parishioner recalled a conversation that took place twenty-five years earlier. This lady had suffered a series of difficulties and told Nevile that she had lost everything except her faith. "He said, 'having that you have everything', and how true that has been."

Those who knew Nevile personally can quote their own examples of how he was ready to help those in need. A Nethy Bridge lady, now in her nineties, acted as a housekeeper at Forest House during several summers in the 1950s and still clearly remembers how he comforted her after the death of her mother, saying "no-one can take the place of a mother." David Beckett recalls one lady in the congregation whose father, a snobbish military officer, never allowed her to mix with other people. Lonely and highly-strung, she would frequently telephone the Davidsons in an excitable state, and sometimes stayed at Hill Street where she was always treated with "endless patience." Similarly, Henry Sefton remembers an elderly couple living in a Townhead tenement and barely able to look after themselves. The Cathedral youth fellowship had done a great deal to tidy up and refurbish their flat as the couple seemed to have been abandoned by their family. When the old lady died her husband was too frail to attend the funeral; the only mourners were from the youth fellowship. In due course the old man also passed away and as there was no money to pay for a funeral the authorities insisted that he could not be buried beside his wife but only in a pauper's grave. Nevile Davidson was furious. He immediately called the appropriate official and told him: "this man must be buried beside his wife and the Cathedral will pay if necessary." The official was so taken aback that he replied, "That will not be necessary. I will see to it."

As Henry Sefton says, "these are not the kind of things that you can read about in Nevile's autobiography."

In the fifties—and, indeed, well into the sixties—church organizations like Sunday school, youth fellowship and the BB (Boys' Brigade[1]) were well-attended. Though staffed by volunteers, these meetings would receive periodic visits from the minister and, although there is no record of Nevile playing Santa Claus as he did in his younger days at Aberdeen, in Glasgow

1. The Boys' Brigade is an international Christian organization for boys, founded in Glasgow in 1883 by Sir William Alexander Smith.

he would attend youth fellowship dances, "hilarious" Hallowe'en parties and Sunday School trips. At one of the latter, held in December 1953, he thought "the children looked very sweet and were all wonderfully clean and well-dressed, even those who came from quite humble backgrounds." What the youngsters made of this tall, patrician figure is not recorded. There is a story of him turning up at a junior Sunday School class and inquiring of the teacher, "Why do the children not have any hymn books?" "Oh, but Dr. Davidson," came the reply, "they can't read!" Members of the choir were similarly awestruck. It was his custom to pray with them on a Sunday morning before the service was about to start. The younger singers would be chatting and giggling; the minister simply stood without speaking until, gradually, complete silence reigned and only then would he lead in prayer, gliding off afterwards in his stately manner without further conversation. At the end of the service, minister and assistant would stand at opposite sides of the crossing to greet the congregation. One visitor—clearly more familiar with Anglican than Presbyterian practice—shook hands with the assistant minister and, pointing to the imposing figure standing opposite in his red cassock asked, "Is that the Dean?"

But Nevile Davidson's role extended far beyond looking after his own congregation. He may not, like John Wesley, have said that "the world is my parish" but he certainly made himself available to the to the whole of the city. After all, the minister of the Cathedral was the "Minister of Glasgow."

May 4 1949 saw one of those tragedies which occur periodically in large cities. That afternoon fire broke out in Grafton's fashion shop in Argyle Street and thirteen young female garment workers between the ages of fifteen and twenty-three lost their lives. Nevile was approached by a Salvation Army colonel who suggested a memorial service in the Cathedral, to which he readily agreed and, characteristically, he also wrote personal letters to the mothers of the thirteen girls. Four days later, 700 people thronged the churchyard and square in front of the Cathedral; the building was soon filled and even though the nearby Barony Church opened its doors to accommodate 1200 more for an overflow service, 100 people were still left in the street. Eleven years later, Glasgow suffered an even worse fire when a whisky warehouse in Cheapside Street went up in flames in March 1960 with the loss of nineteen lives, including fourteen firemen. Once more, the Cathedral served as the focal point for a city's grief.

Similarly, when a prominent citizen died, the Cathedral was the natural venue for a memorial service, whether it was for King George VI in 1952 or Sir Harry Lauder, the famous music hall singer and comedian in 1950, when a congregation of 500 gathered to hear Nevile say that "through all his life, beneath the glinting laughter and rippling fun, like a deep, strong river there ran a steady and strong religious faith, one expression of which was his refusal to sing or act on Sundays."[2]

Cultured, well-acquainted with the writings of figures like André Gide and Franz Kafka, and a lover of drama and films, Nevile Davidson was always ready to open the doors of Glasgow Cathedral to figures from the world of entertainment. One of his novel ideas was to send out letters in November 1948 to the managers of local theaters and cinemas inviting them to a special Christmas service. Then, a week before the event, he and Peggy visited the managers of the King's, Alhambra, Pavilion and Empire giving them the final details. Such personal attention paid dividends and the service, held on the afternoon of Boxing Day, attracted a crowd of 1100. Lessons were read by producer and director John Casson of the Citizens' Theatre and Jack Anthony, currently starring in the Pavilion's pantomime "Goldilocks and the Three Bears." Never averse to a bit of theater himself, Nevile started the service with a processional hymn round the quire and finished with choir and clergy processing through the nave to the triumphant singing of *O Come All Ye Faithful*.

The minister of the Cathedral may have earlier expressed his strong reservations about cinemas opening on Sundays but this did not stop him maintaining warm relations with the showbusiness world and when a service was held in St. Giles' Cathedral to inaugurate the 1948 Edinburgh Festival he was the obvious choice as guest preacher. Speaking to a congregation that included four lord provosts and nine lord mayors, he said that art at its best always had something of a spiritual quality and that "we have been content for too long with a divorce or separation between art and religion." But he also warned that "nothing is more dangerous than to think of music or art, or science and philosophy, as a substitute for religion."[3]

Relationships with newspaper editors were of mutual benefit too, and yet another innovative Christmas event in 1948 came about at the instigation of the *Daily Express*. The idea was that three Christmas Eve carol services for children would be held simultaneously in Cardiff, Glasgow and St. Martin-in-the-Fields in London with ten minutes broadcast from each center.

2. *Glasgow Herald*, March 17 1950
3. *Dundee Courier*, August 23 1948

1951 was the year of the Festival of Britain, a way of celebrating the country's post-war recovery and moving on from the gray years of austerity. The event centered round a huge south bank site in London, but there was also a complementary "Exhibition of Industrial Power" in Glasgow's Kelvin Hall which ran for thirteen weeks, although attendances proved disappointing. Nevile served on the organizing committee and after going round the exhibits, wrote that "It is splendidly laid out and full of interest but perhaps too technical and 'educative' to appeal to the masses." Nevertheless, he believed that the church had something to contribute in every field of human activity and held a dedication service in the Cathedral as well as offering a prayer at the opening ceremony which was performed by Princess Elizabeth.

This was not the first time Nevile Davidson had met the future Queen. At the special request of King George VI, he had been invited to be King's Chaplain in Scotland and in September 1948, while Peggy was busy arranging for the Hill Street flat to be painted and taking measurements for furniture, her husband spent a weekend at Balmoral. He took the train to Ballater where he was met with a car sent by His Majesty and at dinner sat between Princess Elizabeth and her mother, both of whom he found "very charming and easy to talk to." On the Sunday he preached on "Ye are all the children of God" and had a long talk with the King in the evening. Late that night the company played a game called "Murder" and did not get to bed until 1.30 a.m. He was taken to the station the next morning where the driver "was obviously shocked at my getting out of a royal car and into a third class carriage!"

The coronation year of 1953 naturally involved further contact with royalty. Nevile traveled by sleeper train to a dress rehearsal at Westminster Abbey and, as a royal chaplain, was a member of the procession on June 2. Elizabeth also had a separate coronation as Queen of Scotland in St. Giles' Cathedral, followed by a garden party at Holyrood Palace attended by 8000 guests. In October Nevile was again at Balmoral where he sat beside the new Queen at dinner on both evenings. Chaplain and sovereign talked about the coronation, the Queen saying that she had been too nervous to enjoy it, but at Balmoral she was far more relaxed: Nevile recorded in his diary that after dinner "we all played a new American game 'Scrabble' (like a crossword puzzle) round a small table in front of the fire."

In addition to innumerable special occasions and anniversaries, there was the customary round of annual civic services in the Cathedral and by now Nevile Davidson had an unrivaled network of contacts in all these or-ganizations. The "Kirking of the Council", the Trades and Merchants House services and the annual University of Glasgow service continue to this day, though they are more muted occasions than in the past. Nevile relished the color and ceremonial of such events. At the 1952 University service, attend-ed by about twenty academics and nearly two hundred students, he noted that "the church looked magnificent with the sunlight streaming in on the coloured gowns and hoods and red altar cloth and masses of flowers." Still more elaborate was the service held in the Blacader Aisle for members of the Order of St. John of Jerusalem, a British order of chivalry constituted by Queen Victoria in 1888 but tracing its origins back to the Middle Ages. "We robed in Provand's Lordship[4] and then walked in procession across the square with cross-bearer, standard-bearer, a sword-bearer and the knights in their long black capes while the police held up all the traffic." One fellow minister who was not quite so enthusiastic about ritual and ceremonial re-ferred to this as "the sort of dressing up for irrelevance that Nevile enjoyed."

These events would invariably be preceded or followed by a lavish lunch or dinner and Nevile's diaries are full of references to "sumptuous feasts": a banquet for 600 members of the Institution of Chartered Accountants of Glasgow at the Central Hotel, annual dinners for the Ship Owners' and Ship Brokers' Benevolent Society, the Royal Faculty of Physicians and Surgeons, and many others.

A one-off occasion was the 400th anniversary of the Scottish Reformation in October 1960, marked by a "Solemn Service of Thanksgiving" at St. Giles in Edinburgh, conducted by Nevile, with the Queen in attendance. Glasgow Cathedral celebrated the event in a different way, with an open-air "Reformation Rally" in the Cathedral Square in which all the ministers from the local Townhead area participated, with the music taking the form of unaccompanied psalms led by Wilfred Emery, the director of music, in the role of precentor.[5] This drew a crowd of about 1200.

The grand occasions would be fitted in with more routine tasks in the course of a single day. This, for example, was Nevile's program for October 13 1948:

4. Located opposite the Cathedral, Provand's Lordship is said to be the oldest sur-viving house in Glasgow.

5. In the days before organ accompaniment, the tradition in Scottish Presbyterian worship was for a precentor to lead the singing of psalms. The practice continues today in some churches, particularly in the Highlands.

Went to City Chambers to discuss arrangements for the service in George Square on Remembrance Day. Took 12 o'clock train to Dumfries to address members of the Synod at luncheon. Meeting had been delayed by a difficult piece of business. Sat down to lunch at 2.35! I spoke for about twelve minutes (on Public Worship Today) and then had to dash to the station to catch the 3 o'clock train to Glasgow. Changed quickly and then to the Trades House for the Annual Dinner.

Sundays, of course, were the busiest days of all. The general routine was an 11 a.m. service, a monthly afternoon service for children, and an evening service at 6.30 p.m. often followed by a class for new communicants. But there were frequently other special services on top of all that:

> October 29, 1950. Preached at University Chapel at 11 a.m. Lunch with Principal and Lady Hetherington. Special Cathedral service for the Glasgow Society of Organists p.m. 1 hr. at home for tea. Preached at 6.30 service. Soon after, people began to arrive for broadcast of Sunday Half Hour. Splendid choir representing 26 churches.

Often on a Sunday there would be no time for lunch and Nevile and his assistant would sustain themselves in the Sacristy with sandwiches and cider.

Sometimes, though, he just had to say no. Invited to be Chaplain to the High School of Glasgow in 1951, he declined on the grounds that he could not do the role justice but suggested that the whole school might come to the Cathedral for a service once a year. The service continues today, as do similar annual commemorations for Hutchesons' Grammar School and The Glasgow Academy. He seems to have been less enthusiastic about Freemasons' services and although these were regularly held in the Cathedral he did not always participate. In spite of strong pleas during 1954, he turned down an invitation to move to St. Giles' Cathedral and when asked in 1960 to be moderator of Glasgow Presbytery felt he could not take this on as he had so many demands on his time.

If Nevile was in his element at royal occasions, dedication services and opening ceremonies, he was less at home in the world of politics. It was not his style to adopt a partisan stance or make provocative political statements in the manner of George MacLeod. Even in the privacy of his own diary, any remarks he made about figures in government were balanced and re-strained. After VE Day in 1945, for example, he wrote that "it seems a great pity that the National Government couldn't have continued a little longer before a resumption of 'party' warfare." In the election in July he voted for the Conservative candidate for Glasgow Central, Colonel Hutchison (who won the seat), as he felt that "Winston Churchill is really the only leader adequate to deal with problems of foreign policy." But the result was a La-bour landslide and Nevile felt it "rather tragic that Churchill has not been able to lead the country until the end of the war with Japan," though he acknowledged that Churchill's "rather aggressive and unworthy conduct during the electioneering period had . . . lowered his personal prestige a great deal." He further admitted that there were widespread doubts about whether the Conservatives were genuinely committed to tackling urgent social problems, especially housing, and that this gave the Labour party "a wonderful chance if only they have the necessary breadth of outlook." While he admired some individual politicians (praising Sir Stafford Cripps' "magnificently Christian address" to the 1948 General Assembly, for exam-ple) Nevile found party politics an unpleasant and ungentlemanly business. After offering the opening prayer at the first meeting of the newly elected town council in November 1945, he came away depressed by the rudeness of the speeches he had heard, saying that "we sorely need a finer type of man and woman" in local politics.

These were private reflections rather than public pronouncements but he felt it legitimate for churchmen to lay down broad principles that should govern political decision making and elaborated on this theme during a sermon at a service of preparation and prayer for the General Election of 1950, attended by representatives of various political parties:

> A good many people who say "Keep politics out of religion" also mean, though they might not always say it, "Keep religion out of politics." That view was based on a fallacy. If a man was a Christian then his citizenship should be tested at every point by Christian standards and inspired by Christian motives . . . Christianity of-fered by way of guidance not plans or policies but principles and motives. The primary standard of judgment to be applied by Christian citizens must be the creation of a truly Christian social order in the land. [6]

6. *The Scotsman*, March 20 1950

Voters, he said, should ask themselves which policy was most likely to lead the nation, not only towards economic recovery, but moral recovery.

There were nevertheless two contentious issues in the early 1950s on which Nevile Davidson took a more specific public stance: home rule and atomic weapons.

The question of Scottish home rule was hotly debated in the post-war years and a Glasgow lawyer, John MacCormick (1904–61), took the lead in forging a diverse coalition of Scottish interest groups to press for devolution, sensing that there was a national hunger for a Scottish parliament which did not translate into a desire for separation from England. He reckoned his approach was a more effective one than party political action and he was able to bring together parliamentarians normally as far apart as the Communist MP Willie Gallacher and the Unionist T. D. Galbraith. In 1947 a Scottish Convention was formed and in March 400 delegates representing burghs, counties, the church, law, industry and cultural institutions as well as politicians met together to press the government to give Scotland legislative control of domestic affairs.

Nevile contributed to these discussions, spoke at many rallies and took part in a radio debate with MacCormick, Gallacher and Galbraith in June. MacCormick's efforts culminated in the launch of a Scottish Covenant in 1949 demanding the setting up of a Scottish parliament within the framework of the UK with powers to deal with matters such as industry, agriculture, education, broadcasting, marriage and divorce, food regulations and immigration.

Nevile's position was clear: "This assembly," he declared at a conference in Glasgow in March 1948, "takes for granted that to-day Scotland is to be thought of, not as one of the provinces but a nation." However, unlike the more extreme Nationalists, he also believed that "separation would be disastrous." There were protests from some in the hall when he declared that "Scottish Nationalism in its extreme form has always been regarded as a small and negligible movement in Scotland" and Nevile was obliged to apologize for hurting anyone's feelings.[7] The Covenant eventually received two million signatures but Nevile was uncomfortably conscious that within the Convention there was "a distinct cleavage of opinion between the more moderate of us and the more extreme"—or, as the *Sunday Post* termed it, the half-hoggers versus the whole-hoggers.

---

7. *The Scotsman*, 22 March 22 1948

These tensions reached their height during the Stone of Destiny incident. This venerable object had been used for centuries during the coronation of Scottish kings until it was removed by King Edward I in 1296 and taken to England. Four Scottish students, ardent supporters of home rule, decided it was time to bring the stone back to Scotland and broke into Westminster Abbey to steal it on Christmas Day 1950. In the course of removing it, the stone split in two and the students temporarily hid it, returning to collect it a couple of weeks later, dodging roadblocks on the journey home. Rumors and alleged sightings filled the newspapers for months until, in April 1951, the stone was ceremoniously deposited in the ruins of Arbroath Abbey where Scotland's Declaration of Independence had been signed in 1320. Naturally, reporters wanted Nevile to give his opinion "which I did rather cautiously," saying only that he welcomed the return of the stone and that decisions regarding its resting-place remained entirely in the hands of the authorities. He was more forthcoming in the privacy of his diary, where he condemned the "extraordinary foolishness" of MacCormick in supporting the theft. After discussion at the Church and Nation Committee, Nevile clarified the position of the Kirk in a further statement: "After disapproving the removal from the Abbey, we recommended that it should now be voluntarily returned to Scotland and committed to the custody of the Church." The Stone of Destiny was eventually placed in Edinburgh Castle—but not until 1996.

An infinitely greater problem on which the Church and Nation Committee expressed a view was the spread of nuclear weapons and the fear of a future war. Nevile Davidson was no pacifist like George MacLeod who, at the 1954 General Assembly, declared to a hushed auditorium, "I for one cannot press that button. Can you?" MacLeod earned the Assembly's utmost respect, but not its support. "The pacifist position is logical but utterly unrealistic," said Nevile when presenting the Church and Nation report to the following year's Assembly. "To give superiority in armaments, however terrible, to a potential enemy, might be to surrender the very safety of civilisation, to betray the future of mankind. It is for this reason, and for this reason alone, that we cannot, dare not, condemn the manufacture of nuclear bombs by our own country."[8]

At the same time, he was deeply uneasy at the proliferation of such weapons and felt that the conscience of mankind could not be satisfied with "an attempt to build the structure of world peace on a foundation of fear."

8. *Falkirk Herald,* June 4 1955

"The achievement of peace is the greatest task confronting our time," said Nevile at the unveiling of a war memorial in Glasgow's Royal Technical College (now the University of Strathclyde). "War as a method of settling international disputes must somehow be outlawed" and in the longer term that could only happen by fostering contact and friendship between nations at all levels, in the arts, literature, education, scholarship and science. Ultimately, though, the only solution was a spiritual one, "a new flowering of love in the hearts of men and women of every land . . ." War was essentially bound up with the streak of evil that was in human nature itself. "The most dangerous threat to civilization came not from the atom bomb or the hydrogen bomb but from the evil desires and passions hidden in human hearts."[9]

Nevile considered himself justified in making such pronouncements so long as he stressed the moral and spiritual dimension, but even this got him into a certain amount of bother. Speaking at the annual Kirking of the Council service in 1955, he strongly condemned the lack of decent housing in the city which, he told the rows of elected representatives sitting in front of him, "should be a weight on the conscience of every Christian citizen and the urgent concern of all those in authority." He used his 1956 Remembrance Day sermon to attack the British government for acting alone in the Suez crisis rather than with the United Nations. Defending the country's material interests was not the be all and end all of policy: "Better lose the Suez Canal and all its advantages tomorrow than lose our moral integrity as a nation." Reactions to that intervention filled the correspondence columns of the *Glasgow Herald* for the next week, the general feeling being that, as the cobbler should stick to his last, so the clergy should not pontificate on political matters.

This did not stop the Church and Nation Committee from continuing to express views on subjects as diverse as pensions, industrial relations, unemployment, road safety, commercially sponsored television, gambling, smoking, tuberculosis, runaway marriages, capital punishment and homosexuality. Today the church feels increasingly marginalized from public life, but in the 1950s the views of the Church of Scotland counted; the committee's reports were fully covered by the press and copies sent to senior government ministers and all Scottish members of parliament.

The Church and Nation was the most prominent committee on which Nevile Davidson served, but it was only one of many. Whether it was the

9. *The Scotsman*, March 8 1950

National Bible Society, Church of Scotland Prayer Union, the Glasgow Presbytery Social Problems Committee, the Hospital Sunday Fund, the Marriage Guidance Council, the Society of Indigent Gentlewomen, the Scottish Church Society, the Glasgow Islay Association, Save the Children Fund, or even the Glasgow Tree Lovers' Society, at one time or other Nevile Davidson would have been listed as a committee member, governor or president. For her part, Peggy was the honorary president of the Glasgow Society for the Prevention of Cruelty to Animals and in March 1956 the Society marked its centenary with a Cathedral service in which Nevile, a life-long lover of animals, condemned the treatment of circus animals and, at Peggy's behest, called for a "campaign of greater kindness to cats." On that occasion, the Davidsons would have scarcely recovered from the loss of their beloved dachshund Dingwall at the end of the previous year. Dingwall had suffered heart problems for some time, and after further complications resulting from kidney trouble, "had passed peacefully away with Peggy and me and Flora all beside him. He has been a most perfect little companion and a member of the family for eleven and a half years and we shall miss him terribly."

Still another committee in which Nevile Davidson took an active part dealt with the subject of spiritual healing, an interest perhaps stimulated by his friendship with Rev. Alan Boyd Robson who for many years ran a week-night service of laying on of hands for healing at his church in Kelvinside. Medical representatives were involved in the discussions as well as church-men, and cases of possible physical healing as a result of prayer carefully examined. The committee nevertheless concluded that bodily and mental healing was normally the task of the physician, and that the primary task of the minister was to cure men of the affliction of sin and bring them to reconciliation with God, which would enable them to face suffering and the ultimate experience of death with "complete faith and serenity."

As anyone who has served on a committee knows, meetings can be lengthy and unproductive. Nevile came away from a foreign missions' policy meeting in December 1951 feeling that there had been "too much concentration on the need to reduce expenditure in every field instead of formulation of constructive policy." However, the cause which produced the greatest amount of frustration, and the one to which Nevile Davidson devoted the greatest amount of time and energy, was that of ecumenical co-operation. He was a member of the Inter-Church Relations Committee for many years and convener for five. "I am convinced," he wrote in his autobiography, "that the ecumenical movement is the outstanding feature of religious life in our century."[10]

At an informal level, the churches were already working together in many ways. At Glasgow Cathedral, Nevile was able to work well with representatives of other (Protestant) denominations, and willingly invited preachers from the Baptist, Congregational and other Presbyterian churches to participate in services. On his frequent visits to his wife's family in Surrey Nevile would take part in services with the local vicar and in July 1953 he preached at Crosthwaite Parish Church in Cumbria on the 1400th anniversary of St. Kentigern, to whom the church was dedicated, and even administered the chalice to communicants at the Eucharist, something that was most unusual for a Presbyterian in an Anglican church at the time.

The 1947 trip to witness the reunion of the churches in South India had demonstrated the possibility, not only of informal co-operation, but institutional unity. Nevile was keen "that all may be one" and he was instrumental in building up good relationships with European churches, being one of a group of distinguished Church of Scotland clerics who attended the Faith and Order Conference in Lund, Sweden, in the summer of 1952. Nevile helped chair a section which considered "Fundamental Points of Agreement" and it was to the seeds sown at the Lund Conference that he attributed many subsequent contacts between churches in Scandinavia, Germany and Scotland, one result being the establishment of full communion between the national churches in Sweden and Scotland. That, at least, was his verdict in his autobiography; from the account of the Lund visit in his personal diary, he seems to have spent more time sightseeing than attending meetings!

The formation of the World Council of Churches in 1948 was a landmark event which brought about increased contact with Orthodox Churches as well as European ones, but relationships between the churches of England and Scotland remained more problematic.[11] Essentially, the main stumbling block was the same as it had been in the seventeenth century: episcopacy. In 1947, the Archbishop of Canterbury, Geoffrey Fisher, suggested that as a first step to reunion other churches should introduce bishops. "Not very promising," wrote Nevile dryly. Discussions between the two national churches took place sporadically during the fifties, but

---

10. Davidson, *Beginnings,* 69

11. For a detailed account of the Church of Scotland's role in ecumenical developments in this period, see Louden, *The True Face of the Kirk,* 87–102

a proposal for the institution of "Bishops in Presbyteries" had been rejected by 1959. The Anglicans had, moreover, adopted an attitude of what Nevile called "dogmatic exclusiveness" with a statement from the Lambeth Conference reaffirming their belief that communion could only be dispensed by someone ordained by a bishop. Institutional union was impossible when "full sacramental inter-communion" had not yet been achieved. Nevile strongly condemned both sides: in his pastoral letter for June 1959 he wrote that the General Assembly's decision not to seek further steps towards integrating Episcopal and Presbyterian church government was "tragic," not only because

> it may well cause a deadlock in conversations with our Anglican brethren, but because it seems to indicate a complacent clinging to our own traditions and doctrines as unalterable. If rigid Anglicanism is arrogant and unchristian, no less arrogant and unchristian is rigid Presbyterianism. And in such a situation any hope of reunion or inter-communion becomes faint and indefinitely far-off.[12]

It was not until 2016 that the "Columba Agreement" was signed, under which both denominations agreed to allow ordained ministers to exercise ministry within the existing discipline of each church. "Nevile was broken-hearted by some diehards who would not work with other denominations," says Rev. David Beckett, "and he remained on good terms with Archbishop Fisher."

"Inter-church relations" in these days did not include the Church of Rome but in 1961 there was a tentative step towards lowering what Nevile called "the centuries-old barbed wire barrier between Roman Catholic and Protestant" when that year's moderator, Archie Craig, became the first holder of the office to visit the Pope. John XXIII and Craig did little more than exchange courtesies but it was seen as a momentous event—though the story that at the end of the visit Archie said "I'll be gone, John" and His Holiness replied "Arrivederci, Erchie" is certainly apocryphal!

The dream of a truly united Christian church continues to elude even the most ardent ecumenists. But a major opportunity arose in the mid-1950s for the churches to put their differences aside and work together in Scotland's biggest ever evangelistic campaign: the Billy Graham "Tell Scotland" Crusade of 1955.

12. *Chronicle*, June 1959

# 8

# "Tell Scotland"

## THE 1955 BILLY GRAHAM CRUSADE

THE SLICK, DYNAMIC AMERICAN approach combined with the traditional reserve of the Scottish churchman: that was the verdict of the *Evening Times* on the opening night of Billy Graham's "All Scotland Crusade" which took place in Glasgow's Kelvin Hall over a six week period in March and April 1955. The campaign was the culmination of months, even years, of preparation as the Scottish churches came together as never before in a united effort to reach those outside their walls.

Its roots lay in the growing recognition of the need for evangelism in the post-war years, a process in which Nevile Davidson played a leading role. Nevile was chairman of the BBC's Scottish Religious Advisory Committee and his voice was frequently heard on air—so frequently that by 1961 his BBC colleague Ronnie Falconer was telling him excitedly of the "quite staggering" total of three-quarters of a million people who had listened to his broadcast Christmas Eve service from the Cathedral. As early as March 1948 the Advisory Committee had decided on a significant change of policy: religious broadcasting should be aimed, not at churchgoers, but at those who did not attend, "since wireless can often reach such people more easily than the person working through ordinary channels of evangelism." One fruit of this approach was the Scottish churches' radio missions of 1950–52, the climax of which was a broadcast communion service from the Cathedral on Easter Sunday.

One of the speakers in the radio mission was the Rev. Tom Allan (1916–65), a minister in the North Kelvinside area of the city where he was revolutionizing the concept of parish mission. In 1946 and 1947 Allan had led summer missions organized by the Church of Scotland evangelist D. P. Thomson (1896–1974) and he began to extend a "missional" approach to his own parish through systematic visitation which revealed that 36% of homes had no church connection. The basis of his strategy was to encourage lay church members, through the formation of small groups or cells, to witness to their faith by serving those within the community. Allan publicized his ideas through his involvement in the World Council of Churches and in his book entitled *The Face of My Parish* (1954).

No longer was "mission" something that only happened in far-off foreign lands. The parish church had a mission field on its own doorstep.

These efforts gave rise to the "Tell Scotland" movement in 1953. Nevile Davidson was involved at an early stage but the response was slow at first: when he spoke to a gathering of East End ministers in November on the background and policy of the new movement, he found the discussion that followed "rather desultory." Tom Allan was appointed for a five year secondment to lead Tell Scotland and it gradually gained the support of most Scottish Protestant denominations and of important churchmen like Professor John Baillie and George MacLeod. There was even, to a considerable extent, a shared outlook by Allan and MacLeod on the question of whether Christian commitment meant individual salvation or social action. It was not a case of "either—or" but "both—and." Both could agree that faith without works is dead and both agreed on the centrality of the parish church in reaching out in service to its local community. MacLeod himself had been a pioneer of parish visitation with his "Message of Friendship" campaign in his Govan parish as far back as 1933.

A harmonious blend of evangelism and ecumenism was within grasp—or so it seemed. Then came the Billy Graham Crusade in London's Haringay Arena in the spring of 1954. Enthused by this, Allan saw a similar crusade as the way forward for Tell Scotland, whereas Macleod objected to what he called "a tip-and-run raid into enemy territory" which would undermine the outreach work of local churches. But Allan's charisma won the day; misgivings were, if not overcome, at least laid aside. Tom Allan and D P. Thomson met together and decided that at a meeting of Tell Scotland's "Parent Committee" on May 3 1954 Allan should start off the discussion and Thomson formally move that Graham be invited to Scotland. MacLeod was not present but he had put forward a Memorandum with his objections, which several others at the meeting shared. Nevile Davidson, however, was one of those who spoke in favor and the committee agreed to send a deputation to London (by air) to invite Graham to conduct a campaign in Scotland.[1] Later in the month the General Assembly of the Church of Scotland approved Tell Scotland's invitation which was, moreover, a genuinely ecumenical one, being backed by the Congregationalists, Baptists, Methodists, Episcopalians, the United Free Church and some other smaller denominations. Nevile gave the move his personal endorsement by joining the Crusade sponsoring committee.

Controversy about the Billy Graham campaign was not confined to ecclesiastical circles. Two weeks before his arrival, the *Glasgow Herald* published a hostile piece by Alistair Cooke (1908–2004), the journalist and broadcaster of "Letter from America" fame, giving his impressions of a Graham rally in Madison Square Gardens, New York. The show, he said, moved on as slickly as a Republican rally. As for the speaker and his message, "For all his microphone suavity, the gorgeous contour of his hair-do, he is one at last with the grizzled rustics who bark damnation over the hillbillies down by the river."[2] Nearer to home, correspondents of the *Evening Times* had their doubts too. "The teenagers who are criticized for their emotionalism over the current singing stars can take heart," maintained one W. E. McCulloch. "Their elders and supposed betters are going to emulate them at the Kelvin Hall and with a lot less justification." Others objected to what they assumed the evangelist would be preaching about. "People cannot see the relevance of a 'pie in the sky' approach," said another letter writer, adding that "the only thing that will possibly influence them is seeing Christians putting their beliefs into action"—a sentiment to which Graham and his supporters would hardly have taken exception.[3]

None of this deterred 1000 hymn-singing admirers from gathering to greet the evangelist when he stepped off the overnight train at St. Enoch Station to be met by Tom Allan. From there he was taken to his hotel and to a reception in the City Chambers, followed by a meeting in the Kelvin Hall with 7000 counsellors, choir members and stewards. The next morning— Sunday—he slipped quietly into the service at Dowanhill Church, Hyndland but could not escape being asked by the minister to say a few words. In his

1. Bardgett, *Scotland's Evangelist*, 308
2. *Glasgow Herald*, March 7 1955
3. *Evening Times*, March 7 1955

"easy conversational style" he chose to strike an ecumenical note: he said that his wife and children were Presbyterians and he was a Baptist but that made no difference to how they got on. Ironically, the service that morning happened to include an infant baptism.

Nevile Davidson with Billy Graham outside Glasgow Cathedral on the occasion of the dedication service for the 1955 Kelvin Hall Crusade. (Photo: Herald and Times Group).

Later that day, Graham made his first appearance at Glasgow Cathedral where the campaign dedication service took place. Snow started falling at lunchtime but by the start of the service at 4 p.m. an estimated 1500 people had crowded into the church. Respecting the formality of the ancient venue, Billy Graham wore the gown and hood of his honorary Doctor of Divinity degree from Baylor University in Texas, though at his request he was addressed simply as "Mr. Graham." Nevile chose as his text the description of the Day of Pentecost in Acts:2: "they were all with one accord in one place and suddenly there came a sound from heaven" and delivered an address structured round three simple points: the moment, the man and the message. The moment had come in Scotland, when there was such evident need in the hearts of men for "the Faith once delivered to the saints." The man God had raised up for the task, and set His seal on his ministry.

> Mr Billy Graham is a man with a message. We here know what that message is. It was defined by the greatest of all Christian evangelists a long time ago—"I am determined to know nothing among you save Jesus Christ and Him crucified." . . . There is the good news which Mr Graham has come to preach to us—the old, old story, but in new words, with new settings and by new methods, through the medium of a new voice and consecrated personality.[4]

After the reserved Scot, the dynamic American stepped up to the microphone and spoke for five minutes, giving a foretaste of the passionate preaching style that would pack the Kelvin Hall for the next six weeks:

> We stand and pray that the fire from heaven will fall and that the wind will scatter it across Scotland and that all Scotland will be aflame and the impact will be made on a world that desperately needs Christ.[5]

The next evening, a huge crowd turned out in cold, sleety weather to fill the Kelvin Hall, the largest ever attendance for the first night of a Graham campaign. Along with Dr. E. D. Jarvis, the moderator of the General Assembly, Nevile Davidson was on the platform and afterwards he told journalists that "this was Biblical preaching in the real Scottish tradition." In private, his impressions were just as positive. His diary entry for March 21 1955 reads:

> An absolutely amazing sight, the huge arena crowded with an audience of 18,000. Brilliant lights and elaborate broadcasting apparatus. Tom Allan spoke, the choir of 120 voices sang some mission hymns and the 23rd Psalm and then Billy Graham preached for about 40 minutes (on Faith) finishing by making a personal appeal for "decision for Christ." While the choir sang softly *Just as I am* about 340 men and women came forward [other reports said 470] and were then directed to a side hall for personal talks with "counsellors." No undue emotionalism and all very impressive.

Nevile attended the Kelvin Hall on three subsequent occasions, on one of which he took the opening prayer, and he was also present at the

4. *Glasgow Herald*, March 21 1955
5. *Glasgow Herald*, March 21 1955

closing rally for an estimated 100,000 people at Hampden Park stadium. In between, there were various private functions. Hugh Fraser of department store fame invited 400 guests to a lunch in the Central Hotel in honor of the evangelist, but Nevile did not appear because of "some kind of gastric infection" and Peggy went alone. However, a few days later Nevile gave "a little luncheon party" where he and Graham discussed the Crusade. "In spite of the amazing blaze of publicity in which he lives, he is completely humble—unspoilt—and attributes all the success of his missions to the power of God and to prayer." Four days later, they lunched again at the North British Hotel, in the company of E. D. Jarvis, James Pitt-Watson (Professor of Practical Theology at Glasgow University), Tom Allan and Dr. Paul Rees, one of Billy Graham's associates. Before he left for home in early May, Billy again attended the Cathedral and recorded some television talks from Broadcasting House, where Nevile went to say goodbye to him. The two would meet up again during Nevile's tour of America in 1957.

Of course, Cathedral duties continued as normal during the period of the Crusade. April 6, for example, was a typically busy day. Nevile traveled to Edinburgh by train for a Foreign Missions committee meeting; at 1 p.m. Peggy met him at the station and drove him to the Cathedral to discuss patterns for a new rug under the communion table; at 5.30 his Secretary Miss Stewart came for two hours' dictation and in the evening he preached in the Barony Church at a joint Holy Week service. But the day was not over yet. He had just started on a late supper when the phone rang with the message that one of his elders was in hospital unconscious. "So I went there at about 10.30 p.m. and said some prayers and recited some Psalms with him, or rather beside him." After Easter, Nevile attended the annual Dunkeld Retreat as usual where, in the aftermath of the Crusade, there were several addresses and discussions on "Conversion: the Psychological Approach."

If the Billy Graham Crusade had an impact on the minister of the Cathedral, it also involved the congregation. Volunteers could sign up to be stewards and choir members, and three elders represented the kirk session at preparatory meetings. Buses were hired to take people to the Kelvin Hall, three being required on one occasion, and during the weeks of the Crusade a short period of prayer was held in the East Chapel after the morning service. One long-standing Cathedral member, Patricia Miller, remembers being caught up in the excitement as a teenager:

> This was a truly wonderful event, with thousands attending and crowds queuing round the Kelvin Hall. I was very fortunate to

shake hands with Dr. Graham and with Cliff Barrows, the choir-master. I was also fortunate that my father managed to get for me the autographs of Cliff Barrows and of George Beverly Shea—the soloist—when they visited Yarrows Shipyard. I sang joyfully in the Crusade choir, although I wasn't old enough, but used my aunt's ticket when she wasn't going!

Nevile's pastoral letters in the monthly *Chronicle* sought to win over those who were less enthusiastic. "[Billy Graham's] methods, his presentation of the Gospel, his attitude to the Bible may not seem to all of us in line with the modern outlook. But it was felt by the great majority of the General Assembly . . . that God works in many ways and that we have no right to limit the Holy Spirit by our own ideas."[6]

After the thrill of the Kelvin Hall came the follow-up. The names of eighteen converts had been given to the Cathedral and either Nevile or one of his assistants visited them to invite them to an evening service followed by a tea-party afterwards to meet some of the church members. To keep up the momentum, a big "reunion" event was held in June at the St. Andrew's Hall at Charing Cross at which hundreds were left standing while a film of one of the Crusade services was shown, after which Nevile spoke. So many were still waiting outside that afterwards a second meeting was held.

When Tom Allan left Tell Scotland to become minister of St. George's Tron Church in Glasgow city center, the movement lost its figurehead and gradually ran out of steam, though Allan himself went on to lead other missions and—as Sandy Forsyth's recent book *Mission by the People* shows—a hugely successful parish ministry which combined evangelism and social action.

Since 1955 there has been much discussion of the long-term effects of Tell Scotland and, in particular, the Graham Crusade. Tom Allan felt that there had been an immediate ecumenical benefit: "The first result . . . of the Graham Crusade, under God, has been the breaking down of denominational barriers and the unifying of men of goodwill consecrated to one compelling purpose."[7] To this day, many older church members—and ministers—can testify to the profound effect of the Crusade on their spiritual lives, but critics have questioned how many of the "conversions" proved to be genuine and lasting. "Tell Scotland" did not end with the Crusade—an estimated 600 parish visitation campaigns took place in the winter that

6. *Chronicle*, June 1954

7. *Life and Work*, March 1955, 57

followed it—but there were indications that the feelgood factor was wearing off. When representatives of churches in the Townhead area met in October to consider a joint "Tell Scotland" visitation of the area, Nevile Davidson was frustrated by the attitude of his colleague Roy Sanderson of the Barony church who insisted that any campaign should be on a parish basis rather than a combined effort. So much for the hope expressed by Billy Graham towards the end of the campaign: "Wouldn't it be grand and wonderful if we could continue to work together?" After 1955 the movement which had started by promoting outreach at "grassroots" level was, rightly or wrongly, compromised by its association with mass evangelism, as MacLeod had feared. Even the Church of Scotland's full-time evangelist, D. P. Thomson, felt that mass rallies were not the right approach.[8]

One recent scholar has attributed the churches' lack of commitment to further evangelism to "many-layered institutional inertia."[9] Too many ministers were simply unwilling to face the radical changes in their role that a mission-oriented church would require; congregations were ill-equipped to welcome new people and the converts themselves were hardly likely to experience the same "buzz" at a Sunday morning service as they had at a mass rally. As Sandy Forsyth puts it, "There was a naïve assumption that someone drawn to Christianity by the 'Kelvin Hall' experience would be equally drawn to the 'damp church hall' experience."[10]

Billy Graham made a return visit to Glasgow in June 1961, but the atmosphere was noticeably different from 1955. The theological divisions which the churches had managed to put aside six years earlier returned to the surface and, in an address to 700 ministers in the St. Andrew's Hall, the evangelist was outspoken in his criticism of the ecumenical movement and the theories of German theologians, attacking those who prioritized other issues such as ecumenism and world peace above the preaching of the gospel. The Bishop of Manchester, who had opposed the crusades on the grounds of ecumenicity, was singled out for particular criticism by Graham: "He might not have agreed with the method and message. But if you care for ecumenicity, can't we work together even if we don't agree with each other?"[11] This meeting was followed by a mass rally at Ibrox Stadium which did not attract as big a crowd as those of 1955. Tom Allan and Nevile

8. See Bardgett, *Scotland's Evangelist*, 318–19

9. Bardgett, *The Tell Scotland Movement*, 150

10. Forsyth, *Mission by the People*, 53

11. *Glasgow Herald*, June 26 1961

Davidson were on the platform and Nevile gave the benediction, but he noted in his diary that "I imagine the great majority of those present were church members."

In his Cathedral sermon the next morning, Nevile heaped praise on Billy Graham as a prophetic figure for the twentieth century, comparing him to John the Baptist, but added that "he was sorry Dr Graham had seen fit to criticise certain aspects of the ecumenical movement . . . The goal of the ecumenical movement was to restore the lost unity of the Church in order that the Church might better fulfil its great task of evangelism."[12] This balanced assessment is typical of Nevile's pronouncements on many issues. While there do not seem to be any references to Graham in the diaries after this date, it is unlikely that the Scottish ecclesiastic and the American evangelist fell out over their differences of opinion for Nevile adopted a gentlemanly approach to everyone he met and, unlike some of his clerical brethren, tended not to become involved in acrimonious disputes. At least, the Graham family continued to send him Christmas cards, one of which survives in his correspondence files!

The combined effects of all the missionary endeavors of the 1950s produced a temporary rise in church membership but did not inaugurate the religious revival and transformation of society for which so many had hoped and prayed. Church of Scotland membership peaked at 1.3 million in 1956 but has been declining sharply ever since, especially from 1964 onwards. At the time of writing it is barely 350,000.

12. *Glasgow Herald*, June 26 1961

# 9

# "This Secular-minded Age"

## THE CHURCH OF SCOTLAND IN THE 1960S

THE BEATLES, THE PROFUMO affair[1], Vietnam protests, the Pill
. . . everyone can compile their own list of factors which contributed to the
seismic social changes of the "Swinging Sixties". At the time, though, the
transformation of Scottish society wasn't quite so apparent. Journalist and
academic Gerry Hassan, in a 2017 article entitled *When were the Swinging Sixties in Scotland?* maintains that, while the younger generation grew
increasingly dissatisfied and listened to the same pop records as teenagers
everywhere else, there was as yet no direct questioning of institutions like
the Kirk or the Labour Party.[2] The irreversible decline of the old heavy in-
dustries and their associated working class culture, the rise of nationalism,
the loss of influence of the Church of Scotland and the spread of secular
values were all happening but the extent of these changes was not always
clear at the time and, indeed, was probably not fully appreciated until the
eighties. In the sixties Scotland had as Secretary of State Labour's Willie
Ross, once described by BBC journalist Andrew Marr as "a stern-faced and
authoritarian Presbyterian conservative," and the average Scot got his values and opinions from *The Sunday Post* which in 1969 was read by 80% of
the country's adult population.

1. A political scandal in which John Profumo, Secretary of State for War in Harold
Macmillan's Conservative government, at first denied and then admitted his sexual involvement with nineteen year old Christine Keeler.

2. www.gerryhassan.com/blog/when-were-the-swinging-scottish-sixties/

How far was Nevile Davidson aware of the changes in society, and how did he respond?

There is ample evidence from his public pronouncements that the minister of Glasgow Cathedral was concerned that Scottish society was drifting from its Christian roots. In 1956 he caused a stir in the press when, in an address at the annual meeting of Glasgow City Mission, he claimed that "Glasgow was a city of astonishing contrasts, partly Christian and in other aspects pagan." Young people could tell you all about well-known film stars but scarcely knew the name of Jesus Christ; middle-aged men could repeat the names of any football team but did not know the Lord's Prayer. What is needed is the re-christianizing of twentieth century Glasgow, he said. A few days later, opening an exhibition at the Kelvin Hall, Lord Provost Andrew Hood registered his strong disagreement, saying that 95% of the city's population were "honest-to-goodness men and women" and even pointed to an attendance of 3000 young people at a "Tell Scotland" rally the previous night as evidence of interest in the Bible. But the minister of the Cathedral stuck to his opinion. At a St. Andrew Society service the following year, with Hood and other magistrates sitting in the pews in front of him, he called Scotland "a half-Christian land." In another sermon, he said that society was going back to the pre-Christian philosophy of Hedonism: many people thought "a good time"—fun and games, parties, money, clothes— should be pursued at all costs, "even if it means the break-up of marriage or the neglect of duty or the repudiation of responsibility, even if it means sometimes heartbreak for someone else." Preaching at the annual service of the Trades House in October 1961, he asked, "At this crucial point in the life of our nation, what are we doing? We are playing bingo. We are reading the newspapers in bed on Sunday mornings. We are filling up football coupons and agitating for ever higher wages and bank accounts."[3]

Changing times were reflected in the topics coming up for discussion at the Church and Nation Committee. In 1958, for example, there were the questions of hire purchase, artificial insemination, divorce and homosexuality as well as the ongoing issue of the ordination of women. In general, Nevile's stance on such issues was to defend the status quo. When Glasgow Presbytery discussed proposed legal changes to allow divorced persons

3. *Glasgow Herald*, 16 October 1961

to remarry, "I spoke strongly in opposition, but the vote went heavily the other way. It seems to me a disastrous policy virtually to give up having any general rule." Similarly, he thought artificial insemination was "a violation of the Christian doctrine of marriage." The Church and Nation Committee could not altogether condemn the practice of buying goods on hire purchase but it pointed out the dangers to families of getting into debt and put forward a solution: as women were tempted to go out and buy items they could not afford, the law should be changed so that a husband's signature was required in any hire purchase agreement.

Homosexuality proved to be the most controversial moral issue, and it still continues to cause deep divisions within the church. At the 1958 General Assembly Nevile delivered the report of the Church and Nation Committee which decisively rejected Lord Wolfenden's recommendation that "homosexual behaviour between consenting adults in private should no longer be a criminal offence." The committee was convinced, he said, that this would only serve to accelerate what Wolfenden himself described as "a general loosening of formal moral standards." It might be objected, he continued, that it was illogical to class one form of immoral behavior as a criminal offense while others, such as adultery, were not. However, the committee considered that "homosexual conduct was so essentially unnatural a vice and so obviously injurious to the social welfare of any community, as to require special legislation to discourage and, if possible, eradicate it."[4] Anticipating that such a view might invoke the charge of being reactionary, Nevile added: "If to be reactionary was to stand fast by the great traditional standards of the Christian ethic then there were occasions when we must be ready to face such aspersions rather than acquiesce in the easy-going moral relativity of the age in which we were at present living." Nevertheless, he strongly believed that the church must show more understanding and compassion towards those afflicted with this "constitutional abnormality" and claimed that many men who had "sublimated such wrong inclinations instead of giving way to them had . . . enriched the world with works of creative art and literature, or had dedicated their lives to the service of God's Church and Kingdom."[5]

This reasoning was by no means shared by all on the committee and at the General Assembly a past moderator, Professor James Pitt-Watson, and a future one, Rev. G. T. H. Reid, spoke out in support of the Wolfenden

4. *Glasgow Herald*, May 27 1958
5. *Glasgow Herald*, May 27 1958

recommendations, with Reid criticizing the committee's "fussy preoccupation with homosexual sin and its complete disregard for the simple principle of justice."[6] However, the Assembly endorsed the committee's disapproval of decriminalization by "a large majority." [7]

If there was a single event that symbolized the changing moral climate of 1960s Scotland it was the incident of the "nude in the trolley." At the end of an Edinburgh Festival drama conference in September 1963, a twenty-one year old model called Anna Kesselaar was wheeled naked in a trolley across the gallery of the McEwan Hall—a stunt which was supposed to illustrate the notion of "action theatre." Predictable outrage followed: Edinburgh's Lord Provost described it as the work of those "sick in mind"; Miss Kesselaar was denounced from the pulpit of St. Giles and was charged with indecency, though the case was thrown out of court. The press dubbed it "the Lady MacChatterley" trial.[8]

The furore had died down by May of the following year when the General Assembly fanned the flames. In the light of the incident in the McEwan Hall, Edinburgh Presbytery asked for a special committee to be set up to "examine the foundations on which ethical judgments on contemporary issues are based." Even making that request suggests a certain amount of perplexity within the church about how to react to rapidly changing social mores. This was echoed by Nevile Davidson who, in support of the motion, said that "young people were deeply bewildered and were longing for a new word of enlightenment to be spoken."[9] But it wasn't only the young who were confused. Presenting the overture, one minister said that while they were agreed about "the necessity for the Church to say something significant" they were unclear about the nature of the problem or the precise way to respond to it. The Assembly ducked the issue, deciding not to appoint a special committee and lamely instructing Edinburgh presbytery to "examine the question in consultation with such persons, inside or outside the Church of Scotland, who might be helpful to them."

6. *Glasgow Herald*, May 27 1958

7. Homosexual acts in private between two males aged twenty-one or over were decriminalized in England and Wales in 1967, but not until 1980 in Scotland.

8. *Glasgow Herald*, September 14 1963. This was a reference to the trial at the Old Bailey in London in 1960 when Penguin Books was prosecuted for obscenity after publishing an unexpurgated edition of D. H. Lawrence's novel *Lady Chatterley's Lover*. The verdict was "not guilty."

9. *Glasgow Herald*, May 21 1964

But the "nude in the trolley" wouldn't go away. The subject was raised yet again at the 1965 Assembly because London publisher John Calder, one of the organizers of the 1963 drama conference, had been invited to take part in a discussion at a Church of Scotland youth meeting. This, suggested one delegate, was like inviting Al Capone to address an audience of police commissioners. Opinion was split between those who complained that the church was providing a platform for anti-Christian views and those who said that the young should not be subjected to strictures about who they could listen to. "This is not the place for closed minds or fearful hearts," said one speaker. Nevertheless, the Assembly voted 478 to 341 to withdraw the invitation to Calder.

Another future moderator, Dr. Hugh O. Douglas of Dundee, dismissed the trolley stunt at the drama conference as "a silly piece of pretentious vulgarity and nothing more."[10] On the other hand, to the journalist and broadcaster Bernard Levin it marked the birth of the permissive society. The church faced an unpalatable choice: stick rigidly to its traditional moral values and be increasingly seen as irrelevant to the modern world, or loosen its stance and be thought of as compromising on its principles. As Professor A. M. Renwick of the Free Church—always much more rigid than the Kirk—put it, "there was nothing courageous in shouting with the crowd, or allowing oneself to be carried helplessly downstream by the current."[11]

Even Nevile Davidson sounded a less certain note at times. While he was "against any form of condoning unchastity, whether before or after marriage,"[12] he added that it was neither the only sin nor the worst sin; moreover, as chastity before marriage was a Christian injunction, the church had no right to impose a moral standard on those who did not accept the Christian faith. He believed that the church must be "alive to the movements and needs of the present" but had few specifics to offer. Endeavoring to understand the mindset of the younger generation, he maintained that, "Teddy-boys should not be blamed for their restlessness, rebelliousness and discontent; indeed, they could do a service if only by starkly challenging our smug complacency and careless superficiality."[13] Preaching in Peterhead in September 1962 during his moderatorial tour,

10. *Glasgow Herald*, May 21 1964
11. *Glasgow Herald*, May 25 1960
12. *Glasgow Herald*, December 10 1962
13. *Glasgow Herald*, October 16 1961

he lamented a past when the Bible was read in every household, and said that "the church, deeply disturbed about many things in the social and religious situation, was searching for answers, but had not yet found them. The search must go on."[14]

Slowly, the national church began, reluctantly or otherwise, to adapt to the moral revolution that was occurring round about it. The 1968 Assembly finally endorsed the view that homosexuality should be decriminalized and urged greater sympathy and understanding. By 1970, the Kirk had accepted that giving contraceptives to unmarried women was the lesser of two evils, and an overture opposing this view from the leading evangelical Rev. James Philip of Holyrood Abbey Church, backed by Nevile Davidson, was rejected. To those who argued that such a move was simply being realistic, Nevile countered that "if it meant compromise with a changing and alarming situation in the country, then he did not think the Church should be led into that kind of realism."[15]

It was inevitable that as society changed the earlier opposition to the ordination of women would crumble, and the acceptance of women elders in 1966 naturally intensified the call for women ministers. As the *Glasgow Herald* put it, "the walls of Jericho have fallen though it has taken about thirty-five years of intermittent trumpeting to do the trick."[16] Addressing the Women's Home Mission annual meeting in May 1966, Nevile spoke diplomatically of the "significant decision" of allowing women elders and predicted that by the time of the next Assembly "some of you may have emigrated to the Mound to give us the benefit of your counsel"[17]—a remark that sounds very much like it was made through gritted teeth. But by 1968, when the General Assembly agreed to ordain women as ministers, he seems to have accepted the situation; his diary for May 22 says: "The Assembly resolved by a considerable majority to admit women to the ministry!! Inevitable, perhaps, but justifiable, I think."

Unable to do little more than protest about the direction in which society was moving, the Church of Scotland began to retrench, and much time at the general assemblies of the sixties seems to have been spent discussing such operational matters as ministers' stipends, proposals to streamline administration and avoid over-centralization, and, of course,

14. *Glasgow Herald,* September 6 1962
15. *Glasgow Herald,* May 21 1970
16. *Glasgow Herald,* June 26 1966
17. *Glasgow Herald,* May 27 1966

stewardship campaigns to increase congregational givings. The early post-war enthusiasm for evangelistic outreach had noticeably waned and, with the rejection of the idea of bishops in the Kirk, ecumenical progress stalled too, though the acceptance of Roman Catholic observers at the Assembly in the early seventies was an innovation. Predictably, this aroused a good deal of protest from hardline Protestants but it was welcomed by Nevile who had already described the thaw in relationships with the RC Church under Pope John XXIII as a cause for rejoicing. Nevertheless, by 1966 Nevile was conceding that his dream of a reunion of Protestant churches in Scotland would not be achieved in his lifetime though he never gave up his belief that the way forward lay in "the continuance of conversations at every level of church life."

Politically as well as morally, the world was undergoing profound changes and the impression given by press reports is that the General Assembly debated the international situation with more passion than it did the problems in its own backyard. George MacLeod continued to grab the headlines. In the era of the Campaign for Nuclear Disarmament (CND) and Polaris missiles, he was more convinced than ever of the pacifist case and tried to persuade the Assembly to appoint a commission to study the doctrine of pacifism as "God's word to his church in the twentieth century." The Iona Community founder was equally vocal about developments on the African continent and there is no clearer example of the contrast be-tween the radicalism of MacLeod and the caution of Davidson than the debate over Africa at the 1961 Assembly. MacLeod had delivered a typi-cally passionate speech urging whites in central Africa to hand over power speedily to Africans and become a "guiding light" to all of Africa south of the equator. He had been in charge of a special committee on the subject since 1958 but resigned his position in the belief that he would then be free to demand more rapid acceptance by the white minorities—a move that caused an unprecedented outburst at the Assembly from Melville Dinwiddie, Nevile's friend from the early days of religious broadcasting, who attacked MacLeod by saying "we're a' wrong but oor George." This did not go down well with the fathers and brethren, and Nevile sought to lower the temperature with a carefully balanced statement:

> The future politically belonged to the Africans and, naturally, they were impatient to achieve complete independence. Equally naturally, the white minority were deeply apprehensive about the effects of these great changes on their own position and future . . .

> The proper word for the Christian Church to speak at this moment was a word of reconciliation—not taking sides, not trying to force the pace, and not trying to say anything so radical or provocative as further to inflame passions or make more difficult the delicate tasks of the Minister for the Colonies.[18]

On this occasion, though, it was MacLeod's radicalism that won the day and the Assembly decisively endorsed his stance.

It would be hard to overestimate the long term consequences of the moral, social and political changes of the 1960s for the Church of Scotland. Looking back at the General Assembly debates of the period, it is painfully clear that the Kirk struggled to know how to respond to changing times, and for those of a basically conservative disposition like Nevile Davidson, that response frequently seemed the wrong one. Speaking on "The Church in This Secular-minded Age," he said that the church "had lost passionate conviction in its own message."[19] Nor—if Professor Gordon Donaldson, Her Majesty's Historiographer, is to be believed—was that conviction recovered in the decades that followed. The concluding chapter of his book *The Faith of the Scots*, written in 1990, offers a withering condemnation of contemporary spokesmen for institutional Christianity:

> If the church . . . has lost its way so far as religious and moral teaching is concerned, yet, by a curious paradox, some leading churchmen are supremely confident about everything else. They may regard the events of Our Lord's life and death as no more than metaphors . . . Yet they dogmatise with easy assurance on what are often called political and social questions . . .[20]

Nevile Davidson avoided falling into such a trap as he was careful never to make pronouncements on public matters at the expense of his firmly held belief in eternal truths: "Only in so far as the Church is both loyal to 'the faith once delivered to the saints' and at the same time sensitive to the spirit of the age, and the urgent new problems and movements of our time, will its voice be listened to and its influence felt."[21]

While few would disagree with these sentiments in theory, in practice they represent a balance that churchmen have found well nigh impossible to achieve.

18. *Glasgow Herald*, May 26 1961
19. *Glasgow Herald*, June 19 1963
20. Donaldson, *The Faith of the Scots*, 142
21. Davidson, *Reflections*, 65

# 10

## "The Right Man gets the Right Thing"

### MINISTER AND MODERATOR, 1956–1967

THE SOCIAL TRENDS OF the sixties affected every local church congregation and Glasgow Cathedral was not exempt. In the remaining years of his parish ministry Nevile Davidson and his kirk session considered how best to respond to challenging new circumstances while maintaining the Cathedral's historic role as mother church of the city. On a personal level, these years also brought Nevile a number of public honors, including the highest accolade his denomination could offer: appointment as moderator of the General Assembly.

In 1960 the kirk session of the Cathedral expressed concern at the decline in the number of children attending Sunday school and Bible class and undertook an investigation of the causes and remedies. One significant factor was the demolition of tenements in the Townhead area and the movement of the population to housing schemes on the outskirts of the city. Ian R. Mitchell, a writer on the history of Glasgow life, points out that, unlike some other parts of the city that were redeveloped, in Townhead "not most, but all"[1] the tenements were demolished. So radical was the transformation that many of the streets disappeared too, including the main thoroughfare, Parliamentary Road. The building opposite the Cathedral, Provand's Lordship, the oldest house in Glasgow, is one of the few surviving landmarks.

---

1. See http://www.glasgowwestend.co.uk/people/joaneardley's-townhead.php

It was also noted that most of the children attending Sunday school were from homes not connected with the congregation and that a lack of parental encouragement led many to fall away when they left primary school as they considered themselves too old for Sunday school. Suggested solutions included asking the Sunday school teacher to pay a home visit when a child had been absent for two or more weeks, the introduction of more visual material into the lessons and an attempt to recruit more male teachers but the small numbers of children on the roll continued to crop up in kirk session discussions in subsequent years. All this, of course, was part of the wider problem of the emergence of a youth culture which increasingly saw the church as old-fashioned and irrelevant. Attending a BB (Boys' Brigade) party in February 1958, Nevile noted with some astonishment that "some of the older boys were dressed almost in 'Teddy Boy' garb!" Later that year, the BB had to be disbanded as there were only a dozen boys left, who joined up with the company at the neighboring Barony church instead.

Problems were not confined to the younger generation. Concern over finance led to a stewardship campaign in 1963, with elders visiting members and urging increased giving but the overwhelming response turned out to be one of indifference. This, said the minister, indicated that there was "an urgent need for a spiritual re-awakening of the congregation." At various meetings, Nevile was also disappointed with the poor attendance of elders and in 1958 he failed to find any volunteers from the kirk session to go to a "Tell Scotland" conference.

In times of rapid change people tend to hold onto tradition, and much of Cathedral life continued as before. The work of beautifying the building was ongoing, together with the associated dedication services. In 1956 HRH the Duke of York unveiled a Scots Guards memorial window, an event followed by both a civic lunch in the City Chambers and a Scots Guards' dinner in the evening. In 1958 the Society of Friends embarked on a new project: the installation of clear glass in the lower church and remaining windows of the nave. A public appeal was launched to finance this and 7000 letters sent out, but the response was disappointing, with donations amounting to only £1200 in the first month.

Fortunately, though, various organizations and prominent individuals continued to approach the minister with gifts in money or kind. In 1959 Sir Charles Hepburn, a wealthy whisky broker and patron of the arts, donated a Persian carpet for the Blacader Aisle and a medieval treasure chest for use as a box for donations which was positioned at a pillar near the south door, where it remains to this day. Lady Weir, wife of another Scottish industrialist, gave Nevile a check for £500 which he put into the "private fund" he kept for Cathedral improvements of his own choice and when, in 1960, the Royal College of Nursing offered to make a presentation to the Cathedral, Nevile suggested furnishing a chapel in the lower church to be known as the Nurses' Chapel.

In January 1961 Nevile regarded the fitting of four small windows in the Blacader Aisle as "an historic occasion in a way because they are the last windows we are installing in the Cathedral" and by the time he retired in 1967 the vision of "much needed improvements to the interior of the church"[2] he had outlined to the Society of Friends thirty years earlier had been largely achieved. But he was looking still further ahead. A deliberate decision had been made not to reglaze the whole of the nave in order to give future generations and artists yet unborn the opportunity to make their own contributions—a far-sightedness which has borne fruit in later additions such as John Clark's "Millennium Window" (1999) and Emma Butler-Cole Aiken's "Tree of Jesse Window" (2018). Nevile quoted with pride a remark made to him by Dr Eric Milner-White (1884–1963) who, as Dean of York, had overseen the replacement of windows at York Minister: "I expect you know that you now have here in your Cathedral the most comprehensive and representative collection of modern stained glass anywhere in Britain."[3] Equally complimentary was the comment of Lionel Stones, Professor of Medieval History at Glasgow University, who once referred to Nevile as "the Eric Milner-White of Scotland."

Perhaps Nevile Davidson was a victim of his own success when it came to stained glass. From the first year of his ministry in Glasgow he had been a member of the Council of the Scottish Ecclesiological Society, formed in 1903 "for the study of the Principles of Christian Worship, and of Church Architecture and the allied Arts which minister thereto." Addressing the Society as its President in May 1957, he commented unfavorably on the "craze" for erecting stained glass windows in churches, criticizing the numerous commercial firms now providing windows of questionable taste.

2. Annual Report of the Society of Friends of Glasgow Cathedral, 1937, p. 10

3. Davidson, *Reflections*, 55. Full details of the window designs, the donors, the artists and the sequence of installation can be found in *Glasgow Cathedral: the Stained Glass Windows*, published in 2009 by the former Cathedral Archivist Iain MacNair, and in the guidebook *A Walk Through Glasgow Cathedral* (revised edition published by the Society of Friends in 2019).

Nevile always maintained that aesthetic and doctrinal standards should not be separated:

> Ministers and kirk sessions intending to restore a new window should consider first of all its theological and devotional possibilities and make certain that if it were a window at the east end of the church the subject should be one of the supreme facts of the Gospel.[4]

Another matter that involved much kirk session time at Glasgow Cathedral over the years was the search for suitable hall premises and when a building formerly occupied by the Discharged Prisoners Aid Society in Cathedral Square became vacant towards the end of 1961, this was purchased at a cost of £5000, the top floor being converted into a flat for the use of an assistant minister.

Some modifications, albeit modest ones, were made to services in the light of changing times. It is said that late in his ministry Nevile started addressing the Almighty in his prayers as "You" instead of "Thou." A hint that even the grand official services were not quite as well supported as in the past came at a meeting in June 1961 with Sir Hector Hetherington, Principal of Glasgow University, when the decision was taken to hold the University service once every three years rather than annually, "to give it more significance and encourage a more worthy attendance," though somewhere along the line the practice reverted to an annual event which continues today, sadly with a mere token turnout of academics.

Even in his last few years of ministry, Nevile was always willing to try something different: two days after his meeting at the University, he was conducting a service for over 300 people at the newly-opened Butlin's holiday camp at Ayr. This was not the first time he had tried to adapt worship to the new forms of leisure: a short-lived experiment in 1957 saw a half-hour service at 8.30 a.m. being held during the summer in the hope of attracting cyclists and hikers setting off for a day's outing. Another attempt to involve the young was a series of discussion meetings held after the evening service in the chapter house. A sermon in November 1963 entitled "Is the Church behind the Times?" produced some "lively discussion." Another time, the subject was "Women in the Ministry" but Nevile's assertion in his sermon that congregations were overwhelmingly opposed to this was disproved by a show of hands at the discussion group. Various assistant ministers

4. *Glasgow Herald*, May 27 1957

organized other activities aimed at younger people—one even took a group for an evening of dancing at the Plaza, a popular dance hall, in 1962 and in 1964 Rev. Hugh Wyllie, a future moderator, started a teenagers' club for those aged fifteen to seventeen. At the other end of the age spectrum, 1964 also saw a special service for old age pensioners attended by 650 and Nevile found "the singing of the old-fashioned hymns *What a Friend we have in Jesus* and *I need Thee every Hour* was most moving." And, even though times were changing, the Christmas Eve service remained perennially popular. In 1962, the church "was filled from end to end, the great majority quite young and many in 'Beatnik' clothes."

Throughout all these vicissitudes, the ancient building—in which, as Lauchlan MacLean Watt once said, every stone is a prayer—remained as a symbol to the city of something enduring which, however briefly, lifts those who enter it above the mundane things of daily life. In a paper read to the Church Service Society in 1965, Nevile addressed the question of the relevance of Glasgow Cathedral to modern life. His closing remarks are worth quoting at length:

> Perhaps it may be asked: has a Cathedral or Mother Church still any significant part to play in a great modern industrial city such as Glasgow? The answer is undoubtedly in the affirmative. It is true that since the Reformation Glasgow Cathedral has been no longer the seat of a bishop, as in medieval times. Yet in many ways it has been able, and still is able, to maintain its ancient role and carry out some of the most valuable of its former functions. More than that, although a constitutionally formed congregation . . . worships regularly within its walls, yet in a very real sense the Cathedral is also the spiritual centre for the whole city . . . On occasions of national or civic rejoicing or disaster, it is to the Cathedral that the people naturally come, from all parts of the city, to join in prayer and to find comfort and inspiration. In a very real sense, the great old church, even as a building, visibly symbolizes the central part which the Christian Faith has played generation after generation in the life of the community, and silently speaks of the prayers, the aspirations and the spiritual longings of countless men and women through the centuries. This sense of continuity in Christian tradition, belief and worship is of very high value in an age which is often tempted to disparage the past. When possible a great church, with endowments at its disposal and contacts with generous friends and patrons, should also give encouragement to artists and craftsmen, whether in stained-glass, wood, wrought

iron, weaving, or embroidery. In this way something practical can be done to bring to an end the arid period of misunderstanding which, peculiarly in Scotland, for so long has separated the arts and artists from the Church. Nor must it be forgotten that a Cathedral Church should be expected to set a pattern of Divine Worship and provide a standard of religious music which cannot be found, and indeed would not be suitable, in the average parish church. The great festivals of the Christian Year can be celebrated with special magnificence. Liturgical experiments, moreover, can be more easily carried out. Distinguished representatives of other Communions, or those engaged in social and evangelical activities of special interest may be invited to preach. At other times, distinguished musicians from other countries are invited to come and give recitals on the great organ. In these and in many other ways the Mother Church of a city can both provide spiritual leadership and also afford opportunities for that peculiarly effective modern form of evangelism: the gathering of different groups, professional, industrial, artistic, athletic, for common worship. For, in spite of contemporary attacks on traditional religious observances and customs, it is above all when men and women come together to worship and pray in one place that the barriers between secular and sacred are found to be illusory; and the worshippers gain not only new glimpses of the splendour and the loving kindness of God, but also new insights into the meaning and the possibilities of ordinary life, in its heights and its depths.[5]

As an explanation of the role Glasgow Cathedral has performed throughout the generations, and which it still endeavors to fulfil, these words could hardly be bettered.

By 1960 Nevile Davidson had been minister of the Cathedral for a quarter of a century, and over the next two years he had the satisfaction of seeing his labors receive considerable public recognition. At the end of January his silver jubilee at the Cathedral was marked by a social function at which he was presented with a check and new robes, while Peggy received some diamond earrings (which she had been given the opportunity to choose for herself). Nevile estimated that by that stage of his ministry he had preached

---

5. *Church Service Society Annual,* 1965, 36–38 (slightly condensed).

2000 sermons and uttered at a moderate estimate 2.25 million words when conducting services.

The closing months of 1961 brought further honors. Every three years the Lord Provost of Glasgow awarded the St. Mungo prize to the person who "had done most . . . to make Glasgow more beautiful, healthier or more honoured" and Nevile was selected, principally because of his work in renovating the Cathedral. The prize was a gold medal and a check for £1000 and, characteristically, Nevile gave some of the money to Miss Stewart, his faithful secretary who had spent so many evenings taking dictation in the Hill Street flat.

The pinnacle of his career, however, was selection as moderator of the General Assembly for 1962, a role which involves chairing the highest court of the church during its annual meeting in May in the Assembly Hall in Edinburgh. The moderator holds the post for a year, during which he relinquishes his normal duties and travels at home and abroad as an ambassador for the national church. The Rev. Tom Kiltie, a former assistant who was now minister at Stepps, wrote to his mentor, "It seems that honours as well as troubles never come singly!"—just one of something like 400 letters of congratulation delivered to Hill Street. Rev. Alan Robson of Kelvinside thought "there will surely be joy in the presence of the angels in Heaven" at the news; back on earth—where those who secure the top jobs are not necessarily the best candidates—a BBC colleague, Andrew Stewart, wrote that "There is such a feeling of happy satisfaction when the right man gets the right thing." In reflective mood on his sixty-third birthday in February 1962, Nevile wrote in his diary: "The days are so crowded, that the years roll by, almost unnoticed. But how full they are of blessing and encouragement and friendship infinitely beyond one's deserts. And above all and through all, the goodness and loving kindness of God."

Nevile Davidson robed as moderator of the General Assembly in 1962.
(Photo: Glasgow Cathedral).

Though the Assembly did not meet until mid-May, preparations began immediately. Being properly dressed was always a priority for Nevile, and in January he was at R. W. Forsyth's outfitters in Glasgow to order his moderatorial gown and a court suit, while Peggy was measured for a suit made of a roll of "clergy tartan" given to her by Charles Warr which his late wife, Ruby, had ordered just before she died. When the *Glasgow Herald* interviewed "Mrs Nevile Davidson" for the paper's "Women's Topics" page on the eve of the assembly, the journalist noted she was wearing her new "well-tailored suit . . . in quiet yet telling tones of dark blue and green."[6] During March Nevile was busy drafting his moderatorial address, attending

6. *Glasgow Herald*, May 16 1962

meetings to make arrangements for the Assembly and planning his itinerary for the year. Dr. A. J. Boyd took over the Cathedral pulpit during
Nevile's absence and Hugh Wyllie was appointed as a full-time second assistant who would move into the top floor flat in the new halls. Once again,
the congregation gave the Davidsons an affectionate send-off at a social
gathering at which Peggy was presented with a new handbag and Nevile
with a "splendid leather case." Representatives from his previous charges
in Aberdeen and Dundee traveled down to be present, "which touched us
both deeply." "Somehow," he reflected, "the event seemed to summarise and
fuse the memories of my three happy ministries."

The couple then moved into the Roxburghe Hotel in Edinburgh,
which served as a base for the next ten days. At his first press conference,
Nevile spoke on two matters which he saw as priorities: the need to update
the Westminster Confession of Faith and relationships between the various churches, particularly the delicate issue of a hoped-for improvement
in relations with the Roman Catholics in the light of the meeting between
the previous moderator, Dr. Archie Craig, and the Pope. Then at 10.30 a.m.
on May 22 the formal proceedings began with the arrival of a vintage Rolls
Royce to take the new moderator up the Mound to the Assembly Hall. Dr.
Craig offered a prayer of consecration and placed the ceremonial ring on
his successor's finger, a message from the Queen was read out and the Lord
High Commissioner, the Earl of Mansfield, made a speech. There followed
a hectic week presiding over lengthy debates, delivering addresses to various public meetings, and attending social events and dinners, among the
highlights being the reception at Holyrood Palace and the royal garden
party. But Nevile had been brought up to such a high-profile role and took
it all in his stride.

The General Assembly was only the start of the moderator's duties.
Once the ceremonies and debates had finished he immediately set off on
his tours, starting with a visit to the Assembly of the Presbyterian Church
of Ireland in Belfast followed by engagements in the south, and later in
the north, of Scotland. It was the custom for the moderator not only to
visit churches but schools, hospitals and places of work; at Stranraer, for
instance, he went to a maternity clinic where he "inspected" the babies after
which he attended the cattle market, where proceedings were stopped for
ten minutes to allow him to address the farm workers. At Dounreay in the
very north of Scotland he saw the nuclear power station, "the most exciting incident being taken inside a great steel sphere in which the uranium

is processed." At Glasgow's Barlinnie Prison he led an act of worship in the chapel attended by about 190 prisoners and spoke on "Is Life Worth Living?" and was particularly moved when he preached at Blackadder Church in North Berwick from the pulpit once occupied by his father. Yet all of this was but a prelude to the world tour which occupied the first three months of 1963 [see chapter 11].

During this period Nevile found himself coming into ever closer contact with the royal family, though there were occasional mishaps. In August 1962 he was invited once again to stay at Balmoral Castle where he spent much time socializing and dining, finding the young "Prince Charles and Princess Anne both quite talkative and she very lively." However, after preaching at Crathie Church, he was climbing into the royal car when he gashed his head on the sharp edge of the door. Press photographers pounced and he covered his head and face with a towel until, back at the castle, the wound was stitched up by the Queen's doctor and Nevile enjoyed much sympathetic concern from the royals. Later in the year, a phone call came through from Buckingham Palace to inquire why the moderator had not responded to an invitation to a state banquet at Holyrood; the letter was later found in a pile of mail awaiting opening at Hill Street as he had been away on his travels.

Moving in such exalted circles was now almost part of Nevile's daily routine: his diary for June 1963 records his attendance at yet another royal reception at Holyrood, casually adding: "a delightful party of about 250, of whom we knew the majority." In fact, on some of his visits abroad, the Church of Scotland moderator was taken to be such an important person that he was virtually considered to be royalty himself. After going to dedicate the new premises of the Scots church in Brussels, Nevile kept a cutting from an unidentified Belgian newspaper which reported that "le moderateur est considéré comme le plus haute personalité Écossais . . . Son rang le place en Écosse juste après la Reine et le prince Philip."[7] He now knew the Queen so well that in June 1964 she fitted in a visit to a Sunday morning service at the Cathedral during a tour of Scotland—the first monarch to do so since Queen Victoria in 1849. Nevile preached on the theme of "Life: a Land of Hills and Valleys" and the choir sang an anthem composed by the former organist and choirmaster, Wilfred Emery, which had a special poignancy as the previous month Emery had died very suddenly one Sunday

---

7. "The moderator is considered the most important person in Scotland . . . after the Queen and Prince Philip."

morning while waiting for a bus to take him to the Cathedral. Nevile had also taken the risk of including in the order of service *Summer Suns are Glowing*—a hymn which, said the *Glasgow Herald* in a rare flash of humor, "in Glasgow often heralds the beginning of the monsoon season."[8] After the service, the Queen was shown round the lower church and St. Mungo's tomb and met with officebearers.

Yet, amongst all the high living, Nevile Davidson still found time to offer pastoral care. Briefly back at the Cathedral during his tour of Scotland, he made a point of visiting the father of one of his assistants in the cancer hospital, and while carrying out official engagements in Caithness spent time with a young woman who had suffered a stroke and was in need of spiritual help. And, like the rest of the population in the 1960s, he would relax on free evenings by watching television. On various occasions he followed the rugby, football, the Grand National and the Oxford and Cambridge boat race and he and Peggy never missed their favorite program, *Dr Finlay's Casebook,* which became as much a part of their Sunday routine as morning and evening worship!

Nevile Davidson had many hobbies but the one he took most seriously in the early 1960s was his art collection. Even in his youth he used to buy prints and wherever his travels took him he would look for paintings as well as antiques. His best find had occurred in 1944 in a shop run by John Yates in Stirling where he saw a very old oil painting of the Nativity which had been in the shop for some years. His initial idea had been to purchase it and use it as a reredos in a side chapel for children, perhaps situated in the lower church, but he either changed his mind or, as had happened years earlier in Aberdeen, encountered some opposition, as by January 11 1945 arrangements had been made with the architect of H.M. Office of Works to have the picture hung in the nave instead. Once in position, Nevile thought it looked beautiful but nervously confided to his diary: "I hope there will be no protests from ultra-Protestant-minded people as it is probably the first picture that has been hung in the Cathedral since the Episcopal period in the seventeenth century." Naturally, this provided the pretext for a choir procession and dedication ceremony which took place on Saturday January 13—St. Mungo's Day—prior to the annual meeting of the Society of Friends. Dr Tom Honeyman, Director of Glasgow Art Galleries had the painting expertly restored and pronounced it to be "a work of extremely fine quality, probably painted in Italy and almost certainly of the early seventeenth

8. *Glasgow Herald,* 29 June 1964

century."[9] Sir Kenneth Clark, at that time Director of the National Gallery, also viewed the work on a visit to Glasgow and expressed the view that it was possibly painted by a Flemish artist living and working in Italy. It was later identified as a studio copy of "The Adoration of the Shepherds" by Camillo Procaccini (c.1551–1629) which is in the Brera Gallery, Milan.

The seventeenth century copy of "The Adoration of the Shepherds" by Camillo Procaccini discovered in an antique shop by Nevile Davidson and gifted to Glasgow Cathedral in 1945. (Photo: Jack Stevenson).

Perhaps as a gesture of gratitude for the cleaning of the painting, Nevile donated another canvas to the Art Galleries, a still life by a nineteenth century artist, David Horn, which had previously hung in the Oakfield Avenue

9. *Glasgow Herald,* January 15 1945

house that he sold in 1945. There was more room to display works of art in the Hill Street flat so that by the late 1950s he and Peggy were regularly attending art auctions in Glasgow and sometimes further afield. They were present in November 1963 at a sale run by Morrison McChlery of Sauchiehall Street when a flower painting by Fantin-Latour sold for £17,000; on that occasion, the Davidsons made two more modest purchases by Dutch artists, a street market (£20) and two peasants in a landscape (£12). Nevile seemed to favor the Dutch school and the following month at Dowell's Fine Art auction he bid up to £210 for a seventeenth century version of "The Flight to Egypt" but it sold for £230. He dabbled in selling paintings, too: six months after buying the Dutch market scene for £20, he put it back into another sale at Dowell's where it fetched twice what he paid for it.

The Cathedral minister was a patron of art as well as a collector: in 1963 he commissioned a painting from his Hill Street neighbor, the Scottish writer and artist Alastair Gray, long before he became well-known for his novel *Lanark*. Gray had been painting a mural of the Garden of Eden in Greenhead Church, Bridgeton, and Nevile asked him to produce a smaller work based on this entitled "A Corner of the Garden of Eden." The commission resulted as much from Nevile's kindness as from his appreciation of art, for he was aware that the Grays had just had a newborn son and they were struggling financially at the time.[10]

Round the corner from the Hill Street flat was the famous School of Art designed by Charles Rennie Mackintosh and Nevile called on the Director, Douglas Bliss, to suggest holding a special service to forge a link between the students and staff and the Cathedral. Bliss cordially approved of the idea and the service took place in May 1964, bringing yet another institution into contact with the mother church of the city.

The first hint that Nevile was thinking of withdrawing from his demanding public role came in January of that year when he met with some of his officebearers and shared his intention of finishing his active ministry by moving to a small country parish. "Kindly and affectionately" they urged him to continue a little longer and it was not until October 1966 that he announced that he would retire the following Easter. "I believe it will be good that a new voice should be heard from this cathedral pulpit," he told the congregation, "and a new and younger mind turned to the problems, the responsibilities, and the opportunities of the rapidly changing social scene."

10. www.theskinny.co.uk/art/interviews/autopictography-a-study-in-gray

Spring 1967 was accordingly taken up by a succession of farewell lunches and dinners as the many organizations with which Nevile had been associated all wanted to show their appreciation. The Davidsons were showered with gifts: "two beautiful silver grouse" from the Trades House, "a silver Iona cross" from the Society of Foremen Engineers, "a Doulton china ornament" from the Sunday School, a check for £179 from the Society of Friends, and much else. The climax was a huge gathering held in the Banqueting Hall of the City Chambers where an audience of 500 said farewell to the Davidsons with a generous check for £1,200 and gifts of a food-mixer for Peggy and a lawnmower for Nevile, which, to much amusement, he pushed up and down the aisle for the benefit of the press photographers present.[11]

Yet, what meant more to Nevile than all the public tributes were the many private expressions of gratitude from ordinary members of his congregation. A simple and genuine sincerity shines through the letters he received. One elderly parishioner wrote:

> My heart is just broken at the thought of losing you and Mrs Davidson. I know Dr we all have faults but I want you to know you had none in my eyes. My late hubby and I were your first bride and groom and the first and only ones to be married in your manse at Oakfield Avenue. I know the time comes to us all and we must accept it that we are getting older and must give way to the younger generation coming up. But there will never be another minister in my eyes like you.

A Sunday School teacher reminded Nevile of an incident many years earlier during an outing to Largs when a small girl who had climbed onto rocks near the sea started to cry as she had left her shoes behind on the grass and the rocks were hurting her feet.

> As soon as you spoke to her she stopped crying immediately as though because you were there she knew everything was all right. I think that memory stayed with me because that is how I've always seen you, Dr. Davidson, as always being there and always ready to help and knowing, like that little girl, as long as you were there everything would be all right.

11. See *Chronicle*, May 1967

Nevile Davidson chose Easter Sunday as his final service and as he ascended the pulpit steps to preach his last sermon as Cathedral minister was conscious of "an extraordinary feeling of stillness, attention and affection."

On Thursday 30 March, thirty-two years of ministry at Glasgow Cathedral officially came to an end. But in the years that lay ahead, Nevile Davidson would do much more than use his new lawnmower.

# 11

## Peaceful Retreats and World Travels

"EVERY NOW AND THEN," recommended Leonardo da Vinci, "go away, have a little relaxation, for when you come back to your work your judgment will be surer." That advice was certainly followed by Nevile Davidson, a practitioner of the notion of work/life balance long before the term had been thought of. Though his commitment to his duties was beyond question and often involved a grueling program of engagements, he also took frequent short holidays and each summer insisted on a two month break from the Cathedral, which did not altogether please his office-bearers as he sometimes left no forwarding address. Throughout their married life the Davidsons rented or owned numerous holiday properties where they could completely escape from the strains and stresses of their public role. In addition, they clocked up thousands of miles traveling abroad on official trips representing the Church of Scotland which also provided opportunities to see different parts of the world.

While staying in a remote cottage on a holiday in Lochinver, Sutherland in the summer of 1946, the recently married couple first acquired a taste for even greater solitude than the family house at Nethy Bridge could offer. "We have the whole of the little bay to ourselves. It is wonderful to wake and see the water and rocks from one's bed. And, except for the lapping of the flowing and ebbing tide, and the occasional scream of a gull, the silence is complete." Having spotted a similar property that was empty, they approached the factor of the estate with a view to purchasing it, but the

135

owner's response was non-committal and the idea came to nothing. That winter, however, they came across Caldwell Tower in East Renfrewshire, the only remaining part of an earlier castle, and "fell in love with it at once." There was a possibility of buying it from the farmer who owned the land, but his asking price was exorbitant and, once more, nothing materialized.

Then a friend recommended another tower in an even more attractive location: Hallbar, a sixteenth century tower house beside a stream in a wooded glen near the village of Crossford in Lanarkshire. The landowner was again reluctant to sell but agreed to lease it for the nominal sum of £1 per annum, so long as he should be involved in no further expense. As it was uninhabited and virtually derelict, total restoration was required which would involve much time and money, but Nevile relished the challenge of a project like this in a spot that was secluded enough for complete privacy yet within easy reach of Glasgow.

The tower had three rooms, one of top of the other, and furniture for the upper levels had to be slung up on ropes let down from the battlements and taken in through the windows. The Davidsons would take a day off whenever they could to work on clearing out rubble and making the house habitable and, by the end of March 1947, they were able to sleep there for the first time. The windows lacked glazing and the hooting of an owl kept them awake but these minor drawbacks did not detract from the "marvelous sense of peace." It was difficult to get building work done so soon after the war, but Nevile managed to find someone to fit locks and glaze the windows, though even basic household items like a doormat and a pail remained unobtainable in local shops. He and Peggy did some painting themselves, and during the summer spent much time clearing the grounds, cutting down so much bracken that it made a pile eight feet high, creating the problem of how to dispose of it all. Not until 1951 was Peggy able to turn her attention to stocking the garden with flowers, and in May she was pleased to find out that 200 of the 230 daffodil bulbs she had planted were in full bloom.

Hallbar Tower, a sixteenth century tower house situated near the village of Crossford in South Lanarkshire. The Davidsons used it as a holiday retreat between 1947 and 1969.

Conditions were primitive at first: lighting was provided by paraffin lamps and cooking done on an open fireplace but that made staying there more of an adventure. Milk and eggs for breakfast had to be fetched from a neighboring farm and even running water was lacking until mid-1949 when a supply pipe was installed at a cost of £30 which Nevile reckoned "money well spent." "You know, we live there under fifteenth century conditions. Isn't that wonderful?" he told one of his Cathedral elders, who failed to see the attraction. But hard work over the years brought the tower up to a habitable standard without destroying its character and when the landlord was invited for tea to view the progress, he was so impressed that he not only offered a twenty year lease but provided a supply of oak to install a staircase between floors.

The Davidsons now had an added reason for visiting antique shops and auctions. After the local council acquired Castlebank House in Lanark there was a sale of furniture where they bought "some nice old-fashioned pink curtains and four large cushions and a painted iron garden seat for Hallbar, all of which we got for marvelously low prices." Peggy and Nevile could even be found going round the Barrows in Glasgow, looking (in vain) for a suitable brass door knocker.

Hallbar Tower was just over twenty-five miles from the center of Glasgow, a journey which can be covered by car in under an hour, though it would have taken longer in pre-motorway days. The Davidsons now had a place to which they could retreat every week, as well as the house at Nethy Bridge, which was not only less accessible (in 1952 it took them eleven and a half hours to get there by road, including stops) but was also frequently let to tenants. Most years, however, they continued to make their way north after Easter, usually setting off as soon as the Holy Week services were over in a car crammed with luggage. "On top of the suitcases, baskets, golf-clubs, wireless, coats, etc. Dingwall was ensconced on his rug!" At Nethy Nevile would relax, read, go fishing, saw logs, play croquet on the lawn and bridge in the evenings, and spend a good deal of time paying visits or going on picnics. There would invariably be friends or relatives staying too. Peggy's sister Diana, her brother Peter and his wife Felicia and their children David and Fiona were frequent visitors. Nevile loved playing with children and the adjacent forest provided a perfect playground: at various times he talks of trying to retrieve a model aeroplane stuck in a tree, playing a "vigorous game of quoits in the garden until we were driven indoors by a host of midges" and even daring the children to swim across the River Dulnain while the adults were having a picnic on the shore, offering a half-crown [about 12.5 pence in today's British currency] as a reward. Today, David Martin says: "They treated my sister Fiona and I as if we were their own children and we were thoroughly spoilt by them. I have happy memories of playing golf, cricket, fishing, walking and sawing logs with Uncle Nevile at Nethy Bridge."

Nevile Davidson relaxing on holiday at Nethy Bridge. (Photo: David Martin)

A busy schedule sometimes meant that Hallbar Tower was not visited for some months, and in November 1953 the Davidsons returned to find a large brown owl had been roosting in one of the rooms upstairs where, as Nevile delicately put it, "he had left unmistakable evidence of his occupation." Human visitors were more welcome and children found it exciting to climb the steep staircase and "emerge from darkness into moonlight on the battlements." In the later fifties and sixties, when the tower had been left unoccupied for long spells, there were numerous break-ins, though nothing much was ever stolen.

When it came to property, the Davidsons acted on impulse: if they liked something, they would immediately go for it. The one thing lacking at Nethy Bridge and Hallbar was a view of the sea and when, on a trip to the East Neuk of Fife in May 1955, they saw a small house for sale in the picturesque village of Crail they arranged for an architect to look at it. The house cannot have been suitable, for the next month they were viewing another in Anstruther which turned out to be in "a state of great dilapidation." After one or two other disappointments, they found what they wanted in a part of the world very familiar to Nevile from his childhood: a small terraced house called "Sea Point" in Dunbar. They put in an offer the same day.

Its location on the shore with the incoming tide visible from the back windows was the main attraction but another consideration in Nevile's mind was that it might be a suitable place for his sister Cois to settle. Her life certainly seems to have lacked stability. In October 1946 she left her job in Aberdeen and moved to London to join the Order of the Good Shepherd in Finchley so that she could take part in social and rescue work. Nevile immediately went to discuss this decision with her. "She is convinced she has a vocation (although I can't help being doubtful) and the only course seems therefore for her to try it." After only a few weeks, however, she left the convent and returned to Aberdeen. By 1948 she was back in London working as a nurse but planning to move to the Carthusian Monastery in Cowfold, West Sussex to look after the Guest House. From the early 1950s onwards she lived in the Wavertree district of Liverpool, working with boys from disadvantaged homes, but by 1956 she had returned to nursing. All this took place against a background of poor health and periods where she was recommended to take rest. Throughout her life, her brother kept up a lengthy correspondence with her, most likely provided financial support and when traveling in England would call in to see her. Cois was rarely in Scotland during this period and it seems she did not make her first, and perhaps her only, visit to Sea Point until Christmas 1959.

Sea Point, a small terraced house in Dunbar owned by the Davidsons between 1955 and 1965. The back windows look onto the rocky shore below. (Photo by the author).

Peggy and Nevile began New Year 1956 at their new hideaway at Sea Point where they took the first of many walks along the sands to the lighthouse, picking up driftwood for the fire. "We felt very comfortable in front of the fire while the storm roared round the house and the waves boomed on the rocks just below." Towards the end of January Nevile suffered an attack of shingles and, always excessively concerned about his health, retreated to Sea Point to recuperate for almost the whole of February. Inevitably, for the rest of that year Hallbar Tower was visited less often. A lifelong lover of nature, Nevile drew satisfaction from the simple pleasures of his new sea-side location: "A beautiful Spring morning. We drove to the lighthouse and had a delightful walk along the edge of the sand dunes and back along the sands. The larks were singing and curlew calling and one corner of the bay was full of eider duck. And we actually saw a rabbit." The proximity of the cottage to Edinburgh also made it easier to attend, and recover from, tense committee meetings. In May 1956, after an Inter-Church Relations meeting where he was faced with opposition to the idea of continued discussions with the Anglicans, Nevile found Sea Point helped restore his peace of mind: "Late in the afternoon, Peggy and I left the heat of the debating arena behind us and drove peacefully to Dunbar and the endless familiar flashing of the waves."

But all good things come to an end. In 1964 the boarding house behind Sea Point built a large extension looking straight into the back of the house and the Davidsons felt the time had come to part with it. They accepted an offer in June of the following year and vacated it in October but felt "very sad at letting it go." Even at Nethy Bridge, change was in the air: in 1963 Nevile tackled the factors of the Seafield Estate over plans to cut down three-quarters of the forest around the house and tried to persuade them to leave some of the best trees, but the timber had already been sold in advance. While staying there in July 1965 the Davidsons "woke to the ominous sound of sawing and the periodical crash of a falling tree." It was not long before new housing encroached on the isolation of Forest House.

If holiday properties were bought on impulse, the same was true of the cars that Nevile used to reach them. New cars were hard to come by after WWII as the British motor industry, at the insistence of the government, prioritized export and when Nevile's garage offered him a new Vauxhall Wyvern in September 1950, he jumped at the chance. Three years later, he traded it for another of the same model which took the Davidsons on a European driving holiday in the summer of 1955—quite an ambitious undertaking in these days. It began with a sail from Harwich to Holland, followed by a drive through Belgium into Germany, where much war damage was still "tragically obvious" at Coblenz and Munich. The Davidsons then moved on to Salzburg, Vienna and the sharp gorges and mountain passes of Kitzbühel. They did not trouble to book accommodation in advance and usually managed to find a small hotel, though at Zell am See in Austria they spent an hour and a half in pouring rain looking for a room before they eventually found one at midnight. Adventurous as ever, they tackled the challenging two and a half hour drive on hairpin bends leading to the glacier on the eastern side of the Grossglockner, Austria's highest mountain. In Austria, "The churches are always open as God's House ought to be," reported Nevile in the September issue of the Cathedral *Chronicle,* adding that he had completed the 4000 mile trip without so much as a puncture.

In 1957, Nevile acquired his third Wyvern, a black 1956 model, having first done the rounds of the local dealerships to make sure he secured the best price. By 1960 this car needed expensive repairs and he decided to change it but the American-inspired styling of the new generation of Vauxhalls was not to his taste and this time he went for the more dignified lines of a 1958 Humber Hawk. "Hope we have made the right decision!" he wrote in his diary, but it turned out to be a mistake: a couple of months later, the clutch burnt out and a gearbox repair was needed. By the following year, his mechanic advised against spending any more money on the car and it was replaced with a 1960 Humber Super Snipe "in perfect condition" with 22,000 miles on the clock. While driving this car in wintry weather on the road between Forfar and Brechin in December 1962, Nevile miscalculated when trying to overtake and had what he described as a "semi head-on collision with a small shooting brake." Nearby road workers helped pull the other car out of a ditch and, although no-one was injured, a good deal of time had to be spent in the police station before continuing on the journey to Aberdeen to record a television interview.

By this time, the Davidsons had yet another place to stay in addition to their holiday homes at Forest House, Hallbar Tower and Sea Point. After the death of Colonel Martin in 1949, Peggy's mother Margaret had been spending an increasing amount of time traveling north to be with her daughter and in 1957 she decided to move permanently from Surrey to Scotland where she purchased a house called "Fair Fields" in Newton Port, Haddington. An amusing incident in connection with this occurred in April 1959. Nevile had been in London for a meeting of the British Council of Churches and was returning by express train from King's Cross to Edinburgh.

> Suddenly I noticed that the train had stopped in open country near Longniddry and as I wanted to join Peggy at Haddington it seemed too good a chance to miss so I jumped out of the train with my case. Marvellously, found a small car which had been stopped at the level crossing and the driver kindly drove me to the main road where I caught the last bus to Haddington! Peggy and Margaret were astonished to see me as they hadn't expected me until tomorrow morning.

He may have been sixty years of age, but there was still something of "Nevile the Devil" left in Peggy's husband.

The Davidsons' restorative breaks in the "silence and solitude" of Nethy Bridge, Hallbar Tower or Dunbar alternated with packed itineraries taking them all over the world. Often these came about through an official visit of some kind which also allowed plenty of time for sightseeing and socialising.

In June 1951, for example, an invitation to provide summer pulpit supply in the USA allowed a welcome respite from the austerity of post-war Britain. After a leisurely journey to Liverpool, with Nevile and Peggy sharing the driving, they set off on the M.V. *Britannic*, while Peggy's sister Diana took the car down to Yateley and kept it there until they returned in September. Being on board during the Independence Day celebrations of July, Nevile acted as one of the judges of a fancy dress parade. The Davidsons were based in Montclair, New Jersey, where Nevile was to conduct the joint summer services for the First Methodist and First Congregational Churches and their host, Dr. Morgan P. Noyes, laid on a full program of sightseeing and dinners. They visited the museums of New York, saw Harlem and Broadway and went to the top of the Empire State Building which prompted a thought for a sermon: "how tiny looking are man and all his works even from 1448 feet up." Keen as ever to see as much as possible, the Davidsons sat and passed their American driving tests "without difficulty" and were given a loan of Noyes' Chevrolet in which they drove through New Hampshire and Massachusetts, visiting Vermont, Boston and Princeton, and calling in to see Dr. Hugh Black, now a frail 83 year old, who had left Scotland forty years previously to become a Professor at Union Theological Seminary. They also tasted hamburgers and strawberry ice-cream sundaes for the first time!

An invitation to represent the Church of Scotland at the General Assembly of the Presbyterian Church in Canada resulted in another trip across the Atlantic in June 1957, this time on a BOAC flight from Prestwick Airport. At Toronto Nevile met up with two of his colleagues from the "Tell Scotland" movement, Tom Allan and William Fitch, who were over working with Billy Graham. A visiting cleric might pass unnoticed today, but on arrival at Vancouver Nevile was greeted by the press and had to give a television interview. As always, the Davidsons were well looked after by church people and they met many expatriate Scots. At Toronto they experienced the excitement of staying in "a modern hotel [which] had a private bathroom, telephone and television set!" Nevile preached at several churches and addressed the General Assembly on current concerns of the Church of Scotland, such as nuclear weapons, the place of women in the church and ecumenical conversations with the Church of England. In early July he crossed the border to New York where Billy Graham was leading his Madison Square Gardens Crusade. Nevile was given "a delightful welcome" in his private room and "Billy made me sit with him on the platform." Evidently the formal Scottish cleric was adapting to the easy-going American ways and was now on first name terms with the famous evangelist. But Nevile also went out of his way to visit humbler acquaintances, paying a call on the daughter of the Cathedral beadle who had emigrated to Canada and was feeling rather homesick.

In April 1961 he and Peggy again flew from Prestwick, this time to Copenhagen where they caught another flight to Stockholm in the company of a group of other Scottish church delegates for a conference on the theme of inter-communion conducted by the Archbishop of Uppsala. Afterwards, the Davidsons stayed on for three days of sightseeing in Stockholm. A trip to Germany in 1964, taken at the invitation of the Germany government, provided a similar opportunity to build relationships with the Lutheran church, though things got off to a bad start: on arrival at Hamburg by air, the Davidsons discovered their luggage was missing and the normally immaculate Nevile must have been mortified when he had to attend his first meeting with leading churchmen dressed in his traveling clothes instead of his clerical black. The tour took in a number of modern churches erected in cities destroyed by wartime bombing and "everywhere one got the impression of vitality" but crossing the border to the East revealed "a different world with an atmosphere of sadness, suspicion and sordidness." What impressed Nevile most about the Lutheran church was its emphasis on pastoral care: in the largest central church in West Berlin there was at least one pastor on duty day and night to talk to anyone who needed a sympathetic ear.

Nevile's most extensive travels took place during his year as moderator in 1962–63 when he undertook what was virtually a world tour representing the Church of Scotland. As he had been invited to preach at Melbourne he put in an advance request to the British army authorities that he might be allowed to visit Scottish troops stationed in the Middle East before traveling on to Australia. This epic journey commenced on January 6 1963 with a 2,300 mile flight to Khartoum via Geneva and Rome. *Beginnings but no Ending* dutifully catalogs each stage of an itinerary that covered Aden, Dhala, the Yemeni border, Nairobi, Australia and New Zealand, listing the military bases and churches visited, but the unpublished diary entries are far more successful in bringing these locations to life. Equally interested in both the wonders of nature and in human technological progress, Nevile marveled at "the wondrous smooth and quiet" of the Comet jet airliner, recounted the types of planes which took him across "mile after mile of treeless, waterless savage desert" from Khartoum and over the "snow-streaked rocky summit of Mount Kenya, looking superb in the clear light of early morning," and described his fascination with "Arab fishing craft, camels, salt-pan windmills, goat-crowded bazaars."

In spite of the usual packed schedule of engagements, social events and church services, the Davidsons would always find time for shopping expeditions, even for bulky items like an electric toaster, a trout rod and a "lamp shade made of camel skin in the shape of a large fat duck"—a rare lapse in their usually impeccable aesthetic judgment.

Flying via Singapore, the moderator and his wife arrived for their month's stay at Melbourne's Royal Commonwealth Society Club on February 2, where they could be forgiven for "feeling rather tired after all our journeying." Many of the talks used in Africa received a further airing in the Antipodes, with a sermon entitled "What is Man?" cropping up several times. A special service in the Scots Kirk at Melbourne was the occasion of another encounter with the Queen and Prince Philip, with whom Nevile was now on quite familiar terms, and the Queen unveiled a new stained glass window. The official tour ended in New Zealand with the first ever visit from a Church of Scotland moderator during his year of office and it was here that the only misadventure of the whole trip occurred when Peggy slipped and broke a bone in her foot which then had to be put in plaster for three weeks.

Having traveled so far round the world, the Davidsons decided to return via the United States to catch up with the many friends made on previous trips. They visited New York, New Jersey, San Francisco and Los Angeles, where they saw the Forest Lawn Memorial Park with its "Wee Kirk of Annie Laurie". Nevile found "the sentimentality and pseudo-religion of it all quite incredible" and he must have been relieved to be back in the familiar surroundings of Glasgow Cathedral in April for the solemnity of the Holy Week services. Recounting their adventures in a talk to the Women's Guild that winter, Peggy said that in three months they had traveled 32,000 miles and taken forty different aeroplane flights.

As well as serving as a figurehead for the Church of Scotland, Nevile Davidson was a prominent representative of national and international organizations such as the BCC (British Council of Churches) and WCC (World Council of Churches). Making one of his regular trips to London for a BCC meeting in April 1965, he notes in a matter of fact way in his diary that "the Archbishop of Canterbury wasn't able to be there so I presided all morning." His role as a WCC delegate took him to conferences in Denmark and Geneva, and sometimes further afield, as in January 1965 when he and Peggy flew to Nigeria where the Central Committee was debating such matters as the appointment of a new general secretary, a review of the structure of the World Council, and the needs of the African nations. As usual, this trip was also combined with many visits to schools, theological colleges and hospitals, a highlight being the opportunity to preach at an open air service commemorating the fiftieth anniversary of the death of the Scottish missionary Mary Slessor (1848–1915), held on a hill looking across at a dense forest of palm trees just below the site at Use Ikot Oku where she had died. Visiting Lagos, he was struck by the contrast between "the incredibly sordid slums with open drains and uncleared rubbish and 90,000 people living one family to a room and then the sumptuous club, swimming pool, houses and gardens laid out by Shell for their staff." Throughout their tour the Davidsons enjoyed unfamiliar foods like antelope meat and local fruits, even if the heat was often unendurable.

Nevile Davidson's appetite for travel and adventure was insatiable, but by the time he returned to Hill Street in February to be greeted by a blazing fire and a dinner cooked by Flora, he had decided that, after all, it was "good to have one's permanent home in the 'Temperate Zone.'"

# 12

# "The Consecration of the Commonplace"

## THE THEOLOGY AND ECCLESIOLOGY OF NEVILE DAVIDSON

NEVILE DAVIDSON DID NOT consider himself to be an academic theologian. "The parish minister," he said, "is never concerned only with abstract ideas, but always with ideas, convictions, beliefs as they affect men and women, in the myriad ordinary situations of life."[1] Nevertheless, a clear view of his position on questions of belief and practice emerges from his various writings and public statements. In particular, he had much to say about the conduct of worship and the role of the church, and as minister of Glasgow Cathedral was uniquely placed to put his ideas into effect.

The nearest he came to composing a theologically-flavored work was his 1965 volume *Reflections of a Scottish Churchman*. From the outset, it was clear that this was not going to be a book that challenged traditional thinking like *Honest to God* by the Anglican bishop John A. T. Robinson which, two years earlier, had argued that secular man required a "secular theology." Robin Denniston, a director of the publishing firm Hodder, offered Nevile a rather lukewarm acceptance of his proposal:

> One's palate is to some extent jaded by the Robinson school, and
> your own measured and more traditional approach to the great

1. Davidson, *Reflections*, 7

matters of which you speak is a very different one. Consequently, we are not sure that your views will carry a great deal of conviction amongst the younger generation of theologians nor will there be any startling press impact made by the publication of *Reflections of a Scottish Churchman*, but this does not invalidate in any way the fruit of a lifetime's Christian thinking and doing, which is what you are planning to give us. So do please keep going."

When *Reflections* went on sale in May 1965, Peggy took a walk round some of Glasgow's bookshops and was pleased to see that three of them had devoted a window display to it, together with a portrait of the author. But Denniston was correct in predicting that the book would make comparatively little impact: in its first year, 841 copies were sold which, as Nevile noted in his diary, was "not a result to encourage vanity!"

In spite of the title, *Reflections* was not a book of memoirs but an eclectic collection of sermons, articles and addresses prepared for specific occasions some of which are, inevitably, dated in certain respects. In his Introduction, Nevile considers he is being slightly controversial in describing ministry in Europe and America as being "exercised in a semi-pagan society," qualifying the statement by adding optimistically that "things may not be so serious with us in Britain."[2] While he concedes that "the Church no longer exercises the authority and influence it once had" he reckons that his clerical colleagues had shown willingness to adapt to changing times and become involved in the wider life of the community. "That is why the Christian minister today has discarded his long coat and top hat and ebony cane: symbols of status."[3] It is hard to credit these words were written in 1965 and not 1925!

The theological views expressed in *Reflections of a Scottish Churchman* are fairly typical of what could be heard from many Church of Scotland pulpits at the time. Church historians talk of a "liberal evangelical tradition which was dominant in Scottish theology from the late nineteenth century until the 1960s"[4]: "evangelical" in its upholding of the basic tenets of the Christian faith as contained in the ancient creeds of the universal church, and "liberal" in its broad if sometimes skeptical acceptance of the methods of biblical criticism and of general theological enquiry in the context of advances in contemporary thought. As the famous Alexander Whyte of

2. Davidson, *Reflections*, 10
3. Davidson, *Reflections*, 14
4. Forrester, *Truthful Action*, 180

Free St. George's, Edinburgh, once said, "the theological mind will stand still at its peril . . . I find no disparity, no difficulty, in carrying much of the best of our past with me in going out to meet and hail the new theological methods."[5]

At a farewell social at his first charge in Aberdeen, Nevile was described by one of the speakers as "sound to the core" and he remained so throughout his long ministry. In a communion address he expounded the orthodox view of the Atonement:

> He, the sinless One, hanging on that Cross, was voluntarily suffering for us; bearing our guilt, accepting our punishment, taking upon his own shoulders our sins, that he might set us free from sin.[6]

In an Easter sermon, he similarly stressed the centrality of the resurrection to the Christian faith:

> [The first Christians] took pleasure in thinking about [Jesus'] love of children, his sympathy with the poor and oppressed, his courage in the face of danger or unpopularity. But in a sense all these things were secondary. What was central and dominating was the incredible fact that he had faced death and let it do its uttermost, had actually lain in the tomb, and then on the third day come back alive, victorious . . . That was the distinctive thing about the Gospel: it was the Good News because it proclaimed Christ Jesus crucified, risen, and alive for evermore, and because it proclaimed that the man who accepts and holds to Christ shares in this victory over death.[7]

Nevile Davidson's 1962 moderatorial address can be taken as a distillation of some thirty years of theological reflection and practical experience and in this, too, there is nothing unconventional or original. Entitled "The Vocation of the Church," the address is structured around two points: "a looking upwards to God in faith and expectation, and a reaching outwards to the world in compassion and concern"[8]—an idea used by many a preacher before and since. He made a powerful plea for the church to follow the earliest Christians by constantly looking upwards in prayerful expectation. "If the Church in our land becomes in fuller degree a praying

---

5. Quoted in Cheyne, *The Transforming of the Kirk*, 171
6. Davidson, *Reflections*, 155
7. Davidson, *Reflections*, 14
8. Davidson, *Reflections*, 19

Church and an expectant Church, then there may be granted to us such a fresh outpouring of the Holy Spirit as will bring us that dynamic revival and renewal for which we long."[9]

With all that, Billy Graham would have heartily agreed, but the two differed in their views of Biblical inspiration. Whereas Graham and most "Biblicist" Christians espoused an unequivocally fundamentalist stance on the Bible, believing that the human authors were kept from error by the inspiration of the Holy Spirit, Davidson thought the church required to "escape from the arid conception of an infallible book."[10] As he explained in a presidential address to the Scottish Theology Society,

> Modern biblical scholarship has made such a position no longer tenable. We can no longer think of the whole collection of biblical documents as a once and for all furnished storehouse of doctrines, finding "proof texts" whether for theological dogmas or ecclesiastical customs. Rather we see them as the record of a continuously developing process of Divine revelation and human response.[11]

If Nevile rejected the notion of Biblical infallibility, he was equally hostile towards "those who dogmatically reject the very possibility of miracle and frankly refuse to accept any event that appears 'supernatural.'"[12]

> Ultimately rationalism of this sort cannot recognize any kind of revelation. The very pretentiousness of its claims constitutes its fatal spiritual limitation. Christianity has no answer for those who remain unbelievers because they cannot satisfactorily measure the vast and fathomless truths of the Gospel by the little yardstick of their own intellectual apparatus.[13]

It is unlikely that Nevile would have had much sympathy with those within the church today who take such a line. He was not impressed by Robinson's book *Honest to God*, describing it as "a strange plea for a kind of 'religionless Christianity' based on Tillich and Bonhoeffer." A few months before he died in 1976, he was still keeping up with theological developments and expressed his dismay at a report he had read from the Anglican Commission on Doctrine which, as he saw it, left "almost no room for any

9. Davidson, *Reflections*, 25

10. Davidson, *Reflections*, 55

11. Davidson, *Reflections*, 53

12. *Church Service Society Annual, 1950*, 23

13. *Church Service Society Annual, 1950*, 23

concept of Revelation in the Scriptures—permitting an almost complete subjectivism."

Nevile's conception of "the upward look" was based on a conviction that "the Holy Spirit would lead us into ever new and fuller insights into God's purposes."[14] By the same token, "the outward reach" of the church should be as wide as possible. If there is a key to understanding all the varied aspects of Nevile Davidson's life and career it is surely his belief that "the proper domain of the Church is the whole arena of human life." [15] In one of the most eloquent passages of his moderatorial address, he says:

> Let us give no heed to those voices which declare that the Church must keep to its own domain; that it may concern itself with the solemn Coronation of a queen, but take no concern for the wages of a crossing-sweeper; that it may encourage the satisfactory singing of hymns on Sunday, but not the satisfactory using of tools on Monday; that it should have something to say to the devout worshipper in his pew, but need have nothing to say to the scientist in his laboratory or the financier in his boardroom, the journalist in his newspaper office or the politician in the council chamber.[16]

Hence, the preacher has the right and duty to speak about art, literature, politics, economic and social conditions provided that he is giving a Christian perspective on these subjects. The theme recurs in sermon after sermon: religion is not to be confined to church on Sundays; Christian standards must be reflected in public life; our faith must be the basis of our family life, working life, decisions and personal relationships; gifts and talents should be used in the course of everyone's daily calling as a way of serving God. In another address to the Church Service Society, Nevile said that

> it is above all when men and women come together to worship and pray in one place that the barriers between secular and sacred are found to be illusory; and the worshippers gain not only new glimpses of the splendour and the loving kindness of God, but also new insights into the meaning and the possibilities of ordinary life, in its heights and its depth.[17]

14. Davidson, *Reflections,* 54

15. Davidson, *Reflections,* 32

16. Davidson, *Reflections,* 32

17. Davidson, "The Cathedral Church of Glasgow," *Church Service Society Annual,* 1965, 38

Nevile's efforts to relate religion to everyday life (which, in a memorable phrase, he described as "the consecration of the commonplace"[18]), together with his "liberal evangelical" theological stance, owe much to the wide and pervasive influence of John Baillie (1886–1960), Professor of Divinity at Edinburgh University, and his brother Donald (1887–1954), who held the Chair of Systematic Theology at St. Andrews. Both provided an accessible alternative to the more dogmatic presentations of Karl Barth and Thomas F. Torrance who were also influential in Scotland.[19] The Baillies used to visit the house at Nethy Bridge and Nevile worked alongside John in inter-church negotiations and on various committees, notably the Church of Scotland's Commission for the Interpretation of God's Will in the Present Crisis which Baillie chaired in the 1940s. Nevile greatly admired John Baillie and considered his 1961–62 Gifford Lectures, delivered in Edinburgh and published as *The Sense of the Presence of God*, to be

> a very fine book, illustrating his amazingly wide range of knowledge and also his balanced and clear judgment. Very moving in parts, declaring his personal beliefs and convictions about the ultimate verities.

It has been said that John Baillie was "concerned to maintain a proper balance between faith and culture, the gospel and society, in which extremes of liberalism and conservatism were avoided."[20] The description could just as easily be applied to Nevile Davidson.

Nevile was also friendly with Donald, whom he found "more human and approachable, probably because he had been a parish minister before going to a chair, whereas John had been an academic all his life."[21] Their friendship dated from the late 1920s when Nevile had reviewed

---

18. *Chronicle,* November 1959

19. Throughout his life Nevile Davidson recorded in his diaries the titles of books he read, and while there is little evidence that he systematically studied the works of theologians which had appeared after he completed his Divinity course, he did have some familiarity with their views. He occasionally quotes from writers such as Barth and from 1937 onwards he attended meetings of the Glasgow University and Trinity College Theological Society at which he and fellow ministers gave papers of an academic nature. In November 1960, for example, he listened to a paper on theories about the resurrection put forward by the German theologians Bultmann and Tillich, both of whom regarded it as an existential experience rather than a literal, physical event. A diary entry for March 3, 1965 records that he was reading "a volume of striking sermons" by Paul Tillich.

20. Blackie, *A Time for Trumpets,* 22

21. Davidson, *Beginnings,* 80

one of Donald's books. Donald had then written to his brother, "I know Davidson—a first class philosophy man, but a very high church catholic type of UF [United Free] minister, who swears by such things as ecumenical councils."[22]

It was a perceptive comment, for it is in his ecclesiology rather than in his theology that Nevile Davidson's main contribution to church life can be found.

When it came to the conduct and content of worship, Nevile Davidson was firmly in the high church "Scoto-Catholic" camp. A. C. Cheyne provides a useful, if sometimes scathing, list of the characteristics of those involved in this group:

> Ministering often in large, prestigious churches of the cathedral or collegiate type; devoted to seemliness and dignity in worship, and by no means averse from a little pomp and circumstance; seldom noted for their preaching ability but deeply concerned to magnify the part played by the sacraments in parish life; zealous for church unity, and especially for closer relations with the Church of England; clerical in temper, and inclined to speak much of "clergy" and "laity" . . . [23]

These are all boxes which Nevile Davidson could tick, though Alec Cheyne is perhaps being a little dismissive of the preaching abilities of notable post-war figures who favored a high church approach such as Charles Warr, Ronald Selby Wright, Leonard Small, George MacLeod, Stuart Louden, and indeed Nevile himself.

Efforts to improve the "seemliness and dignity" of Scottish worship date back to the mid-nineteenth century and are particularly associated with Rev. Robert Lee (1804–68) of Greyfriars Kirk, Edinburgh. Compared to the beauty and order of an Episcopalian service, Lee considered Scottish Presbyterian worship to be drab and uninspiring, with far too much emphasis on long, dry and sometimes overly-intellectual sermons, unaccompanied psalms often sung in a tuneless manner and rambling extempore prayers. At his services from 1857 onwards Lee therefore began

22. Quoted in Newlands, *John and Donald Baillie*, 142. Donald Baillie officiated at the wedding of Nevile Davidson in January 1944 alongside Charles Warr.

23. Cheyne, *The Transforming of the Kirk*, 195

to introduce written prayers, with the congregation kneeling, responses, chants and organ music and he published his own service book in the hope that it might be more widely adopted.[24] Such things were unheard of in Presbyterian churches at the time and many a humble Scottish churchgoer must have reacted like the female servant of a noble Episcopalian family who was taken by her mistress to hear a full choral service for the first time. On the way back, the lady asked her servant—a Presbyterian of the old school—what she thought of it. "It's verra bonny, verra bonny," replied the old woman, "but oh, my lady, it's an awfu' way of spendin' the Sabbath."[25]

The cause of liturgical reform was taken up by other ministers who founded the Church Service Society in 1865, not to impose a fixed liturgy on the Scottish church but rather to prepare a variety of forms of service and aids to worship on which ministers might draw.[26] As the late Douglas Murray[27] points out, the intention was to further the "practical improvement" of worship in the Kirk rather than to advocate any particular point of view or position.[28] However, in 1892 a more conservative group of high churchmen within the Society formed a separate organization, the Scottish Church Society, which had an avowedly doctrinal aim: "to defend and advance catholic doctrine as set forth in the Ancient Creeds, and embodied in the Standards of the Church of Scotland."[29] The founders of the Scottish Church Society took as their starting point the belief that the Kirk was "part of the Holy Catholic or Universal Church" and adhered to "the fundamental doctrines of the Catholic faith"—principles that were later to be affirmed in the first clause of the Articles Declaratory of the Constitution of the Church of Scotland. By "Catholic" they meant the heritage originating in Scripture of core beliefs and practices of the members of the universal church, past and present, and not confined to one church or denomination.[30] Although the Scoto-Catholics never formed a large party within the

24. See Robertson, *The Place of Dr Robert Lee*, 31–46

25. Ramsay, *Reminiscences,* 19–20

26. Parsons, *Religion in Victorian Britain*, 134

27. Rev. Dr. Douglas M. Murray (1946–2001), senior lecturer in ecclesiastical history at Glasgow University and principal of Trinity College, Glasgow.

28. Cameron, *Dictionary,* 186

29. Cameron, *Dictionary,* 756

30. Wotherspoon and Kirkpatrick, *A Manual of Church Doctrine*, 9, states: "The Catholic Faith means the Faith, which, being guaranteed by the Holy Scriptures (the Rule of Faith) has been continuously and permanently held from generation to generation . . . A Catholic practice is one which is rooted not in local or temporary use, but is

national church, their most significant achievement was probably *The Book of Common Order* of 1940 whose prayers for weddings, funerals, baptisms and other special occasions were widely adopted by ministers across the theological spectrum.

During the 1940s and 1950s Nevile Davidson played a prominent part in both the Church Service Society and the Scottish Church Society and served as president of each of these organizations at various times. In his presidential address to the Scottish Church Society in 1946, he outlined his vision for Scottish worship: it should be "more colourful, more sacramental, more varied and more relevant to ordinary life."[31] He felt that Presbyterian worship had become "too much of a one-man show" whereas public worship should be a genuinely corporate act; the congregation might participate in responses, and more use should be made of ceremonial and symbolism, especially at key seasons of the Christian year. Above all, as Calvin and Knox had wanted, communion should be celebrated more frequently. Nevile believed that the importance placed in Scotland on preaching made worship too cerebral and the practice of holding communion services only twice a year accounted for the "comparative poverty" of Scottish worship from a devotional point of view. Instead, he told the Church Service Society in his 1950 presidential address,

> if we can recover a sense of the inestimable value and comfort of the Sacraments, as ways by which God directly communicates to us His strength and peace, equipping us for the battle of life and arming us against its temptations, its sufferings and its testings, I believe the whole life of the Church of Scotland would be lifted to a new level of spiritual power and confidence.[32]

In another address, Nevile Davidson argued for the continuing value of the creeds in the modern church. The Nicene and Apostles' Creeds were, first and foremost, of great theological value. "As a short, simple, and compendious statement of what a Christian believed on the doctrinal side, [the Apostles' Creed] would be almost impossible to improve on. Here again are proclaimed, in plain unmistakable phrases, the great essential facts and truth of the Christian Gospel: the nature of God, the reality of sin, the

---

immemorial in the church generally."

31. *Falkirk Herald,* July 10 1946

32. Davidson, *The Place of the Sacraments,* 13

redemptive mission and work of Christ, the fact of forgiveness, the world-wide fellowship of the Church, the certainty of the life after death."[33]

The doctrinal validity of the creeds had already been the subject of much lively debate in the columns of the *Glasgow Herald* after a speech in Aberdeen in October 1948 by Rev. Dr. J. T. Cox, a former principal clerk to the General Assembly, who claimed that many no longer believed in the virgin birth or the resurrection of the body and that these concepts should be dispensed with if the church was to appeal to the modern intellectual. Several correspondents attacked Cox's views but Nevile waited a fortnight before joining in, with a letter sent on behalf of the Scottish Church Society. Stating that he was "astonished" by Cox's "strident if superficial" comments, Nevile pointed out that "Creeds have preserved the great central doctrines of the Christian Gospel through the centuries against dangerous liberalizing tendencies which might otherwise easily have robbed the Gospel of its essentially supernatural character and genius."[34]

The creeds were equally valuable from a liturgical point of view: the "stately, solemn phrases" of the full Nicene Creed of A.D. 381 conveyed the sense of the numinous that should accompany the celebration of communion, while the simpler language of the Apostles' Creed was more suitable for repetition at regular services. When a congregation joined in reciting the creed, it became united with that great company of believers across the earth which no man can number.

To some, such opinions only confirmed their suspicions of Nevile Davidson's "Roman" tendencies. The *Free Presbyterian Magazine* launched a vigorous attack on him in 1951 for his attendance at a luncheon in Edinburgh to mark the appointment of a new RC Archbishop. It was bad enough that "Rev. N. Davidson inclines towards Anglican practices in his own church" but his "deplorable conduct" in "bowing to the Man of Sin" was, said the Free Presbyterians, "calculated to weaken Protestantism in our beloved land."[35] But Nevile Davidson (unlike his sister Cois) was never tempted by the doctrines of the Church of Rome and always distinguished between its dogmas, of which he disapproved, and the devotional and aesthetic aspects of its services, to some of which he responded warmly. He once had a long discussion over lunch with one of his more eccentric assistants at the Cathedral, the Rev. David A. R. McGregor, who flirted

33. Davidson, *The Ancient Creeds*, 19

34. *Glasgow Herald*, 23 October 1948

35. *Free Presbyterian Magazine*, November 1951, 181

with aspects of Catholicism and even went on a pilgrimage to Assisi and Rome. "I put forward what would seem to me certain intolerable beliefs and practices of their communion—in spite of its many great and wonderful features." On the other hand, when visiting the Benedictine Community at Pluscarden Abbey near Elgin in 1953, Nevile stayed for a service on the Feast of the Assumption of the Virgin Mary and noted in his diary that he found it "simple, impressive and moving, even for those who cannot accept the whole doctrine implied."

Far from being a step on the road towards Rome, Nevile regarded his liturgical reforms as a return to original Reformation practices which had been lost sight of. He approved of the achievement of the reformers in stripping away the "semi-magical" elements of the Roman mass and restoring the simplicity of the Sacrament and in May 1956 celebrated the Lord's Supper in Glasgow Cathedral according to the old English version of the Genevan Reformed rite of 1556 (*The Form of Prayers*)[36] to mark its 400th anniversary, reading an exhortation by John Calvin accompanied only by metrical psalms. Similarly, he believed that reviving the Apostles' Creed was in conformity with the wishes and practice of the reformers, pointing out that the 1647–48 Westminster Confession of Faith endorsed its doctrinal value (though the Confession did not actually specify that the creed should be included in services).

However, there were other aspects of the Westminster Confession about which Nevile was less enthusiastic. Drawn up as a statement of belief by the Westminster Assembly of Divines during the conflict between Royalists and Parliamentarians, this document is rarely read or understood today and many a General Assembly has discussed proposals to rewrite it or dispense with it altogether. Its Reformed orthodox doctrines of predestination and election, stipulations about Sabbath observance and hostility towards the Roman mass and papacy have long been considered out of date and in his moderatorial year Nevile spoke for many when he said that

> the time has come for a new "Assembly of Divines." Our leading theologians would go very carefully through the old documents and see if we should not have a rewriting in the light of the changes in thought and scientific discovery in the last one hundred years.[37]

36. Basis of the later Book of Common Order ("Knox's Liturgy")

37. *Glasgow Herald*, May 7 1962

At the 1964 General Assembly he planned to introduce an overture asking for a special commission of this kind to be set up, but abandoned the attempt in case it harmed the cause of ecumenism. The subject has been debated at many subsequent General Assemblies but the Westminster Confession—technically at least—remains the principal subordinate standard[38] of the Church of Scotland, though the Assembly of 1986 decided that office-bearers need no longer accept the clauses which condemn Roman Catholicism.[39]

Nevile's preferences in the conduct of worship were introduced into Glasgow Cathedral and many of his innovations, such as frequent celebration of communion, the recitation of the creed and occasional choir processions, have been continued by his successors. He liked prayers to be prepared in advance and read out, but did not think sermons should be scripted word for word, and he expected junior colleagues to do things his way. Rev. Dr. Johnston McKay, who served as an assistant at St. Giles' Cathedral in his youth, remembers taking part in a service conducted by Nevile while the minister was on holiday. Nevile intended to lead the whole proceedings himself but the young assistant told him he had been left strict instructions to open the service and pronounce the benediction. Nevile did not appreciate this display of independence and called McKay "a young puppy"!

38. Subordinate, that is, to "the Word of God, which is contained in the Scriptures of the Old and New Testaments, . . . the supreme rule of faith and life." (Articles Declaratory of the Constitution of the Church of Scotland)

39. See Macdonald, *From Reform to Renewal,* 191–94

# 13

## "The Upward Look"

### THE PREACHING OF NEVILE DAVIDSON

DURING THE DECADE BEFORE Nevile Davidson's ministry, the pulpit of Glasgow Cathedral had been occupied by Dr. Lauchlan MacLean Watt, famed for the poetic eloquence and passion of his delivery. Congregations sat in awe as "cascades of running, sparkling words are poured out." When the grand old man died at the age of nearly ninety, his successor gave a memorial address in the Cathedral in which he tactfully referred to his "unusual and pungent preaching."

Scottish congregations had traditionally expected this kind of pulpit performance from their ministers and at one time going to hear celebrity preachers was almost a national pastime. In the nineteenth century vast crowds would gather to listen to great pulpit orators like George MacLeod's grandfather, Norman (1812–72), Thomas Guthrie (1803–73) and Thomas Chalmers (1780–1847), moderator of the first assembly of the Free Church in 1843. One of Chalmers' greatest orations was delivered at "the Preaching Brae," Cambuslang, to commemorate the centenary of the address by the famous eighteenth century evangelist George Whitefield during the revival there in 1742. One account records that

> Burning eloquence, flashes of genius, side glints of humour and pathos marked this discourse, which lasted about three hours; but the audience wearied not all that time, and when [Chalmers]

ceased the cry arose from everywhere around him, "Gie us mair, gie us mair" [i.e. "Give us more"].[1]

Even at the beginning of the twentieth century crowds would queue up to attend the evening service at Free St. George's, Edinburgh, to hear preachers such as Alexander Whyte and his successors, Hugh Black and his brother James, to whom Nevile served as assistant. Sometimes the church was so full that people had to sit on the pulpit steps.

But Nevile had been rather put off by Black's flamboyant style of delivery, later writing that "Perhaps fortunately, the day of the 'popular preacher' seems to have passed. It was a slightly artificial phenomenon, not acceptable in this more critical and questioning age."[2] Early in his ministry at the Cathedral, a fellow minister wrote to Nevile asking: "Has anyone warned you not to be as excitable and explosive as your remarkable predecessor?" He need not have worried: Nevile Davidson had no intention of trying to imitate MacLean Watt. Nevile's former assistant Henry Sefton described his mentor's preaching as "invariably useful and edifying but without conventional eloquence or histrionics." Rev. Alfred Brown of Maxwell Parish Church referred to "his deep, and therefore, simple and earnest preaching", while Rev. Thomas McDougall, an Australian minister paying a visit to a morning service in September 1948, thought "Dr. Davidson's address was good, but no better than would be given, I think, by sixty per cent of Australian Presbyterian ministers."

Some sense of what Nevile's preaching was like can be gained from the text of surviving sermons published from time to time in the Glasgow Cathedral parish magazine, *The Chronicle*. They generally begin with a Biblical text and seek to persuade listeners by reason rather than directly appealing to emotion. One (unidentified) writer who clearly watched the preacher closely described how he would gradually get into his stride:

> At first there would be for the observant members of the congregation signs of that nervousness so common among great orators—the hands moved slightly, he fingered his spectacles—and then the message, always simple, direct and magnificently articulated, took over and he carried his audience along on waves of inspiration.

Although the sermons make comparatively little use of anecdote, illustration or quotation, the preacher would always seek to relate the

1. Aird, *Glimpses*, 281
2. Davidson, *Beginnings*, 11

Christian message to the climate of the times and incorporate references to current affairs. A 1946 Epiphany sermon, for example, focuses on post-war fears and goes on to show how "over against the atomic bomb which speaks of the annihilation of mankind, Bethlehem speaks of the deliverance of mankind." In a series on the Ten Commandments in 1956, he referred to a murder case which filled the local newspapers at the time, the shooting of three females in a house in Rutherglen, later found to be the work of serial killer Peter Manuel who went to the gallows in 1958. In 1963 there was a sermon on "The Challenge of the Profumo Crisis" and in 1965 a consideration of "The Colour Question." At a service attended by 200 members of the Association of British Marketing Authorities the text was Proverbs 11:1: "a just weight is His delight" while man's exploration of space in the sixties prompted a meditation on "God and the Cosmos." Even an exhibition of Picasso's paintings provided a theme for a sermon.

But to Nevile, contemporary relevance was not the main purpose of preaching. In his 1962 moderatorial address he said that "the essential thing in true preaching, which marks it off from all other forms of human speech, is the upward look of the preacher, in humble faith and expectancy; so that his own poor words, infused with divine power, become the Word of God. Men and women will recognize such preaching when they hear it."[3] And they recognized it when they heard Nevile Davidson.

Three typical sermons from the later years of Nevile Davidson's ministry are reproduced below: *Towards Belief* (December 1965) addresses "this more critical and questioning age", gently seeking by reasoned argument to persuade the agnostic to consider the claims of the Christian faith; *The Easter Message* (March 1964) stresses the centrality of the death and resurrection of Jesus to the Christian faith; *The House of the Lord God* (January 1961) is one of many addresses delivered at the unveiling of a new addition to the Cathedral's fabric, in this case new windows in the Blacader Aisle, and tackles the issue of the validity of decoration and ornamentation in a place of worship, ending with a powerful plea to modern man to return to God.

3. Davidson, *Reflections*, 22

## "TOWARDS BELIEF"

*[A sermon preached in Glasgow Cathedral on Sunday December 12 1965].*

> *And the warder said, "What must I do to be saved?" And Paul and Silas said, "Believe in the Lord Jesus Christ and you will be saved."*
> *(Acts 16: 30–1)*

Earlier that day the chief warden of the prison at Philippi had accepted under his charge two unusual prisoners. Their crime was that they were proclaiming a new religion; telling everyone about a person called Jesus of Nazareth; His wonderful teaching and miracles of healing, and claims that He had come back from the dead.

The two men were put in a cell, and chained hands and feet. At midnight they could be heard singing praises to God. Then the whole prison was shaken by an earthquake, but after it they were still sitting in their cell, and making no attempt to escape.

It seemed to the warder that the two strangers had some secret of serenity and happiness, and when the tremors of the earthquake subsided he asked that question, "What must I do to be saved?"And they replied, "Believe in the Lord Jesus Christ and you will be saved."

If the same question were put today to any Christian preacher, we should have to give the same reply. And there, for many people the difficulties begin. Because the twentieth-century questioner, conditioned by the scientific approach and scientific criterion of judgment, finds difficulty in believing in One who is said to have performed incredible miracles, contrary to the laws of Nature, and who is supposed to have come back from the grave. He will say, "If that is Christian belief, then with the best will in the world, I cannot believe."

A good many people, who are so to speak on the edge of the crowd, listening, even coming to Church services, wish, with an honest mind, that they could believe in the Lord Jesus Christ, but doubts and uncomfortable questions creep in, and they can't believe.

For these people, may I say a few things.

The first is this: Don't be ashamed of your doubts. To have doubts means you are thinking. Jesus said, "Love God not only with all your heart but with all your mind." And if you have to wrestle your way through doubts and difficulties to belief, then your belief will be all the stronger and more valuable. Honesty of thought is, at least, as important as honesty of action.

But may I say another thing: Go on thinking. Don't be content simply to say, "I'm an unbeliever, I'm an agnostic. So that's that." Religion is far too important a thing to give up lightly. Jesus of Nazareth is far too intriguing a Person to turn your back on so quickly. At least keep on looking at Him.

Begin with Jesus. Not with the doctrine of the Holy Trinity, or the Resurrection or the Virgin Birth. Begin with Jesus. And begin at Bethlehem, even if you think the stories of angels and shepherds, and the star and Wise Men are just fairy tales. Because Bethlehem says, at least, two things which no-one can deny. It says that on a certain winter night in Palestine a baby was born. Like a million other babies He lay helpless in his mother's arms, as she looked down at Him in wonder and love. She was a simple woman, Mary, and she and Joseph brought the baby back to a humble home where He grew up in the small provincial town of Nazareth. Like a million other boys when the time came to leave school, He went to work with His hands, in a joiner's shop. In other words, Jesus of Nazareth was a man like other men living a human life, with all its ups and downs; its happiness and sorrow; its successes and failures.

Bethlehem reminds us also of another fact: that the Baby born on that night grew up into a man whose name was somehow carried from that little land of Palestine into one country and continent after another. Why? That is a difficult question to answer but it is only fair to face up to it. If Jesus was only an ordinary person, how did the Gospels come to be written? If He was no more than an ordinary good man, how was it found possible to bring into existence congregations of believers? If He was no more than an ordinary good man, how is it after 2000 years the New Testament is the best selling book in the world?

When you ask such questions, I think you will feel compelled to say that there must be in the life and personality and words of this man a quality which is unique. And when you read the Gospels carefully you will find that unique quality is there. For in His actions there is a strange mingling of humility and authority. He is master of every situation. Threats of danger cannot move Him from speaking the truth. Malice or hatred cannot shake His charity. Even when being nailed in agony on the cross, He prays for His torturers. The same uniqueness shines out in the words of Jesus. They have a penetrating and lasting quality transcending the passage of time and changing fashions.

Perhaps when you have felt the uniqueness of this man Jesus, His actions and His words, then you find yourself asking, "Mustn't He have been more than an ordinary man?" Then who was He? Well, Christianity declares that in Jesus we see God acting, and in Jesus we hear God speaking. That in Him, we are actually in touch with the living God.

Of course you can't prove it. There is no scientific test or historical demonstration. No philosophical argument can prove that in Jesus we are in touch with God. You have to look at Him; listen to His words, watch His behaviour in the situations of life that came to Him, and in the harshness of His death. Then make your own decision, make, if you are able, the great act of faith. *"Believe in the Lord Jesus Christ and you will be saved."*

[Source: *Glasgow Cathedral Chronicle*, January 1966, 4–5]

## "THE EASTER MESSAGE"

*[Excerpts from a sermon preached in Glasgow Cathedral on Easter Sunday March 29 1964].*

> *Peter said: "Men of Israel, listen to this: Jesus of Nazareth was a Man duly accredited to you from God. This Man you have put to death. But God raised Him up again, releasing Him from the pangs of death. God has made Him Lord and Christ, this Jesus whom you crucified."*
> *(Acts 2:22).*

That was an extract from the first Christian sermon ever preached: the wonderful sermon of St. Peter spoken in the open air on the Day of Pentecost. It is significant to notice that the central note in that sermon is the Resurrection. Significant and natural, because Christianity stands or falls with the truth of the Resurrection of Jesus Christ from the dead. To the Disciples the Resurrection meant supremely one thing: Jesus their Master, their Leader, their Divine Friend whom they had imagined dead and defeated and buried, was alive, eternally alive, and would always be with them; still able to heal men's bodies and souls, still active in the world. St. Paul makes it plain that he regards the whole fabric of Christian Faith as resting on the fact of the Resurrection: "If Christ be not risen, then is our preaching vain, and your faith is also vain. But now is Christ risen from the dead."

The strange institution which we call the Christian Church, which has outlived so many secular institutions, and which seems to hold within it the secret of perennial life and powers of growth, is founded on that one fundamental belief: the belief in Jesus Christ crucified, dead, and risen.

The central note in its preaching in this year 1964 is the same note that was central in the preaching of that first sermon of Peter nineteen hundred years ago. "This man you have put to death; but God raised him up again, releasing him from the pangs of death. God has made him Lord and Christ, this Jesus whom you crucified."

We in the Reformed Church like to have in our places of worship, on the roof-top or on the Holy Table, the great symbol of the Cross, the symbol of redemption and hope. But always it is an empty Cross. Because He who once hung on the Cross, He who once lay in the darkness of a tomb, is now alive and active, not dead, but loose in the world. Just there on the Cross where everything had seemed hopeless, Jesus had set up the standard of His Kingdom. And when on Easter morning He came back as a conqueror, His Kingdom was seen to be established. The battle is not finished, not by a long way. But the Resurrection is the foretaste of the ultimate victory of that Kingdom.

The late Dr. Dale[4] was writing an Easter sermon, when halfway through, the thought of the risen Lord broke in upon him as it had never done before. "'Christ is alive,' I said to myself. 'Alive!' and then I paused: 'alive!' and then I paused again; 'alive!!' Can that really be true? Living as really as I myself am? I got up and walked about repeating, 'Christ is living! Christ is living!'At first it seemed strange and hardly true, but at last it came upon me as a burst of sudden glory; yes, Christ is living. It was to me a new discovery. I thought that all along I had believed it; but not until that moment did I feel sure about it. I then said, 'My people shall know it; I shall preach about it again and again until they believe it as I do now.'"

Easter Day then proclaims that the Living Christ is not only Lord of Life and of Death, but Lord of History; and still at work in the world which he created and in the Church which he founded. It is that conviction which from the beginning has been and is the strength and the inspiration of Christian believers.

[Source: *Glasgow Cathedral Chronicle*, April 1964, 3–4].

---

4. Dr. Robert W. Dale (1829–95), English Congregationalist preacher and leader.

## "THE HOUSE OF THE LORD GOD"

*[A sermon preached at the Dedication of new windows in the Blacader Chapel, Glasgow Cathedral, on January 15, 1961].*

> *Be it known unto the king, that we went into the province of Judea, to the house of the great God, which is builded with great stones, and timber is laid in the walls, and this work goeth fast on, and prospereth in their hands.*
>
> *(Ezra,5:8)*

With the installation and dedication of these new windows in the Blacader Chapel, this morning, we reach the end of a project begun as long ago as 1935.

No mediaeval glass at all remains in the Cathedral Church of Glasgow. Shortly after the middle of the 19th century a scheme was set on foot for the reglazing of the whole church, and all the windows in the nave and quire, in the chapels and lower church, and even the clerestory, were filled with painted glass, most of it made in Munich. Although considered at that time the best obtainable, unfortunately it was a period when almost no good glass was being made. And after about 100 years, the colours began to fade and the leading to deteriorate.

The twentieth century has seen a remarkable revival of the art and craftsmanship of stained glass in both England and Scotland. And about twenty-five years ago the friends of Glasgow Cathedral resolved to try and take advantage of this revival, and have the windows in the principal parts of the Church filled with fine modern glass.

It was an ambitious and in some ways a difficult project and dependent for its success on co-operation from many quarters. And I should like to take this opportunity of expressing our grateful thanks both to the very generous donors of the new windows and also to the unselfish descendants of former donors who willingly gave permission for their family windows to be replaced in order to enable us to carry out our plans.

Those plans, now after twenty-five years, have been completed—and I think we can say successfully completed. As a result, new stained glass of the finest quality has been installed in all the windows of the quire, in the two transepts, on the west wall of the nave, and in the Blacader Chapel. They represent the work of eleven distinguished artists, Scottish and English. In the South aisle of the Lower Church there are twelve small roundels of sixteenth century Flemish glass, and on the South wall of the Blacader Chapel four panels of seventeenth century German Swiss glass.

I think it is true to say that in no other church either north or south of the Border can be seen so fine and representative a collection of twentieth century stained glass as we now possess in the Mother Church of Glasgow.

But we must never forget what is the motive and purpose which inspires and gives meaning to all this lovely craftsmanship. Its purpose is to do honor to God and to show forth his glory. In the building, adornment and the furnishing of a great Cathedral Church, opportunity is given for artists and craftsmen of all kinds to give of their best for the enrichment of God's House. The architect, the painter, the sculptor, the woodcarver, the silversmith, the embroiderer each can use his own talents, not only to create a thing of beauty for its own sake but to do homage to the great source of all Beauty and Truth. Walking round an ancient church like our own, how often one is struck by the careful perfection of workmanship even in dark or remote corners; showing how the unknown craftsman used his skill as a tribute of love and reverence to God.

But there is something more important still to be said. Because a church, whether it be a splendid Gothic Cathedral or a simple whitewashed Highland Chapel, is bright and furnished for one supreme purpose only: that within its walls men and women may worship God, offer to God their praises and thanksgivings, bring to God their prayers and supplications, listen to his word, find his forgiveness, seek his guidance. How sad would it be if we were ever tempted to think of this ancient church as a splendid historic monument, to be decorated and cherished, rather than a House of God in which "prayer is wont to be made," in which week by week and month by month voices and hearts are raised to God in prayer and thanksgiving, and men and women come to have their faith rekindled and their strength for the tasks of daily life renewed.

In a recent series of articles a university lecturer set out the results of a careful investigation which he had made as to the attendance of church members at Divine Service on Sundays. The statistics showed that less than forty per cent attend with any regularity. And when one takes into consideration the large numbers of men and women whose names are not on the roll of communicants of any Church, it becomes evident that a vast number of people in the Scotland of this twentieth century have largely abandoned the habit of joining in the public worship of God.

Modern Man has little sense of the sacred, and therefore little reverence. The climate of our highly mechanized industrial society is hostile to religion. We live and we are surrounded by machines and the noise of machines. The more popular newspapers, magazines, films, and plays are continually bombarding us with appeals to the senses. Football pools, sweepstakes and gambling opportunities in many forms constantly suggest to us that the chief values in life are to be thought of in terms of money and the things that money can buy. Amusements, entertainments, social activities of every sort, absorb all our spare energy and occupy all our leisure time. We are scarcely ever alone. Many people are almost afraid of being alone. And, as a result, in the feverish racket of modern life, worship has been almost crowded out.

The period of history through which we are living is not an "Age of Faith." It is a period in which men and women are absorbed in material possessions and material comforts and ambitions. A great many people have little sense of the unseen spiritual realities. Many have lost the habit of prayer. Some have even come to question the value and effectiveness of prayer. Is that not the reason why ours is a generation that is morally bewildered, nervously restless, superficially self-confident but concealing behind that self-confident veneer a profound sense of insecurity? Because there can be no true contentment or inner peace for any man who has lost contact with God.

And so a great church like this, with its upward pointing spire, with its bells and its music, with its psalms and its sacred ceremonies, calls them back to God.

For more than 700 years the people of Glasgow have come to this Cathedral Church to say their prayers, to plight their troth in marriage, to have their children baptized, to hear God's Word proclaimed. Sometimes they have passed heedlessly by, impervious to the bell. But in time of need and stress, they have felt again that deep need which is hidden in the heart of every man: the need of God.

My friends, let us not stifle that need, that inner voice which cries out for "God, even the Living God." Because we shall find no true satisfaction without Him.

[Source: *Glasgow Cathedral Chronicle*, February 1961, 3–4]

# 14

## "Retirement is the Wrong Word"

### FINAL YEARS, 1967–76

Nevile and Peggy Davidson photographed outside Glasgow Cathedral in 1967 (Photo courtesy of the Herald and Times Group).

ON HEARING THAT NEVILE Davidson was planning to leave Glasgow Cathedral, Charles Warr wrote to say, "There is much left for you to do, both for Scotland and its church; if you think there lies before you a life of leisure, you had better think again." But Nevile was not planning on a life of leisure. Throughout his career he had divided his time between preaching and other church activities, social engagements, committee meetings and trips to his holiday retreats or further afield and this routine remained unaltered right up to the day he died.

If retirement involved surprisingly little change of lifestyle, it did mean a change of address. Before leaving Glasgow the Davidsons had already found a new home: Seafield House in the village of West Barns in East Lothian, just ten miles away from North Berwick where Nevile had spent his childhood. This was a pleasant two storey house built around 1780 and situated beside the Biel Burn with an outlook towards the sea and a stretch of open ground where racehorses were often taken to be exercised. As with other properties occupied by the Davidsons, a certain amount of renovation was required and their architect "warned us that all building work is now shockingly expensive," though there was a possibility of a county council grant towards drainage improvements which "of course, would be a great help." By the end of February 1967,

> the damp has been dealt with in the dining room, the electric re-wiring finished, the cupboards in my dressing-room and the kitchen erected—the plumbing almost in order. So at last things are coming in to order.

Just before an earlier visit to look round the house Nevile's Humber suffered a burnt out clutch and it had to be towed away, but fortunately Cathedral friends Alan and Henty Diack, "marvellously kind as always, insisted on driving us through." This led Nevile to think of replacing the car and, on the basis of several recommendations, he ordered a new Volvo 121, the cost of which was serendipitously covered by his farewell gift from the congregation of £1200. Expressing his thanks in the May issue of the *Chronicle,* he wrote that "as our present car is now seven years old and is also extravagantly greedy in the use of petrol we have decided to use your gift to buy a new car."

On April 5 the Davidsons "said goodbye to the beloved old flat where we had been so happy for our whole married life and with which we have so many associations." They could not have stayed on in Hill Street even if they had wanted to, as the building was earmarked for demolition within the next three years. The removal van broke down en route to West Barns and arrived four hours late, so that everything was not unloaded until 8.30 p.m., the cost of the operation amounting to £77 and ten shillings, plus a £5 tip for the men. The following morning the new residents went round to make the acquaintance of the owners of the local village store and post office, and over the next few days introduced themselves to their neighbours.

Seafield House, West Barns, near Dunbar, home of the Davidsons from 1967 onwards.
(Photo by the author).

But Nevile was never one for staying at home for long. By the end of the month he attended, as usual, the annual retreat at Dunkeld Cathedral where he "spent some time in the church giving thanks for so many blessings in my ministry, my life with darlingest Peggy and our move to such a charming little house in such wonderful surroundings." Then in May the Davidsons sailed on the *Empress of Canada* from Greenock to Montreal where they visited the Expo 67 World Fair and attended the General Assembly of the Canadian Presbyterian Church. As on previous trips to North America, they covered many hundreds of miles by road and enjoyed the hospitality offered, making new friends and catching up with old ones. While in Ottawa, Nevile met a man in the hotel lift who calmly informed him that he was going up to the roof to jump off. Nevile persuaded him to come to his sixth floor room and "we had a long talk about his former alcoholism, relationship with his wife and his personal loneliness. Tried to comfort him and give him a new outlook." Nevile believed that it was because he was wearing his clerical collar that the man opened up to him about his problems and often referred to the incident as proof that ministers should always be properly attired, even when they were not on official business.

The Davidsons returned to Prestwick Airport at the end of June, having managed to persuade officials at John F. Kennedy Airport to allow them to board the plane, as Nevile had lost the tickets! No sooner was he back home than he started planning a group trip to the Holy Land for the following year. There was also the matter of appointing a successor at Glasgow Cathedral and, although Nevile was not officially involved in the process, he had made it known that his preferred candidate was Dr. William J. Morris, a 41-year old Welshman who had formerly been assistant to Ronald Selby Wright at Edinburgh's Canongate Kirk and was currently minister of Peterhead Parish Church and chaplain of Peterhead Prison. Diary entries show that Bill Morris and his wife Jean were frequent visitors to the house at Nethy Bridge and the Morrises reciprocated by allowing the Davidsons to use their boat on the River Spey where they had fishing rights. A month after retiring Nevile stayed at the manse in Peterhead where he was to dedicate a new pulpit and stained glass windows in the church and in August the Morrises came to dinner at Nethy Bridge where they talked until midnight about the duties of the Cathedral minister. The next month Bill Morris preached as sole nominee and was duly elected with 182 votes for and two against, a result which Nevile considered to be "very satisfactory and holding good promise for the future." Some felt that Morris was chosen as his style resembled Davidson's. He remained at the Cathedral until the age of eighty and during his lengthy ministry largely followed his predecessor's manner of conducting worship. With a new ministry commencing, the Cathedral kirk session decided that the time had come to purchase a manse and a solidly-built suburban villa in Pollokshields on Glasgow's south side was chosen, but Nevile did not approve as it was "far too far from the Cathedral and the centre of the city."

In August Nevile set off on his travels yet again, this time to Greece for the World Council of Churches Central Committee meeting in Heraklion, Crete. He attended services at St. Minas' Cathedral—one of them lasting for three hours—and received "a fraternal kiss" from the Archbishop. Long sessions of discussions and reports alternated with equally long and leisurely lunches and there was plenty of time for sightseeing, too: Nevile was impressed by "the magnificent remains of the Minoan civilization" at Knossos which revealed an "astonishing standard of civilized living," prompting him to ask, "What is progress?!" The final event was on August 25, a celebration in honor of St. Titus, companion of St. Paul and traditionally considered the first bishop of Crete, where the Scottish Presbyterian entered into the spirit of the two-hour service and the colorful procession which followed:

> Many people, from church dignitaries to small children, came forward and kissed the jewelled case which contained the skull of St. Titus. And finally the sacred skull in its gold case was carried out of the church shoulder high by four priests into the square and through some of the central streets, escorted by soldiers with fixed bayonets and followed by a procession of archbishops, bishops, clergy and members of our World Council Central Committee—a strange and fascinating piece of pageantry.

By the end of 1967 Nevile had settled into a new house, travelled to Canada, the USA and Greece, and had made several journeys south to attend meetings in London and see his sister in Liverpool, in addition to his customary stays at Nethy Bridge and the Dunkeld Retreat. He had also carried out various preaching engagements and taken on several new responsibilities on behalf of the wider church. And he had only been retired for eight months.

Now free from full-time parish and civic duties, Nevile Davidson could devote more time and energy to Church of Scotland committee work, especially as commuting to meetings in Edinburgh was easier from West Barns than it had been from Glasgow.

He continued to play a major part in the General Assembly each year, often taking the chair for some of the sessions. He also remained on the important Church and Nation Committee, whose deliberations evolved in the light of emerging issues such as the ethics of transplant surgery, Britain's proposed entry into the European common market and the status of Christianity in a pluralist society. As ever, Nevile's standpoint was cautious and balanced. When, in January 1968, the committee decided to urge the government to institute Scottish home rule he "voted for the alternative, viz. to set up a Royal Commission to examine all the issues involved" and in October 1970, in a debate on membership of the common market, he argued "that if Britain did join, the Assembly should pray that it brought not only an increased standard of living but led to more generous aid to less-developed nations."

Only weeks after leaving the Cathedral, he joined a new "ad hoc" committee on the subject of Recruitment and Training for the Ministry. In connection with this, he delivered a series of lectures to Divinity students at Trinity College on practical issues such as the role of the minister and the ministration of the sacraments. His calm and instructive approach had a profound influence on many young ministers like Rev. Hugh Kerr, later to be minister of the Scots Kirk in Lausanne, who still vividly remembers one lecture on the topic of holy communion in which Nevile stated that "the people of God prefer the well-worn paths," another indication of his instinctively conservative stance. He was about to give one of these talks in November 1968 when he discovered he had left his briefcase containing the lecture inside his car and had lost the keys, leaving him no alternative to speak without a manuscript on the topic of "The Minister as Preacher"— thereby setting an unintentional example to the students of how to deliver an extempore address.

In addition to his committee work, Nevile Davidson found an opportunity to draw on his years of experience overseeing improvements to Glasgow Cathedral when he became involved with St. Mary's Church in the market town of Haddington. Often referred to as "the Lamp of Lothian," St Mary's is one of Scotland's largest and most imposing medieval parish churches and the reformer John Knox was born nearby and baptized there. Nevile undertook pulpit supply at St Mary's from time to time and in 1970 served as interim moderator during a period of vacancy. In this capacity he joined the executive of the recently formed Lamp of Lothian Trust which launched an appeal to raise £175,000 to fund an ambitious scheme to restore the church and other historic buildings nearby. Peggy, meanwhile, took on a local role of her own as volunteer Red Cross librarian at the town's Roodlands Hospital and was largely responsible for developing a library service covering all the local hospitals.

Though he made a considerable contribution to the restoration project at Haddington, Nevile Davidson did not adopt St. Mary's as his home congregation. In 1972 he decided to join the village church in Whitekirk, a few miles from where he lived. Also called St. Mary's, this was a more modest building than its Haddington namesake, dating from the fifteenth century and restored in the early twentieth. He was in good company, as in January 1973 both he and the internationally renowned theologian T. F. Torrance were formally "associated" with the kirk session at Whitekirk which was unusually privileged for a small rural charge in having two distinguished clerics to call on when pulpit supply was required.

Along with these new responsibilities, Nevile continued to work towards what he always considered the most important issue facing the church: ecumenical co-operation. In June 1964 he had taken over as convener of the Inter-Church Relations Committee and later that year traveled to Nottingham for the ecumenical Faith and Order conference. Optimism was in the air: not only was there "a perceptible drive to understand each other" but the conference even set a target date of 1980 for the reunion of the churches in Britain.

That target was of course never reached but one cannot but admire the effort put into working towards it. Nevile Davidson's records of the endless round of meetings he attended suggest that he must have been able to draw on infinite reserves of patience in the face of so many procedural complexities. In July 1966 a preliminary meeting of the Multi-Lateral Church Conversations decided on recommendations for the first full meeting. In October the list of names put forward to represent the Church of Scotland was rejected as not representative enough, so the committee had to compile another selection—"extremely regrettable since it means that we can do nothing as a church on this matter until next March." Often these "conversations" amounted to little more than meetings about meetings. The committee on Anglican-Presbyterian relations in January 1966 decided to propose to the General Assembly the "dissolution of the present series of talks and the appointment of a new joint committee with open remit." In February 1969 the Inter-Church Relations Committee "spent the whole day in discussing a paper on Governing Principles for Union among Churches" in Scotland prepared by a working party for consideration by the various denominations involved. After the General Assembly the committee "decided to appoint a steering committee to make definite and detailed suggestions." Three months later—by which time Nevile had taken over as chairman—"we decided to set up four working parties." And so it went on.

Any one of these meetings sounds tedious enough, but March 1970 witnessed an event of seemingly Kafkaesque proportions when the Church of Scotland General Administrative Committee and Inter Church Relations Committee joined together to discuss the work of the British Council of Churches and the Scottish Churches' Council.

The very idea of inter-church co-operation aroused protest from some quarters. In January 1967 an ecumenical service at Glasgow Cathedral drew only a small turnout and Protestant extremists demonstrated outside, attacking Nevile Davidson by name. There was internal opposition, too, notably from leading churchmen like Harry Whitley of St. Giles who objected even to "cautious informal" talks with the Roman Catholics. At times even Nevile became frustrated with the ways things were going. When, in August 1969, a scheme in England for the reunion of Anglicans and Methodists did not achieve the required level of support, his diary entry is uncharacteristically gloomy: "This means failure—a great disaster and a grievous setback to the whole ecumenical movement in Britain."

Nevertheless, while organizational unity proved frustratingly difficult to achieve, a certain amount of progress was made towards dismantling the barriers of mistrust at a less formal level. As chairman of the Scottish Churches Ecumenical Committee, Nevile Davidson had been much involved in the mid-1950s with the renovation of some derelict houses near Dunblane Cathedral and in 1961 these became Scottish Churches House, a center for meetings between representatives of different denominations, with Rev. Ian Fraser as the first Warden. Of this venture, Doug Gay says:

> In place of a globally significant ecumenical union within "the household of God" advocates of ecumenism within Scotland had to settle for a row of cottages in Dunblane, where they could construct a more modest project for co-operation . . .[1]

1966 witnessed the setting up of another ecumenical experiment where the Church of Scotland and Episcopal congregations in the new town of Livingston shared the same building. There was also a growing rapprochement between Protestants and Catholics. At a service of Thanksgiving and Dedication to inaugurate the new University of Strathclyde, held in Glasgow Cathedral in May 1965, the presence in the clergy procession of the Catholic Archbishop Scanlon was symbolically significant, being, as Nevile observed, "most certainly the first time since the Reformation that an RC prelate has taken part in a service in the Cathedral sitting in the sanctuary." A year later, Scanlon led prayers at another service in the Cathedral, marking the 250th Anniversary of the Royal Regiment of Artillery. By this stage Nevile was frequently meeting the Archbishop at social events, and he even proposed a toast to the Society of Jesus at a dinner for former pupils of the RC St Aloysius' College in Glasgow. A further step forward was the General Assembly's agreement in 1968 to invite the RC authorities to

---

1. Gay, *A Practical Theology of Church and World,* 144

send an observer to the following year's assembly, a practice which continued thereafter and by March 1972 it was possible for that year's moderator (Andrew Herron) to issue a joint call to prayer on behalf of Northern Ireland with Cardinal Gordon Gray.

The ecumenical message had also to be communicated at congregational level and here, too, Nevile Davidson had a role to play. He preached at Livingston during the Week of Prayer for Christian Unity, held in 1971 in the RC church, and his conduct of a similar service in St. Mary's Haddington revealed that even in retirement he had not lost his flair for innovative methods of reaching the people. He arranged for four young men and girls to stand outside holding placards attacking the church and at the start of the service these were carried in and placed at the front in sight of the congregation. The cards read "The church is dead!", "Christ cared. Does the church care?", "One Lord, why many churches?" and "Give us life, not religion" and these four issues were addressed during the sermon.

Nevile's hopes rose after an ecumenical meeting at Scottish Churches House in Dunblane in November 1971 where there was discussion about "a new structure" which would include "the office of superintendent and bishop, presbyter, elder, deacon and various lay missionaries. If it is acceptable by the constituent churches it will mean a real ecumenical breakthrough." The following year the General Assembly discussed a new reunion plan centred round the supervision of parishes by "superintendents" who would also carry out duties as parish ministers. But many saw this as just another attempt to bring back "bishops in the kirk" under a different name—something which had already been decisively rejected, though Nevile assured the Assembly that superintendents would be "quite unlike the pompous prelates of certain past ages." The matter was sent down to presbyteries to discuss but by the end of 1973 the Inter-Church Relations Committee had received many replies expressing hostility to the idea of superintendents. Nevile was left clutching at straws: "fortunately, no suggestion that multilateral conversations should be abandoned."

Not for the first time in inter-church discussions, the role of bishop—under whatever name—proved the stumbling block. There is no doubt, however, that Nevile Davidson was in principle in favor of episcopacy, though for obvious reasons he did not often draw attention to that fact. In one of his files there is an undated "Paper on the Catholic Tradition in the Scottish Church," a rather plodding piece of work which leans heavily on the writings of theologians such as T. F. Torrance and Lesslie

Newbigin, a Church of Scotland minister and missionary who became one of the first bishops in the United Church of South India. The conclusions reached are twofold: the claim that episcopacy is the essential test of catholicity is rejected on the grounds that the earliest records give no evidence the apostles had true successors; nevertheless, "episcopacy as an institution is deeply rooted and widely accepted throughout a large part of Christendom and is likely to furnish the most hopeful form of government for a reunited church." That would have been a step too far for most of Nevile's Presbyterian colleagues. Of the Anglican insistence that a bishop in the apostolic succession had to be present at all ordinations of ministers, Andrew Herron said, "It is not just that I don't like this idea, it is that I find it repugnant, in flagrant contradiction to all that the faith means for me."[2] In his memoirs Herron, who possessed a degree in law, highlighted the flaws in the bishops-in-presbytery plan in his inimitable way:

> It is all a little like saying: we have here a square peg, while yonder you have a round hole; why should they continue in lonely isolation; let's pop the square peg into the round hole. "But," some hardy sceptic maintains, "it's well know that square pegs don't go into round holes." "Oh, it's not easy . . . but given a little faith and patience and Christian charity it's wonderful what can be achieved." To me this is poppycock, and the fact that it's pious poppycock doesn't make it any the more palatable.[3]

On the other hand, a friend of Nevile Davidson detected a hidden benefit of the scheme, and wrote to him humorously suggesting that "if the ecumenical spirit quickens the Assembly to adopt the episcopal system in Scotland and I am asked to nominate the first bishop, I shall have no hesitation. You would take the gaiters off most bishops I have known."

One suspects Nevile would not have been reluctant to accept the appointment . . .

When Nevile Davidson told his friend and former assistant James Bulloch that he was retiring, Bulloch responded "probably 'retirement' is the wrong word: 'other activity' would be better." One of these other activities was to write an autobiography, a task which Nevile commenced "very tentatively"

2. Herron, *Record Apart*, 50
3. Herron, *Record Apart*, 57

in October 1972. The lifelong discipline of keeping a daily diary paid off as the source material was readily at hand, and Nevile started re-reading his accounts of events that had taken place up to sixty years earlier. But travel, meetings and a busy social life meant that *Beginnings but no Ending* was not finished until May 1976 and did not appear in print in the author's lifetime.

Though full of factual detail about his numerous official trips abroad, Nevile Davidson's autobiography is reticent in what it says about his personal life, especially when it comes to his sister Cois. Her conversion to Catholicism and the family tensions this created in the 1920s are acknowledged but the book makes little reference to her thereafter. Few people in Glasgow Cathedral were even aware that he had a sister, yet she played a major part in his life.

During the 1960s Cois was living in her own home—"The Little House", Wavertree, Liverpool—with regular visits from nuns who looked after her. The osteoarthritis in her spine worsened during May 1966 when she had to be hospitalized and seven months later she was still "terribly crippled and was not eating." Early 1967 gave some hope of improvement but by October "she had lost the will to live" and a year later her doctors, frustrated by her refusal to go back into hospital, told Nevile they could do nothing more for her. Then suddenly, at the start of 1970, she "marvellously recovered her interest in life" and resumed her favorite occupation of embroidery. Thanks partly to her brother's intervention, Cois secured a newly-built council flat in Liverpool towards the end of 1972 but had a further setback in 1973 when she suffered a stroke and Nevile and Peggy gave up their plans for a trip to Australia and New Zealand as a result. This constant cycle of decline and recovery dogged Cois all her life yet on each occasion Nevile would travel to visit her without complaint and in between had regular telephone conversations with her doctors.

The diaries make frequent reference to "long letters" to and from Cois but Nevile kept only one of these. Dating from a period in 1969 when she was compelled to lie flat on her back and was receiving morphine injections twice daily, this barely legible epistle nevertheless reveals the intimacy that existed between brother and sister.

> It is lovely when you manage to write to me often. It is like a sheet anchor in a storm for a little boat. I feel lonely sometimes and love to see you writing and know you pray for your poor cowardly old sister who loves you so dearly.

In spite of so many years of pain and suffering, Cois lived to the age of eighty-eight and died in Uckfield, Sussex in 1989 where she is believed to have been associated with the Sisters of Mercy at St. Michael's Convent.

The process of writing an autobiography, along with the inevitable tendency to look back on life which comes with aging, understandably evokes a mood of nostalgia. As Vincent van Gogh once put it, "the memories of all we have loved stay and come back to us in the evening of our life." Stopping off at the Hill Street tenement which was still awaiting demolition, Nevile salvaged a section of outside railing and had this installed beside the garden steps at Seafield House. Visiting "our beloved Iona" in September 1975, where "everything looked beautiful in the mellow autumn sunlight," he and Peggy walked to parts of the island they had explored on their first meeting in 1943. The Hallbar Tower days were over, too, as the lease expired in 1969. Passing through Lanarkshire some years later, they stopped to look at "the beloved old Tower, bolted and barred but looking magnificent." An even bigger break with the past occurred with the sale of Forest House which had been such an important part of Nevile's life since his childhood. Now that their permanent home at West Barns was in a rural location, the Davidsons felt less inclined to travel north, while the encroachment of new housing on the surrounding forest and the expense of maintaining the building were further factors in favor of selling. Thus, in July 1970, the newspapers carried an advertisement for a "delightful Country House in secluded position overlooking Cairngorms, consisting of three reception rooms, seven bedrooms and dressing rooms, three bathrooms, usual offices, garage, etc." It took just two weeks for a "very satisfactory offer" of £12,860 to be submitted by an American couple; "we feel glad they are getting it as we liked them." The sale, though "inevitable," was "very sad." Nevile always made quick decisions about major purchases, and the proceeds were immediately used to buy a flat in a Georgian building at 73 Dundas Street, Edinburgh. He justified the move to himself in his diary on July 9:

> Perhaps rather rash but I think, taking the long view, a good move; and we shall be able to furnish it completely from Forest House and shall be able to keep our excellent little library (of about 1700 books) from there, which is a great comfort.

The house at Nethy was finally vacated in November, and after packing up his books on a farewell visit Nevile stayed overnight with friends living nearby with the intention of overseeing the removal the following day. Making his way to the bathroom along a passage in the unfamiliar house in the darkness of early morning, he mistook the door and fell downstairs and broke his wrist. So often ready to retreat to his bed for minor ailments, on this occasion he did not seek immediate medical help as he wanted to deal with the removal and only afterwards did he go to the Royal Infirmary in Edinburgh where his wrist was put in plaster. This did not stop him doing pulpit supply the next Sunday and attending his usual meetings during the following week but a few days later an X-ray revealed he had also broken a finger and he had to stay in hospital for an operation.

In these years Nevile Davidson lost people, as well as places, that had meant much to him. Charles Warr had been ill for some time and died of a heart attack in June 1969. "A true Christian, great churchman and marvellous affectionate friend" was Nevile's epitaph on the man who had been instrumental in his appointments at Dundee and Glasgow and as a royal chaplain. The following year he conducted the memorial service for Steven, 1st Baron Bilsland (1892–1970), the industrialist, banker and early supporter of the Society of Friends of Glasgow Cathedral and, in 1975, took the funeral of Melville Dinwiddie, his friend from Aberdeen days who had introduced him to the world of religious broadcasting. But the most severe blow occurred with the sudden death of his faithful housekeeper Flora on March 9, 1970, which was "a day of great grief. Flora died in a moment when dressing to come to us. She has been with me for 36 years and with Peggy and me all through our married life; a marvellous friend and help every day and in every way."

Such sad occurrences aside, there is not the slightest sign in Nevile's final years that life's little day was swiftly ebbing to its close. Certainly, he often expressed concern about his health and recorded the various prescriptions he received for asthma and bronchitis, but these were conditions from which he had suffered for many years. He was still preaching regularly at Whitekirk, Haddington and occasionally at Glasgow Cathedral, attending Church and Nation sub-committees, chairing meetings of the Friends of St. Mary's, Haddington, helping Peggy with Red Cross fund-raising events and visiting friends and relatives in the south of England. Moreover, his appetite for new ventures and travel was undiminished. In March 1974 he readily agreed at short notice to go to Brussels to take services in the Scots Church which was vacant, remaining there until early June. He returned home to deal with a suitcase of unanswered mail which had not been forwarded and later in the summer set off again, this time to Italy to attend the celebrations of the 800th anniversary of the Waldensian Protestant Church, accompanied by Peggy and her sister Diana.

In November he finished his spell as chairman of the Multi-Lateral Church Conversations, and felt "deeply moved" at the following year's General Assembly after receiving "a wonderful tribute of thanks" for his work from the moderator, James Matheson. Up till that point work on the autobiography had progressed slowly but Nevile began to apply himself in earnest to completing the manuscript and by the spring of 1976 he was ready to hand over a draft copy to James Bulloch for his comments. There are signs in places that he had grown rather bored with the task as some sections simply transcribe entries from his diaries.

Nevile had finished his book but he wasn't finished with his property speculations for, at the end of November 1975, he decided that the Edinburgh flat was too big and started viewing smaller ones. In his seventy-sixth year he still relished the challenge of renovating old properties and when he found a suitable flat at 4 St. Bernard's Row in an "unspoilt Georgian" building was not deterred by its "very bad condition." In spite of putting in a high offer, the Davidsons were unexpectedly outbid by £1000 and "felt very dejected" but Nevile discovered the successful buyer had been a young lawyer hoping to resell at a profit, and by making an increased offer was able to acquire the flat after all. Just about everything had to be done—re-wiring, re-plumbing, eradicating dry rot, installing a bathroom—and much of 1976 was spent supervising the project in conjunction with architect David Stamp. As always, complications and frustrations arose, but by the end of October the building work was finished at last and painters moved in to burn off layers of old paint. A month later the carpets were laid, furniture put in place and the flat was ready to be used for a meeting of the Dunkeld Fellowship Committee to discuss plans for the following year's retreat. When, on December 15, Peggy's mother Margaret came to have a look around, "Peggy had our bedroom all in order and everything looking nice."

Five days later, Nevile was attending one of his routine meetings at the Church of Scotland offices in 121 George Street. As he left home that morning, he remarked to Peggy that he was feeling particularly well but while driving back in the afternoon he had just enough time to pull into the side of the road before suffering acute heart failure.[4] He was found sitting in his car by a passing policeman.

4. Death certificate states cause of death as "acute cor pulmonale" (heart failure secondary to chronic lung disease).

Nevile Davidson once told a journalist that "I can only really retire when finally called to rest."[5] When that call came on December 20, 1976, the policeman who found him told Peggy that Nevile had a smile on his face.[6]

5. *The Penticton Herald* [Canada], September 21 1973

6. The author is grateful to the Rev. David Beckett for this information.

# 15

# "Laus Deo"

## THE LEGACY OF NEVILE DAVIDSON

THERE CAN BE NO doubt that Nevile Davidson was one of the leading figures of the Church of Scotland in the twentieth century, a worthy successor to great Scottish Presbyterian divines like Norman MacLeod, Thomas Guthrie and Alexander Whyte. A fellow minister even described him as "the most Christ-like man I have ever met." But is he simply an interesting personality from the past who deserves to be remembered for his remarkable personal qualities or does he have anything to say to the church of the twenty-first century? What, in short, is the legacy of Nevile Davidson?

At Nevile's funeral—held in the Cathedral on Christmas Eve 1976 with the Christmas tree still illuminated as he would have wished—Ronald Selby Wright's eulogy summed up what he considered to be the late Cathedral minister's most memorable achievements:

> The Church of Scotland remembers with thankful pride his distinguished year as Moderator [and] his Convenership of many important committees . . . but perhaps what he did that so much commands our remembrance and thanksgiving at this time was his great work for inter-church relations. His work for the Ecumenical Movement, his sorrow at disunity and a divided Church, and his constant efforts to bring all more close together was what so many will be most grateful for.[1]

1. *Chronicle,* January 1977

In a private letter of condolence to Peggy, Wright added that "Nevile was the last of our great and humble spiritual statesmen" and it is certainly true that his passing marked the end of an ecclesiastical era.

Any attempt to assess Nevile Davidson's life and work must take into account that he was born into a world which was not only very different from today's but had little in common with the life led by most other church ministers and their families at the time. Domestic tasks in the Davidson household were carried out by maids and from childhood Nevile was accustomed to the gilded lifestyle of his Kinnaird and Agnew relatives at Rossie Priory and Lochnaw Castle. While he witnessed the decline of this aristocratic world and the democratization of society after WWII, and was happy to live in the modest surroundings of a Glasgow tenement, he always had Flora to see to his domestic needs and it never occurred to him that his clerical colleagues did not have similar help. David Beckett recalls Nevile speaking with disapproval of a fellow minister he had recently visited who had been engaged in hoovering the manse carpets, a task which he considered quite inappropriate. In a similar vein is his reputed comment at a meeting where the subject of an increase in ministerial stipends was under discussion. Nevile expressed his opposition on the grounds that he had always been able to manage on his salary, a remark which did not endear him to less well-off colleagues who had not married into money and who did not enjoy the benefits of legacies and inherited property.

On the other hand, Nevile's privileged background, together with his experience as an army chaplain, endowed him with an ability to mix with people from all different classes, from humble tenement dwellers to the royal family. He was the personification of Kipling's oft-quoted ideal of walking with kings while not losing the common touch. He had, moreover, an innate presence that commanded respect and was in perfect harmony with the splendor of the ancient building in which he ministered. As one old lady put it after seeing him lead a service, "My, he's got charm and dignity."

That was the public face of Nevile Davidson, but the gravitas to some extent concealed an inner shyness and only those who got to know him well discovered the surprising sense of fun underneath. Paying tribute to Nevile at the time of his retirement, Roy Sanderson, the former minister of the Barony church, commented on the two sides of his personality: "a natural dignity of bearing mingles delightfully with an appreciation, almost mischievous at times, of what is sometimes called the 'lighter side of life.'" After moving to West Barns, Peggy was distressed to find that mice in the house had been nibbling away at a pair of her best patent leather shoes. Nevile contacted insurance broker Mervyn Hamilton with a view to making a claim but Mervyn told him that would not be possible as the damage was caused by vermin. After that, Nevile always addressed Mervyn as "Vermin"! Although he and Peggy never had children of their own, Nevile was particularly at ease in the company of the young: outdoors at Nethy Bridge he enjoyed playing games with the children of Peggy's brother, Peter Martin, and one surprising diary entry from Christmas 1963 records that "After dinner [the] children did some recitations and songs", other family members played on the violin and piano and "finally Peggy and I gave a brief demonstration of 'The Twist.'"

While Nevile Davidson's diaries record many of these lighter moments, passages of reflection and self-analysis are unfortunately few and far between. One would like to know more about his opinions of the events and people he mentions, but he rarely reveals his inner feelings. However, among his papers there is a list he drew up at the Dunkeld Retreat in April 1976, only a few months before his death, headed "Some personal resolutions or hopes" and this provides an uncharacteristically frank insight into what he saw as his weaknesses:

1. To be less self-centred

2. To think less of health

3. To think less of age and the future

4. To commit myself more completely and joyfully into the safe hands of God

5. To use every day as perfectly as possible

6. To overcome my temperamental laziness

7. To give more time to prayer and reflection

It is true that concern about his health had been a lifelong characteristic, perhaps stemming from over-protectiveness in childhood when he was not enrolled at school at the usual age as he suffered from asthma and bronchitis. The diaries regularly mention minor ailments—colds, headaches, tiredness—and he would take to his bed on these occasions. His wife did nothing to discourage this and he frequently makes statements like "Peggy insisted on my staying in bed today." At the Cathedral it was not unknown for one of the assistants to receive a call on Saturday asking him to take the service the next morning. Doctors were frequently consulted for check-ups—eye strain seems to have been a particular worry—but the answer was invariably that nothing was amiss. In 1965 he was attending a four day World Council of Churches conference in Scandinavia when a headache and temperature made him feel "far from well." Although the conference had only one more day to go, Nevile decided he would have to rearrange his flights and come back early only to experience "a nightmare day" as he missed his connecting flight to Glasgow, forcing him to wait for two-and-a-half hours at London Airport.

Nevile Davidson did think a great deal about his health but it would be unfair to accuse him of "temperamental laziness." Again, this feeling may go back to his youth when, as he acknowledged, he did not study hard enough at school or university and as a result suffered his father's displeasure at his failure to achieve a first class honors degree. In working life, though, Nevile carried out a prodigious range of high-profile public roles, kept up his routine preaching and pastoral duties, made frequent broadcasts and exhibited an extraordinary degree of commitment to an endless round of committee meetings. All this was not done out of a mere sense of duty, as in retirement he voluntarily continued many of these earlier activities and willingly took on new ones. Perhaps James Bulloch was closest to the truth when, after reading the frequent references to perceived laziness in the manuscript of *Beginnings but no Ending*, he commented that "I always regarded you as a person who could get a great deal done while maintaining an air of leisure."

Nevile's desire at the age of seventy-seven "to commit myself more completely and joyfully into the safe hands of God" draws attention to the strong faith which underpinned everything he did. He used the occasion of his final sermon as Cathedral minister to reaffirm the great central truths which he had preached so consistently, and called upon the church to proclaim the message with greater confidence:

> The Church no longer speaks with its earlier authority and conviction. It sometimes even seems to be uncertain about what it really believes about Christ and his Cross and his Resurrection no less than about the precepts and principles about the living of the Christian life. It has lost its confidence. It is too often on the defensive. It is too easily tempted to compromise with the so-called spirit of the age . . . I believe the time has come for the Church to recover the note of triumphant confidence and joy in its own message: to proclaim not doubts but certainties, not questions

but convictions. And conviction can come only through faith and above all through faith in the living Christ.[2]

The sermon touched on one of the central themes of Nevile Davidson's ministry: the need to balance the certainties of faith against "the spirit of the age," and it is here that his example has something to say to the church of today. His successor at the Cathedral, William Morris, noted that "Dr. Davidson was the kind of person who steered his life along a course avoiding [the] extremes of revering tradition to the extent of mistrusting all things new; and of becoming so revolutionary that nothing old is sacred. His life was enriched by both tradition and discovery."[3] A chapter of *Reflections of a Scottish Churchman* headed "Things New and Old" shows how Nevile Davidson applied this principle to every aspect of life. What was necessary, he argued, was "double alertness": an appreciation of the value of both tradition and change. This, he believed, was the approach followed by Jesus himself, who was both a traditionalist steeped in the ancient Hebrew Scriptures and one who "ruthlessly tears down the barbed-wire fences of petty ecclesiastical and social rules which the Pharisees and Scribes had so carefully erected."[4]

This notion of "double alertness" required to be worked out in the practical side of ministry:

> Never had it been more important than it is at this particular hour in history for the Church to be alert to the new situations and problems and needs of the contemporary world. We who are Christians must keep our minds and hearts constantly open to new ways along which the Holy Spirit may be seeking to lead us . . . We must be ready for creative experiment. In the light of rapidly changing conditions of social life, the Church must think out new methods of getting its Gospel across to the man-in-the-street who is often reluctant to listen . . . Only in so far as the Church is both loyal to "the faith once delivered to the saints" and at the same time sensitive to the spirit of the age . . . will its voice be listened to and its influence be felt.[5]

Hence, on one occasion worship at Glasgow Cathedral might follow the Genevan communion liturgy of 1556 and take the form of an informal

2. *Glasgow Herald*, March 27 1967

3. *Chronicle*, January 1967

4. Davidson, *Reflections*, 62

5. Davidson, *Reflections*, 65

"Service for the Man in the Street" on another. His early appreciation of the potential of radio, and later television, is another example of his willingness to use new methods of spreading the Christian message and, had he been alive today, he would undoubtedly have been pleased to see that services of Choral Evensong and notable events such as the national service in November 2018 marking the end of World War I can be accessed via the Cathedral's website. Towards the end of his ministry Nevile was prepared to contemplate not only different types of services and alternative methods of communication but a total reappraisal of how the institutional church operated, anticipating the radical restructuring which the Church of Scotland has required to address in the twenty-first century. Speaking to the Edinburgh Presbytery Ministerial Club in March 1968, he pointed out that the parish system had been planned at a time when parishes were smaller and largely rural and that the pattern for ordained ministry had not fundamentally changed since the end of the seventeenth century. "We have allowed the old conception of the parish ministry to fetter us," he continued. "We have allowed it to become almost the only form of ordained ministry, instead of welcoming and encouraging other forms and modes of ministry." No wonder Nevile's former assistant Rev. Fred Fulton of Dornoch Cathedral told him that "what always fills me with admiration is your still fresh approach after all these years. It can never be said of you that you got into a rut doing the same things endlessly."

With such breadth of outlook, it is not surprising that one of Nevile's heroes was Henry Drummond (1851–97), a prominent evangelical of the Victorian era, but not one who fitted into any conventional category. A revivalist preacher who believed in conversion and worked with Moody and Sankey in their evangelistic campaign of the 1870s, he was unusual in accepting the principles of biblical criticism and holding slightly unorthodox views on the Atonement. Unlike most conventional evangelicals, he was not in favor of rigidly defined doctrinal statements and Nevile Davidson would have endorsed his view that "religion is not a matter of thinking but of living." Drummond had a scientific education and, in an era when religion and science were regarded by some as in opposition to each other, he saw no conflict between the Christian faith and new ideas such as Darwin's theory of evolution. As a result, he enjoyed the respect of churchmen and scientists alike; as David Bebbington puts it, "He was an evangelist, and therefore trustworthy; he was a scientist and therefore authoritative."[6] Nevile saw Drummond's ability to combine these different perspectives as a model for ministers to follow. After reading *The Life of Henry Drummond* by George Adam Smith in 1964 he wrote, "How much we need in the ministry today some men of his quality—his combination of strong Christian conviction and broadminded outlook on the secular world and its achievements."

Nevile Davidson's ability to see both sides of an issue made him an ideal leader of ecumenical discussions. Addressing the General Assembly in May 1967 on the subject of church union, he typically appealed "for mutual respect and courtesy on both sides" and one colleague recalled the many occasions at such gatherings when "Dr. Davidson rescued us from ignominy, or disunity, or crass stupidity with the nobility of his mind, and the rare, persevering courtesy of his address—which even his opponents could not fail to respect." Rev. W. G. Baker who, as Chairman of the Scottish Committee of the Churches of Christ in Great Britain, participated in many ecumenical discussions with Nevile noted that "often we disagreed or held different viewpoints, but if Nevile had to disagree he did so most agreeably or most graciously, and was a genuine reconciler." Few men could show so much patience and optimism in pursuing such an approach over so many years and after so many fruitless negotiations. In spite of all his work on the Inter-Church Relations Committee and in the World Council of Churches, church union was not achieved, but that does not mean that Nevile Davidson's efforts were in vain. His contribution was well summarized in a letter from the RC Archbishop of St. Andrews and Edinburgh, Gordon Gray: "We all realise the problems and we are not trying to push too hard or to move too quickly. We are leaving room for the Holy Spirit to work. But in the preparation of the ground you have done so much."

A similar sense of patience and balance can be seen in Nevile's handling of conflicts between individuals within churches. An April 1966 diary entry describes at some length how an elder came to ask for advice after hearing a "radical and heretical" sermon on the resurrection by his minister, who put forward the theory that Jesus might have been in a coma on the cross, rather than dead.

> I pointed out that there has been no trial for heresy in the Church of Scotland for about 100 years; that certain professors of Theology in our colleges were expressing views almost as radical; and that the best procedure was probably an appeal by the kirk session

6. Bebbington, *Henry Drummond,* 148

to his better judgment—a request that he should consider the consciences of many in his congregation who might be upset.

This could be interpreted as an attempt to "sit on the fence" but it is equally an example of Nevile Davidson's courtesy, his desire to see the best in people and to avoid unpleasant personal confrontations. When publicly attacked he responded on the basis that "a soft answer turneth away wrath." On one occasion he delivered greetings from the Church of Scotland to the General Assembly of one of the smaller Scottish Presbyterian denominations, the United Free Church, and found himself in a "strange and embarrassing situation" when the UF moderator launched a twenty minute attack on the ecumenical movement. Nevile responded briefly with a plea for "conversations" between the churches to continue. The outspoken Harry Whitley of St. Giles was another opponent of aspects of ecumenism, particularly regarding discussions with Roman Catholics. The two clashed during a BBC television debate on church unity in April 1969; afterwards, Nevile wrote that "he was very hostile in his attitude, as always. But before and after the interview we kept on polite and friendly terms." In the thousands of pages of his diaries, there is not a trace of any personal animosity towards those who disagreed with him. Faced with seemingly irreconcilable positions, Nevile's policy was always to keep the lines of communication open. As secular thinking became increasingly dominant in society, he took part in debates with humanists on occasions and at a 1966 World Council of Churches conference in Geneva spoke on the need for dialogue with Marxists. In his personal reading he kept up to date with contemporary writers such as the French existentialists Camus, de Beauvoir and Sartre, even though he thought their work "reflects much of the moral bewilderment and scepticism of the contemporary world."

Thus, throughout his career Nevile Davidson consistently pursued the twin objectives of seeking to understand and reach those outside the church while working for closer co-operation between the denominations. He regarded evangelism and ecumenism as two sides of the same coin and the title of a sermon he preached in 1966 effectively summed up the whole thrust of his ministry in five words:"One Church Renewed for Mission." Nevile would work with anyone in pursuit of that goal and was as happy to serve as President of the Scoto-Catholic Scottish Church Society as he was to sit on the platform at a Billy Graham rally to hear "the old, old story" presented "in new words, with new settings and by new methods." The

Church of Scotland is often talked of as being a "broad church" but few have embodied the idea so effectively as Nevile Davidson.

One expression occurs in Nevile Davidson's diaries more than any other: "Laus Deo" ["Praise be to God"], for at heart his outlook on life was one of simple thankfulness. Again and again he would end a year expressing his gratitude for "innumerable undeserved blessings." The distinguished Doctor of Divinity who loved ceremony and grandeur, dined with royalty and collected antiques and paintings took equal delight in the small pleasures of life, especially in birds and animals. After recording in his diary that he had delivered the eulogy at the funeral of Lord Kinnaird in July 1972, he describes with even more feeling the death of a tame blackbird which had been coming to be fed at the back door at Seafield House for two years. "We buried him close to the garden gate in a little box lined with flowers." His diaries are full of close observations of the habits of wildlife: "Discovered that once again a pair of flycatchers are nesting in the garden—in the same crevice in the wall behind the garden gate where [a] pair made their nest three years ago." Like the poet and novelist Thomas Hardy, "he was a man who used to notice such things."

Peggy Davidson (1918–91), photographed some time during the 1960s.
(Photo: Glasgow Cathedral).

Above all, Nevile was thankful for "darling Peggy." When Principal Rainy, leader of the Free Church of Scotland at the time of the negotiations for union with the United Presbyterians, was asked how he coped with all his heavy responsibilities, he replied, "I have a happy and peaceful home." Peggy provided that same stability for Nevile. As one parishioner put it, "you both seem to radiate a lovely serenity wherever you go." Throughout their married life he loved to buy her gifts; at the age of seventy he came back from an antiques fair in Edinburgh with "a rather charming little Victorian ring for Peggy with seven stones spelling the word 'Dearest.'" The couple observed many affectionate rituals: Nevile liked snowdrops and on his birthday Peggy would always put some in a vase on his desk. A letter to Peggy from a cousin after Nevile's death provides a touching insight into their domestic arrangements:

> He loved everything about you and often told me that your gay laugh gave him such pleasure, and your love of birds and flowers tuned in with his. He often told me how it cheered him to hear you talking and laughing to Mrs Guthrie [the housekeeper at Seafield House] as he attended to his mail and business and how he believed that the Heavenly Spirit had led him to you in Iona.

A friend remembered a conversation in which Peggy said she hoped she would die first as she could not cope with living without Nevile but he replied, "When I'm dead I'll still be with you all the time."

Peggy lived on until March 1991, her last years blighted by ill health. She continued to attend the parish church at Whitekirk until she could no longer climb the steps, and thereafter worshiped at St. Mary's, Haddington, where she was already an active member of the Society of Friends. She lived in the house at West Barns until near the end of her life when she moved to Haddington to be with her mother, who predeceased her by only a few months, and when no longer able to live independently she was cared for in a nursing home at Lymington in Hampshire, near her brother Peter who visited her daily.[7]

Her correspondence files show that immediately after Nevile's death she devoted herself to preserving his memory in every way possible, making strenuous efforts to publish his autobiography in spite of rejections from Collins and Hodder who did not consider it a viable commercial

---

7. Details of Peggy's later years are taken from the eulogy delivered at her funeral at St. Mary's Church, Haddington on March 28, 1991 and kindly supplied to the author by David Martin, son of Peggy's brother Peter.

proposition. She also sought James Bulloch's advice on the possibility of publishing a collection of sermons and distributed some of her husband's valued possessions to those who would appreciate them: a cross thought to be of Spanish Moorish origin went to Nunraw Abbey at Garvald near Haddington and his portable communion set to a minister friend in Ontario.

On the first anniversary of Nevile's death, Bill Morris was able to report that the Society of Friends was installing a memorial window in the Cathedral, designed by Gordon Webster, with the theme of "We praise Thee, O God, we acknowledge Thee to be the Lord." This was unveiled by Peggy at a ceremony on June 3, 1979 and she also left money to ensure that each week in the Cathedral there would be an arrangement of red roses in memory of her husband. The couple lie together in the city's Necropolis in a plot selected by Nevile who said that he wanted to be buried there so that the first thing he would see on the Day of Resurrection would be the Cathedral he loved.

And it is, of course, Glasgow Cathedral that is Nevile Davidson's greatest gift to posterity. As one Cathedral member wrote, "Not only did he breathe life into the fabric of the place, transforming it from an ancient monument into a living thing of beauty, but he breathed life into the congregation too . . . He showed us that God was not only love and truth but beauty too and that every true form of beauty was a manifestation of His presence." The beauty of the interior as it is today, with its remodeled quire and fine collection of stained glass windows, is the result of his vision in the 1930s and his ability to bring together individuals and public bodies in a united effort to ensure that the Cathedral could continue as a focal point for the civic and religious life of Glasgow. It can truly be said of Nevile Davidson and Glasgow Cathedral, as was said of Sir Christopher Wren and St. Paul's, that "if you seek his memorial, look around you."

The grave of Nevile and Peggy Davidson in the Necropolis, Glasgow.
(Photo by the author).

# Appendix

## Scottish Presbyterianism

PRESBYTERIANISM IS A SYSTEM of church government organized around a series of assemblies or courts. A kirk session is responsible for an individual local congregation; kirk sessions send representatives to presbyteries which are responsible for the churches within a larger area; a gathering covering a still wider region is known as a synod, though this level has been abolished in some Presbyterian denominations. The highest court is the general assembly which meets once a year.

These courts are made up of elders and ministers (a minister being, technically, a "teaching elder") and the person who chairs the meetings at each level is known as the moderator. At kirk session level, the moderator will be the minister of the church. The Moderator of the General Assembly holds the post for one year, during which he or she represents the Church of Scotland nationally and internationally.

The story of Scottish Presbyterianism is a complex one dating back to the time of the reformer John Knox (c.1513–1572), under whose influence the Scottish church was reformed in 1560. Andrew Melville (1545–1622) was a significant figure in organizing the church along Presbyterian lines but the Stuart kings attempted to restore an episcopal system with authority vested in bishops as overseers. After a prolonged period of religious and civil conflict, the Scottish church was finally recognized as Presbyterian under the Revolution Settlement of 1690.

The national or established Church of Scotland is often referred to as The Kirk but it is not the only Scottish Presbyterian denomination. In the eighteenth and nineteenth centuries there were various splits or secessions, the issue of patronage (the right of a landowner rather than the congregation to choose the parish minister) being particularly contentious. The most significant division was the Disruption of 1843 when a third of the ministers of the Kirk left to form the Free Church.

Thereafter, a gradual process of reunion occurred. Some of the smaller denominations came together in 1847 to form the United Presbyterian Church. This in turn united with the Free Church in 1900 as the United Free (UF) Church.

Nevile Davidson's father James was ordained in the Free Church and therefore became a minister of the UF denomination after the 1900 reunion. Nevile Davidson was ordained in the UF church but in 1929 a further reunion took place between the UF and the established Church of Scotland; Nevile accordingly became a minister of the latter church.

However, a remnant stayed out of the reunions at each stage, often for theological reasons, and smaller Free, United Free and other Presbyterian denominations continue today.

For a straightforward factual introduction to the history of the Scottish Presbyterian churches, see Andrew Muirhead's *Reformation, Dissent and Diversity* (London: Bloomsbury, 2015). An older work, G. D. Henderson's *The Church of Scotland* (first published by the Church of Scotland Youth Committee, Edinburgh, in 1939 and periodically updated) also provides a useful overview. A summary of the history of the Church of Scotland can be found at https://www.churchofscotland.org.uk/about_us

# Bibliography

Aird, Andrew. *Glimpses of Old Glasgow.* Glasgow: Aird and Coghill, 1894.

Allan, Tom, ed. *Crusade in Scotland: Billy Graham.* London: Pickering and Inglis, 1955.

Bardgett, Frank D. "The Tell Scotland Movement: Failure and Success." *Records of the Scottish Church History Society,* 38 (2008) 127–40.

———. *Scotland's Evangelist: D. P. Thomson.* Haddington: Handsel Press, 2010.

Bebbington, D. W. "Henry Drummond, Evangelicalism and Science." *Records of the Scottish Church History Society* 28 (1998) 129–48.

Blackie, Nansie. *A Time for Trumpets: Scottish Church Movers and Shakers of the Twentieth Century.* Edinburgh: Saint Andrew, 2005.

Bruce, Steve. *Scottish Gods: Religion in Modern Scotland, 1900–2012.* Edinburgh: Edinburgh University Press, 2014.

Burleigh, J. H. S. *A Church History of Scotland.* London: Oxford University Press, 1960.

Calvin, John. *Institution of the Christian Religion* [1536 Edition]. Grand Rapids: Eerdmans, 1975.

Cameron, Nigel M. de S., ed. *Dictionary of Scottish Church History and Theology.* Edinburgh: T. & T. Clark, 1993.

Cheyne, A. C. *The Transforming of the Kirk.* Edinburgh: Saint Andrew, 1983.

Coulter, D. G. "The Church of Scotland Army Chaplains in the Second World War." PhD diss., University of Edinburgh, 1997.

Davidson, A. Nevile. *Diaries, 1912, 1920–29* and *1942–76* (unpublished). National Library of Scotland, Accession nos. 7710, 1–45.

———. *Notebooks and Correspondence Files* (unpublished). National Library of Scotland, Accession nos. 7710, 80–99.

———. *Collection of Press-cuttings.* National Library of Scotland, Accession nos. 7710, 100–110.

———. *Miscellaneous Papers Relating to Dr. Davidson's Parents, 1886–c.1920.* (unpublished). National Library of Scotland, Accession no. 7710, 115.

———. *Beginnings but no Ending.* Edinburgh: Edina, 1978.

———. *Glasgow Cathedral: A Short History and Guide.* Glasgow: privately printed, 1938.

———. *Reflections of a Scottish Churchman.* London: Hodder and Stoughton, 1965.

———. "The Sunday Evening Service." *Church Service Society Annual* 6 (1933–4) 33–38.

———. "Training for the Ministry." *Church Service Society Annual* 15 (1944–5) 17–19.

———. "The Ancient Creeds in the Modern Church." *Church Service Society Annual* 20 (1950) 17–24.

———. "The Place of the Sacraments in the Life of the Church." *Church Service Society Annual* 21 (1951) 3–13.

———. "The Cathedral Church of Glasgow." *Church Service Society Annual* 35 (1965) 28–38.

Dinwiddie, Meville. *Religion by Radio.* London: Allen and Unwin, 1968.

Donaldson, Gordon. *The Faith of the Scots.* London: Batsford, 1990.

Falconer, Ronnie. *The Kilt Beneath my Cassock.* Edinburgh: Handsel, 1978.

Ferguson, Ronald. *George MacLeod.* London: Harper Collins, 1990.

Forrester, Duncan B. *Truthful Action: Explorations in Practical Theology.* Edinburgh: T. & T. Clark, 2000.

Forrester, Duncan B. and Douglas M. Murray, eds. *Studies in the History of Worship in Scotland.* Edinburgh: T. & T. Clark, 1996.

Forsyth, Alexander. *Mission by the People.* Eugene, OR: Pickwick, 2017.

Gay, Douglas C. *A Practical Theology of Church and World: Ecclesiology and Social Vision in 20th Century Scotland.* PhD diss., University of Edinburgh, 2006.

Groome, Francis H., ed. *Gazetteer of Scotland: A Survey of Topography, Volume 6,* Edinburgh: Jack, 1885.

Henderson, G. D. *The Church of Scotland.* Edinburgh: Church of Scotland Youth Committee, 1939.

Herron, Andrew. *Record Apart.* Edinburgh: Scottish Academic, 1974.

Knox, John. *The Liturgy of John Knox.* London: Hamilton, Adams,1886.

Louden, R. S. *The True Face of the Kirk.* London: Oxford University Press, 1963.

McGregor, David A. R. *No Marmalade on Fridays! Memoirs and Memories.* Glasgow: privately printed, 2010.

Macdonald, Finlay A. J. *From Reform to Renewal: Scotland's Kirk Century by Century.* Edinburgh: Saint Andrew, 2017.

Macnair, Iain. *Glasgow Cathedral: the Stained Glass Windows.* Glasgow: Society of Friends of Glasgow Cathedral, 2009.

Marshall, Rosalind K., *Ruin and Restoration: St. Mary's Church, Haddington.* Haddington: East Lothian Council Library Service, 2001.

Morton, A. R., ed. *God's Will in a Time of Crisis: A Colloquium celebrating the 50th Anniversary of the Baillie Commission.* Edinburgh: Centre for Theology and Public Issues, n.d.

Muirhead, Andrew T. N. *Reformation, Dissent and Diversity: the Story of Scotland's Churches, 1560–1960.* London: Bloomsbury, 2015.

Newlands, George. *John and Donald Baillie: Transatlantic Theology.* Bern: Lang, 2002.

Parsons, Gerald, ed. *Religion in Victorian Britain.* Manchester: Manchester University Press, 1988.

Ralston, Andrew G. *Lauchlan MacLean Watt: Preacher, Poet and Piping Padre.* Glasgow: Society of Friends of Glasgow Cathedral, 2018.

Ramsay, Dean. *Reminiscences of Scottish Life and Character.* London: T. N. Foulis, 1912.

Robertson, Alastair K. "The Place of Dr Robert Lee in the Developments in the Public Worship of the Church of Scotland." *Church Service Society Annual* 28 (1958) 31–46.

Warr, Charles L. *The Glimmering Landscape.* London: Hodder and Stoughton, 1960.

Wotherspoon, H. J. and Kirkpatrick, J. M. *A Manual of Church Doctrine according to the Church of Scotland.* London: Oxford University Press, 1960.

# Index